AN IN-DEPTH, IN
REMARKABLE MODE
PHENOMENON: REVELATIONS BY THE ROADSIDE

Searching for *Mary*

- ✤ *The History:* Invaluable insights into the historical context of Mary sightings—from Lourdes to Garabandal—providing a deeper understanding of the centuries-old quest for Mary.
- ✤ *The Mystery:* Eyewitness accounts of flowers raining from the sky, angels floating in the clouds, statues and icons weeping blood tears, and unexplained physical healing.
- ✤ *The Spectacle:* Vivid descriptions of masses of believers gathering in fields of mud, trekking across the country and into remote stretches of desert in a heartfelt communion of the spirit.
- ✤ *The Church:* Results of official Roman Catholic investigations into numerous reported supernatural appearances of the Virgin Mary.
- ✤ *The People:* Meet the prophets and pilgrims themselves, hear their stories, look into their eyes and their scrapbooks. Here are the people selling hope and T-shirts . . . as well as the truly devout believers, convinced that they have been blessed by an audience with the mother of God.

MARK GARVEY is an editor and freelance writer. He lives with his wife and two children in Cincinnati.

Searching for *Mary*

An Exploration of Marian Apparitions Across the U.S.

❧ ❧ ❧

MARK GARVEY

A PLUME BOOK

PLUME
Published by the Penguin Group
Penguin Putnam Inc., 375 Hudson Street,
New York, New York 10014, U.S.A.
Penguin Books Ltd, 27 Wrights Lane,
London W8 5TZ, England
Penguin Books Australia Ltd, Ringwood,
Victoria, Australia
Penguin Books Canada Ltd, 10 Alcorn Avenue,
Toronto, Ontario, Canada M4V 3B2
Penguin Books (N.Z.) Ltd, 182–190 Wairau Road,
Auckland 10, New Zealand

Penguin Books Ltd, Registered Offices:
Harmondsworth, Middlesex, England

First published by Plume, an imprint of Dutton NAL, a member of Penguin Putnam Inc.

First Printing, April, 1998
10 9 8 7 6 5 4 3 2 1

 REGISTERED TRADEMARK—MARCA REGISTRADA

Library of Congress Cataloging-in-Publication Data:
Garvey, Mark.
    Searching for Mary : an exploration of Marian apparitions across the U.S. /
Mark Garvey.
        p.   cm.
    Includes bibliographical references.
    ISBN 0-452-27952-6
    1. Mary, Blessed Virgin, Saint.   2. Mary, Blessed Virgin, Saint—
Apparitions and miracles—United States—History—20th century.
3. Garvey, Mark.   I. Title.
BT652.U6G37   1998
232.91'7—dc21   97-34921
                                                                      CIP

Printed in the United States of America
Set in Galliard
Designed by Leonard Telesca

For Deb, Sam, and Sarah,
with worlds of love

Oh! Blessed rage for order . . .

—WALLACE STEVENS

ACKNOWLEDGMENTS

My gratitude goes out to the many pilgrims, apparition enthusiasts, and visionaries for their candor and generosity. Thanks also to Jane Dystel and Danielle Perez, my agent and editor, respectively, for their efforts and unflagging enthusiasm for this project. And for helpful ministrations of all sorts, ranging from friendly encouragement to research assistance to hot, home-cooked meals hundreds of miles from home, thanks to Greg Albert, Bob and Ann Baker, Stacie Berger, Donna Collingwood, Jack Heffron, Elizabeth Johnson, Alison Kissling, Harvey Rachlin, Connie Springer, Jane Whitehouse, and Mike Willins. Finally, a special thank-you to my wife, Deb Garvey, for her love, support, and astute editorial counsel.

Contents

Introduction

The Call

*B*efore a series of purported apparitions of the Virgin Mary cropped up less than fifteen miles from my home, I had not, for several years at least, given much thought to the subject. I had learned in childhood the stories of Mary's appearances at Lourdes and Fatima, and while I never considered those events important to me in any personal or devotional sense, I accepted their validity as a matter of course. Most Catholics did. In our home we kept a small quantity of blessed water from the allegedly miraculous spring at Lourdes. It was in a small, milky white plastic bottle with a cross on it, and I have a vague, one-time memory of my mother sheepishly sprinkling a bit of it on a chronic and virulent foot rash I had throughout my youth. I don't know how much faith my mother had in the healing properties of Lourdes water (nor do I recall its effect, if any, on my afflicted parts), but it seemed to me, as a child, that there was at least as much magic in that little bottle as there was in the black wood and white plaster crucifix that hung in our dining room.

Later, during my freshman year of college, I viewed a film

about the Virgin's appearance to a group of children in Garabandal, Spain, in the early 1960s. The movie struck me as grotesque and decidedly hair-raising, and I remember being fascinated by it. The visions of the Garabandal children, four prepubescent girls, were filled with apocalyptic imagery and dire predictions about worldwide calamities to come. The visionaries themselves, in their ecstasies, contorted their bodies in dramatic and bizarre ways, sometimes walking backward, swiftly, all around their little village, staring straight up, heads thrown back as far as they would go, mumbling prayers to the Virgin as they went. They looked possessed. The film was black-and-white and silent except for the Wellesian intonations of the narrator. The flickering images of the young girls—their necks extended and taut, lips moving swiftly, eyes fixed and opened wide in what could have been either great love or great terror—have remained with me ever since.

More recently, I had heard of the ongoing series of apparitions (begun in 1981 and, by all accounts, not finished yet) reported by six young people in the town of Medjugorje, in Bosnia-Herzegovina, but knew little about it beyond the fact that the near-constant influx of devotees had transformed the hitherto obscure village into a thriving tourist destination— this in spite of the local bishop's stinging denunciation of the alleged apparitions.

The thought that a phenomenon of this sort might be starting up so close to home piqued my interest, and a few weeks after I had heard about it, there I was, on a clear, warm August night, standing in a church parking lot in northern Kentucky, waiting with 8,500 believers for a predicted appearance of the Virgin Mary. I saw nothing supernatural that night, though many who were there said they had. What I saw were thousands of people ready and willing to believe an anonymous visionary's claim that Mary, the mother of Jesus, would make an appearance, that for a few moments the parking lot in which they were standing would intersect with the portal of heaven and they would witness the wash of physics-defying phenomena that purportedly trails Mary wherever she goes, like the tail of a comet. I did not attend as a believer, nor did I return home a convert, but by the same token, I knew when the evening ended that I had not finished with apparitions.

The experience had affected me in a way I could not have predicted, in a way I was not even sure I understood. My evening among the believers had reached back to my childhood and pulled into the present a cluster of memories—rumors, lore, and legends—that had fringed the fabric of my religious upbringing but that I had somehow successfully relegated to the mental attic years ago. The memories were of some of Catholicism's murkier facets, obscure and occasionally unnerving elements of the Church's mystical heritage that are now, perhaps, felt by most to have little bearing on the question of salvation, but that contributed much to the savor and imaginative heft of the religion as I was growing up. These elements include such phenomena as stigmata, levitating saints, bi-location, weeping statues, the incorrupt and mystically "perfumed" bodies of long-dead saints, and, of course, miraculous visions.

As certain as I was that these phenomena held no devotional relevance for me, I was equally sure they continued to exert a powerful influence on my imagination, whether or not I liked to admit it. And while most marvels of that sort might be easy enough to dismiss as little more than Dark Ages mythology, the question of apparitions had always seemed different somehow. The idea that heaven might wish to communicate with earth is not such an outlandish idea once you've accepted certain basic premises regarding heaven, earth, and the nature of the relationship between the two. Add to that the strength of the devotion they had inspired over the centuries as well as their continuing currency in the Church and among the faithful, and suddenly apparitions begin to seem reasonable, understandable, and perhaps even *possible*.

But did I really believe that?

The more I thought about my experiences that night, the more enthusiastic (I won't say obsessed) I became about following this thread to its end. As difficult as it might be to arrive at answers when the questions spring from the eternal source of all mystery, I felt I at least had to look at the phenomenon long enough and close enough to achieve some kind of resolution, if only to no one's satisfaction but my own. And so I set out.

Apparitions in the United States

It was easy enough to immerse myself in the culture of the apparition enthusiasts. I began collecting literature on the subject and planning trips to other apparition sites around the country, of which, as it happened, there turned out to be an astonishingly large number. Believers are served by a large and expanding media network that includes newsletters, newspapers, magazines, books, and a substantial presence on the Internet. Regional and national conferences on the subject of Mary's appearances are held throughout the year all around the United States.

At the center of every apparition event is a person or persons claiming to have been contacted by a heavenly visitor. Mary has come in the night with a request, or Christ has flickered to life on the crucifix in the bedroom, glowing like phosphor. In some cases, angels and other saints have also made appearances. The messages these luminaries have come to impart are sometimes warm and encouraging but more often dwell on the wickedness of the world and warn of imminent heavenly retribution, or "chastisements," ready to be loosed upon earth should humankind not do a moral about-face, and in a hurry. The prescribed remedy varies among visionaries as to details, but most call for a concentrated program of prayer, repentance, conversion, and sometimes fasting.

Nearly all of the visions and messages are received on a regular basis, whether weekly, monthly, or annually, and for that reason are known as "serial" apparitions. Some visionaries receive the visions and messages in the privacy of their own homes. Most, however, work in front of crowds and, in order to accommodate the faithful, have secured large open spaces or comfortably sizable venues in which all can assemble for the regular meetings. The gatherings follow a general pattern: Believers (sometimes in the tens of thousands) congregate (many travel a good distance to attend, and thus can properly be described as pilgrims); prayers are recited and sung; finally, the visionary or locutionist (the latter being a person whose mystical experience is aural rather than visual) receives her message and, most often, shares it immediately with the pilgrims gathered at the site. Past messages are collected, published, and circulated among believers.

Many of the faithful follow favorite visionaries the way some people follow sports teams, attending all the events and poring over the messages with the same intensity others reserve for box scores. Families and friends travel hundreds of miles to visit their favorite sites. Parents bring their children. Children bring their parents. Large groups of senior citizens arrive in chartered motor coaches. Hotels and motels fill up with out-of-state visitors, and local restaurateurs enjoy a temporary influx of preternaturally cheerful and polite customers.

Of the pilgrims who coalesce around the visionaries, most, but not all, are Catholic. Many are expecting an end to human history sooner rather than later. All are seeking a settled understanding of themselves and the world they live in and the one that comes after.

The Historical Context

Apparition enthusiasts view modern-day visions within the context of a Church history rich in such experiences. Many of today's visionaries draw, either implicitly or explicitly, on famed and tradition-bound apparitions of the past. These influences may be purely stylistic, as in the Virgin's occasional propensity for appearing atop a small cloud, or they may reveal themselves in the messages' content, as when the Virgin speaks against communism or reveals glimpses of hell.

The first recorded supernatural appearance of Mary was to a third-century pagan lawyer turned Christian turned bishop named Gregory Thaumaturgus (Gregory the Wonderworker, so named because apparently on several occasions he caused large stones to move by force of will and once dried up a lake in the same way). One night Gregory was lying awake in bed, worried about the subject of an upcoming sermon. Suddenly, a man stood beside him, "aged in appearance, saintly in the fashion of his garments, and very venerable, both in grace and countenance and general mien." The old man pointed across the room to where the figure of a woman stood, larger than life-size and surrounded by a blaze of light. Gregory could not bear to look upon the woman long and averted his eyes. The woman spoke to the man, whom Gregory understood to be Saint John the Evangelist, instructing him to clarify some matters of Church teaching for Gregory in order to help with the troublesome sermon. Saint John addressed the woman as "the Mother of Our Lord" and then proceeded to straighten out the bishop on the particular doctrinal questions that had been keeping him awake.

Since that first appearance and down to the present day, thousands of apparitions of the Virgin, and other members of the court of heaven (and hell), have been claimed. Most Catholics know of only a handful of these—Fatima and Lourdes, perhaps rue de Bac and La Salette. But those are just the few that have, whether by chance or design, attained some level of popularity and permanence on the devotional scene. Hundreds of visions of the Virgin have been reported in the twentieth century alone, although only a few have ever received official "approval" by the Catholic Church. Many of Catholicism's most enduring devotional aids, including the rosary, the brown scapular, the "Miraculous Medal," and the images of the Sacred Heart and Our Lady of Guadalupe, had their genesis in purported miraculous apparitions.

For the benefit of readers who may be unaware of (or who may have forgotten) the Virgin's past appearances, what follows is a brief introduction to the historical apparitions most relevant to the events covered in this book. All of the incidents outlined below are fascinating studies in their own right and have been written about at book length many times over the years. I urge readers interested in learning more about these apparitions to go beyond my necessarily brief histories here and seek out those books.

1830, rue du Bac, Paris. Sister Catherine Labouré, a novice in the order of the Sisters of Charity of St. Vincent de Paul, was awakened just before midnight on July 18 by a small child dressed in radiant white. The child led her through the darkened convent to the chapel, where Catherine was surprised to see "all of the torches and tapers lit, as if for midnight Mass." The Virgin appeared to Catherine in the chapel and talked with her for two hours. A few months later, while at prayer, Catherine had a second vision of the Virgin. This time she appeared standing, surrounded by an oval frame on which these words were written: "O Mary, conceived without sin, pray for us who have recourse to thee." She heard a voice instructing her to have a medal struck "after this model." The voice promised, "Graces will abound for those who wear it with confidence." With the help of her confessor and her bishop, the medal was struck and distributed. Because of its rumored efficacy in securing heavenly intervention, it became known as the "Miraculous Medal" and remains one of Catholicism's most popular sacramentals. Sister Catherine Labouré died in 1876 and was canonized by Pope Pius XII in 1947.

1846, La Salette, France. Maximin Giraud, age eleven, and Melanie Mathieu, age fourteen, were herding cows on the slopes of the Alps one September day. After waking from a midday nap, the two went in search of the herd, which had wandered off. Looking down into a ravine, they saw a large, glowing circle of light, which opened to reveal a woman seated on a rock, cradling her face in her hands and weeping heavily. She called the children closer, until they too became enveloped in the circle of light. "If my people will not submit," the lady told them, "I shall be obliged to let go my Son's hand, which is so strong and so heavy that I can no longer restrain it." Her son, she said, was upset over the lack of respect shown for the Sunday Mass obligation and the propensity of local workers to invoke his name when cursing. She went on to predict a bad potato harvest and famine to come; then she urged the children to remember their prayers. Afterward, she ascended in the ball of light until she had drifted out of sight. On the strength of a swiftly established popular devotion to the site and mounting reports of cures, the local bishop approved the La Salette apparition in 1851. Following their mystical experience, Maximin and Melanie both tried religious life, but neither stuck with it. Unlike many visionaries connected with apparitions that have been approved by the Church, neither of the La Salette seers ever came close to being canonized by the Church.

1858, Lourdes, France. On February 11, fourteen-year-old Bernadette Soubirous, on an errand to gather firewood near her home in the French Pyrenees, was stopped by an apparition of a lady in white above a hedge in front of a nearby grotto. She knelt before the lady in prayer. Bernadette returned to the grotto three days later, and again saw the apparition. It was not until the third appearance, on February 18, that the vision spoke. She asked Bernadette to come to the grotto to meet with her fifteen more times. The young seer returned each morning from February 18 to March 4. Word spread quickly among the villagers, and on each of Bernadette's subsequent trips the number of curious onlookers grew until, at the March 4 apparition, a crowd of twenty thousand had gathered. During one of the visions the Virgin induced Bernadette to dig with her hands at a muddy spot within the grotto. A spring gushed forth, and almost from the day it first appeared, miraculous powers have been attributed to its waters, which continue to flow to this day. The Virgin identified herself to Bernadette as "the Immaculate Conception." Just four years earlier, Pope Pius IX had defined Mary's Immaculate Conception—the belief that she had been born free of original sin—as a dogma of the Catholic faith. The Virgin also asked that a chapel be built in Lourdes; instead, she got a basilica, which continues to draw hundreds of thousands of visitors each year to one of the world's most popular Marian shrines. Bernadette passed the rest of her life as a nun in the order of the Sisters of Charity in Nevers; she died in the convent on April 16, 1879. Her body was exhumed years after her death, declared incorrupt (preserved, by all appearances, from the normal processes of bodily decay), and can today be viewed in a glass case that serves as an altar at the chapel in Nevers. The apparitions of the Virgin at Lourdes had been declared worthy of belief by the local bishop in 1862, and Bernadette herself was canonized by Pope Pius XI in 1933.

1917, Fatima, Portugal. The appearances of the Virgin to the three shepherd children of Fatima, Lucia Dos Santos and her cousins Jacinta and Francisco Marto, were preceded, in 1916, by visions of an angel, who taught the children a prayer, administered Communion to them, and urged them to make reparation for the sins of the world by means of frequent prayer and sacrifice. May 13, 1917, marked the first of the Virgin's six appearances in a broad basin surrounded by hills and known as the Cova da Iria. The children were tending their sheep when lightning flashed in an otherwise clear sky. A vision of the Virgin appeared in front of them, near the top of an evergreen tree. She told the children she had come from heaven and requested that they return to the spot and meet with her on the thirteenth of each month through October. She advised them to pray the rosary daily and asked whether they would be willing to accept "all the suffering it may please [God] to send you" as a means of reparation for the sins of the world and to bring about the conversion of sinners. The children indicated their assent to this request, and the apparition glided up and out of view. As in Lourdes, word spread quickly within the village and to outlying areas, and the crowds grew with each subsequent apparition. The number in attendance at the final appearance, on October 13, has been estimated at seventy thousand. It was on that day that the famous "sun miracle" of Fatima reportedly took place. The sun was said to have danced in the sky and plummeted toward earth until those in attendance shrieked in terror, expecting to perish at any moment. Instead of striking the earth, though, the sun returned to its proper position in the sky, and the people and grounds, which just minutes before had been drenched by rain, were warm and dry. The Fatima series remained almost unknown outside of Portugal until the release of Lucia Dos Santos's memoirs, written between 1935 and 1941. In her 1941 *Third Memoir* the seer revealed that on July 13, 1917, the Virgin had imparted three secrets to the children. The first secret had been a vision of hell, provided by the Virgin in order to invoke in the seers a proper concern for the fate of sinners. The second secret was the Virgin's desire that a devotion to her Immaculate Heart be established throughout the world. She also requested that the pope consecrate Russia to her Immaculate Heart, thus securing the conversion of that nation, stemming the "spread of [Russia's] errors," and ensuring an era of peace to follow. In the political atmosphere following World War II, the seemingly prescient warning about checking the spread of communism found fertile ground around the world and especially in the United States, where the Fatima apparitions quickly became a devotional favorite. Fatima's third secret, still unrevealed, has been kept under lock and key at the Vatican since the late 1950s and has been the subject of much speculation since its existence was first made known. It is widely supposed that the secret concerns a coming world-wide cataclysm and the approach of the end-times.

1961–1965, Garabandal, Spain. Conchita Gonzalez, Mari Loli Mazon, Jacinta Gonzalez, and Mari Cruz Gonzalez experienced more than two thousand apparitions of the Virgin over a four-year period. The visions were not limited to a particular location, but took place all around the remote village in which they lived. The apparitions were notable for their frequency but also for the behavior of the girls during the course of the visions. Their peripatetic ecstasies have already been mentioned; these sometimes proceeded at speeds that amazed the onlookers who were trying to keep up with them. It was also reported that while in the midst of a vision, the girls sometimes became so heavy they could not be lifted. Like the Fatima children, Conchita is said to have received Communion from an angel, and believers claim this miracle was captured on film. Garabandal is perhaps best known as the source of the Virgin's prophecy concerning the worldwide Warning, the Great Miracle, and the Chastisement. According to Conchita Gonzalez, on an unspecified date in the future, God will reveal to each person on earth the state of his or her soul. This will happen simultaneously around the globe, its purpose to reform the conscience of the human race and prepare it for reception of the Great Miracle. The miracle, as described by Conchita, will take place in a grove of pines near Garabandal. Everyone who is in the area at the time will see it; the sick who are present will be cured, sinners will repent, and Russia will be converted. The second phase of the miracle is to be the establishment of a permanent, miraculous sign in the grove of pines. The sign will be capable of being photographed and touched, its divine origin will be beyond question, and it will last until the end of time. The final leg of the prophecy, the Chastisement, is a global catastrophe held in reserve by God in the event the Warning and the Miracle don't have their intended effects. In spite of frequent and clear denials by Church authorities that anything supernatural occurred at Garabandal, and disregarding the fact that each of the four seers, at one time or another, recanted her testimony, Garabandal remains one of the most popular apparition events of this century.

CHAPTER ONE

✤ ✤ ✤

Vigil Night

Conyers, Georgia, Day One

There was a run on rain gear at Target. Rain had fallen nonstop for two days in Atlanta, and pilgrims from out of town who had not, apparently, considered the possibility of showers had descended on this department store in Conyers, Georgia, a satellite community southeast of Atlanta in the county of Rockdale. Small bands of older women, some with husbands in tow, were scouring the shelves for any kind of material with the potential to repel rain. (A bewildered Target clerk in reply to a query from a pilgrim: "You want *reindeer?*") I was in the store looking for a flashlight. It occurred to me that I should have thought more about rain gear too. A plastic poncho would have been easier to manage than the smallish umbrella I had stashed in the trunk of my rental car. It was too late, though; the ponchos and slickers were gone. People had begun buying plastic garbage bags for makeshift raincoats.

It was six-thirty in the evening on a vigil night, the night before an anticipated apparition of the Virgin Mary to a Conyers housewife on a nearby farm. Tens of thousands of believers from all over the United States and elsewhere had gathered to be present the next day as the Virgin delivered what she herself had promised would be a message of more than typical import. Out of the Target parking lot, it was a right turn and about four miles to reach the apparition site— thirty acres of pastures with a farmhouse, barns, and, that week, 143 chemical toilets. Yellow-slickered sheriff's deputies directed traffic turning left from State Road 138 onto the road that ran beside the farm. Another set of deputies pointed me onto the property. I cantered my white rental up a badly pitted dirt road, a mud road, and through a pasture onto a grassy rise where cars were slotting together haphazardly, log-jam style.

Nancy Fowler, a forty-six-year-old mother of two at the time of my visit to Conyers, first heard from heaven in 1987. A life-size, but silent, Christ appeared to her, dressed in a white tunic with "loose-fitting" sleeves, bathed in supernatural light. That same year Nancy began hearing interior voices, male and female, when she prayed before a crucifix in her room. Sometimes the crucifix would glow. Nancy saw visions of hell ("a dark, black, fiery hole") and heaven ("Angels were everywhere in white robes like Our Lord wears. I could see part of the back of a tall chair. It was the throne of God"). She eventually discerned that both Jesus and his mother were talking to her. Since that time Nancy claimed to have been in almost daily contact with either Christ or Mary. They gave her guidance on everything from the salvation of mankind (Jesus: "Those who refuse to serve me, I will refuse to admit in heaven") to personal consumer decisions (Christ himself had counseled Nancy on buying both a home and a used car). The messages had been alternately comforting and darkly apocalyptic. In the latter idiom, Mary was likely to weep tears of blood as she delivered solemn warnings: "The sins of the country and the sins of the world are increasing God's anger. Please tell my children, come back to God. Return from their wicked, evil ways. I cannot restrain His arm much longer." Jesus once appeared in Nancy's kitchen, near life-size, on a crucifix suspended in air. His head hung on his chest "as if He were dead." Then "the body of Christ lunged forward," and he intoned: "The time has come for God's justice. Nancy, my precious daughter, what else can I do?" Off the subject of eschatology, Jesus was not beyond small talk. Once he called down from a cross as Nancy, her face covered with cleansing cream, passed in front of it. "You look funny," he teased.

From October 1990 to May 1994, Mary appeared to Nancy on the thirteenth of every month with a message "for the United States." The May 1994 message was, according to Mary, the last of her monthly messages, but Nancy received assurances that Mary and Jesus would continue to appear to her and that Mary would return every October 13 with a message. My October visit coincided with the fourth anniversary of Mary's first communication to Nancy, as well as with the anniversary of the last of another, more famous series of Marian apparitions—the appearance of the Virgin to three shepherd children in Fatima, Portugal, in 1917. Mary had told Nancy that on this October 13, she would come "in a special way." The faithful were expecting something extraordinary.

I was there to discover, if I could, why these pilgrims were huddled together out on this limb. The Conyers apparitions are given no quarter by Catholic officials, the local prelate having expressed "grave" doubts and refused even to launch an investigation. Priests who lead pilgrimages there are in direct defiance of the explicit wishes of that same archbishop. None of that seemed to matter, though, to the thousands who arrived there monthly—many priests and nuns among them—to listen to Nancy Fowler tell them what heaven had told her.

A Catholic myself, I cannot deny the possibility of private revelation; it is, after all, what the Gospels and the Church itself were founded on. Still, it seems on the face of it an unlikely way for heaven to accomplish its goals, whatever those might be. People who claim to see visions are considered by most other people, ipso facto, to be delusional—a substantial impediment to successful proselytizing. And the fact that ostensibly vital messages have most often been left in the hands of visionaries ill-equipped to publicize them widely and persuasively—most have been peasants, small children, and teenage girls—seems like particularly haphazard planning. Despite these obstacles, though, many thousands have chosen to believe Nancy Fowler's unbelievable claims.

According to Nancy, Jesus led her to the farm (known among the faithful, pragmatically enough, as *The Farm*) in 1991. It was purchased by supporters and set aside for use as a pilgrimage site in the summer of that year. It is operated by a group of devotees known as Our Loving Mother's Children. The Farm is roughly crescent shaped. At one tip of the property is Nancy Fowler's home and a devotional site in her backyard known as the Holy Hill; at the other is the farmhouse, where apparitions occur and messages are received. In between are unmown fields of high grass, dirt paths, open pastures, and a small woods.

In the forty-eight hours prior to my arrival, The Farm had become a palette of mud, its hues ranging from pure Georgia red clay to chocolate-shake brown to gray to black. It smacked and slurped. Over the course of my two days in Conyers, I would watch as it sucked a shoe off more than one pilgrim. I put my new flashlight in my pocket, stepped out of the car into the muck, picked my way around to the back of the car, and fished my umbrella from the trunk.

The weather on the vigil night was apocalyptic enough for me. It was probably mid-forties, but it was windy and felt much colder. The sky dripped insidiously, and dampness crept in at every chink. I managed my way across the slurried parking pasture to the house in which the apparitions took place, a plain two-story farmhouse with grayish tan siding and white trim. A white-railed porch stretched across the front. Tours were given on vigil nights and on mornings and afternoons of apparition days. Several dozen devotees, mostly Hispanics, and I queued up beside the house and waited to be called in. The people near me, most of them couples in their fifties and sixties, were all engaged in rapid, animated conversation in Spanish. One man in front of me talked to a man directly behind me, both of them acting as if I were not there.

The sun had set and the temperature was continuing to drop, but the rain had at least slowed to a mist. The wind had picked up, though, and was coming in gusts, threatening to invert our umbrellas. After a fifteen-minute wait we were ushered up the steps of the porch, through double doors, and into the apparition room. It was the first room inside the front door, at one time the home's living room, I assumed. Immediately upon entering the room, several of the women in our group turned to face left and fell to their knees before a corner shelf holding a small statue of Mary.

"Do not kneel down, folks," said a volunteer watching the door—a large, athletic, balding man who looked and sounded unquestionably in charge. "We'll have to ask you to stand so we can get enough people into the room. Step right in to the other side of the room. Come right in, folks." He continued to cajole and gently chasten, packing fifty or sixty of us into the room with the skill of a veteran attraction attendant at an amusement park.

It was not a typical living room. In fact, I suspect that if I were left alone in there for more than ten minutes, I would see visions myself. The room was rectangular, about thirty by fifteen feet. The walls were of rough wood paneling, the ceiling stucco and wood beams. The carpet was milk-chocolate brown, turned to black, gray and terra cotta in spots, thanks to the mud and clay we had hauled in on our shoes. There was no furniture, save for a couple of metal folding chairs in the back of the room. What there was was religious art of every description and in every available space. In the fifteen minutes we were in the room, I counted four icons, six crucifixes, thirteen paintings of various sizes, and no fewer than thirty-five statues. Our Lady of Guadalupe; the Infant of Prague; the Rosa Mystica; the Black Madonna of Czestochowa; Saint Michael the Archangel standing on Lucifer, his lance poised over the deceiver's chest; Christ in agony; Christ carrying the cross, rivulets of blood striping his body; Christ crucified; Christ, cinematically spattered with blood, dead in Mary's arms; Christ glorified—white and red rays flaring out from his chest. This room was a living, nearly vibrating, example of an artistic and devotional style I can only think to call Catholic Gothic. It was an ascetic's fever dream. Many of the pilgrims crossed themselves continually the entire time we were in the room.

A statue of Mary holding the child Jesus stood atop a set of shelves in one corner of the room. It was before this image that some of the women had knelt upon entering the room. The wall behind the shelves was white, and it was in this corner, against the white background, that the Virgin usually appeared to Nancy Fowler. The shelves themselves—three of them, triangular, built into the corner—were said to be representative of the Trinity and to have been constructed according to Jesus' own specifications.

Our guide, the door attendant, spoke, echoed in Spanish by a young female interpreter. "Good evening, everyone. I would like to welcome you to Our Lady's apparition room. Our Lady appears up here in this corner, just above the statue of Our Loving Mother [he gestured toward the three-tiered shelf]. Our Lady tells us that when she appears, there are no walls or roof, so she sees us all as if there were no building here. There are petition baskets in the front of the room, and if you just leave your petitions in there, Our Lady has told us that she reads them all. This evening we will say one decade of the rosary, and then we will spend a few minutes in silent prayer. Then we'll move forward, across [he swept a hand in the direction of the corner shrine], and then out the door. And we will pray the rosary in Spanish."

The group embarked on ten beads of the rosary. *"Dios te salve Maria llena éres de gracia el señor está contigo bendita tú eres entre todas las mujeres y bendito es el fruto de tu vientre Jesus. . . ."* It was not long before the dense cluster of bodies succeeded in raising the temperature in the completely closed room. That, combined with the humidity of a rainy night, the stale smell of pilgrims who had been on the road all day, and my own tendency toward claustrophobia, had me glancing toward the door and sending psychic messages to our host to open a window. He was not picking me up. The decade was concluded with a prayer, in English, known as the Fatima ejaculation: "O my Jesus, forgive us our sins, save us from the fires of hell, and lead all souls to heaven, especially those in most need of thy mercy."

To the right of the apparition corner was a fireplace. Above the mantel was a crucifix, perhaps eighteen inches tall. The corpus was meant to look realistic, and it was a bloody mess. Jesus looked as though he had been pulled from a train wreck and *then* nailed to the cross. Blood streamed from his knees, his feet, his waist, his sides, his armpits, his elbows, his hands, his head. He cast a wan look into the distance, his hips canted to the right, and his knees were bent. A section of the wall behind the crucifix, as in the corner where Mary was said to appear, was white. Sometimes, when Christ came alive and talked to Nancy from this crucifix, she saw scenes flashing on the white wall behind him. Saints appeared and disappeared in rapid succession. Maps of the world materialized, often with particular continents portentously colored red.

The stone hearth beneath the fireplace ran nearly the entire width of the room and was filled with statues (eight of the Virgin herself, one with outstretched stumps—no hands), crucifixes, framed religious pictures, flowers, and thousands of petitions, letters, family snapshots, and other personal items left by devotees. The baskets indicated by the tour guide overflowed with envelopes and small folded pieces of paper. Two large plastic garbage bags were also on the hearth, filled with letters and petitions. Among the personal items placed on the hearth—and adding the final shade of surrealism to the room—was a Ken doll dressed in green and gold priest's vestments.

After five minutes of silence, and with nothing in the room left to breathe but muggy carbon dioxide, we were urged to begin exiting. The crowd made its way around the perimeter, each of us filing past the hearth, the crucifix, and the apparition corner itself before stepping outside.

The weather had done nothing but deteriorate while we were in the apparition room. The drizzle had picked up, and the temperature had continued to drop. I took a long breath, deployed my umbrella, hunched my shoulders against the wind, and walked back to my car, glad to be out of that room. In view of the weather and the darkness, I decided to wait until the next day, and daylight, to see the other end of The Farm—the Holy Hill and Nancy Fowler's home. Before driving out of the parking pasture, I took my mud-caked shoes off and threw them on a plastic bag lying on the passenger-side floor.

About a mile up State Road 138 from The Farm, toward Interstate 20, was a long, squat cinder-block building—JMJ's Religious Gifts, a popular stopping-in point for pilgrims. Before getting on I-20 for the drive back to my motel, I decided to pull in and have a look around. I leaned out of my car door in the gravel parking lot, pulled my cold, muddy running shoes back on, and joined the crowd of dripping shoppers elbowing their way through the narrow aisles in JMJ's.

In addition to a full collection of audio- and videotapes documenting the Conyers phenomenon, JMJ's had hundreds of books (on saints, apparitions, visions, miracles, prophecies), devotional pictures and posters, plastic statues, and a wall of at least fifty train-wreck crucifixes. Another wall was covered with "miraculous" photos posted by pilgrims, photos taken in Conyers and elsewhere, most of them Polaroids. The cap-

tions were written out by hand and tacked beneath the pictures:

Picture of Jesus in sun taken September 13, 1992.

Weeping icon at St. Nicholas Greek Orthodox Church Tar-
pon Springs, FL. The 3 candles appeared after developing
the picture. This happened on another picture of the same
weeping icon.

Padre Pio appeared in this after taking a picture of the
Pope's bible in Rome. Fr. Pio died about 10 years ago.

Taken of clouds on the way to Medjugorje. A man's face
appeared after developed.

2:00pm with sun pulsating. Conyers, GA, December 13,
1993.

At the checkout counter were "It's about Time for Jesus
Christ" digital watches, more statues of saints, rosaries, chaplets, scapulars, religious bookmarks, medals and chains, rosary
rings, small white prayer books of the sort first communicants
used to clamp under the thumbs of their folded hands, and
glow-in-the-dark statues of Mary the color of Key lime pie.
Over the sounds of the shoppers (a burble of crisply voweled
Spanish syllables, tumbling like pebbles in a streambed), a
syrupy hymn played on the store's p.a.; the singer sounded
like Dean Martin, but surely could not be. At the register each
customer was handed a ticket and notified that he was now
automatically entered in a monthly raffle for a large plaster
statue of Mary, an example of which stood atop a nearby shelf.
Photos of previous winners, beaming like Olympic medalists,
were taped to a cabinet beside the cash register.

Back at my motel I washed my shoes in the bathtub, scraping
off chunks of red clay mud that looked like puked dog food,

and hung them over a chair in front of the heater. I had picked up a pizza on my way back to the motel, and I spent the rest of the evening reading devotional literature I had bought at JMJ's. Written and published by believers, the books collected testimonials of Conyers supporters as well as past messages given by Christ and Mary to Nancy Fowler. Also included were stories of purported miraculous cures experienced by Conyers believers ("When they went in to remove part of my colon, they couldn't find cancer anywhere") and two indecipherable documents titled "The Scientific Studies" offered as proofs to satisfy hardheaded empirical types. The author of one of the studies, Dr. Philip Serna Callahan, asked Nancy to hold his "recently invented PICRAM (Photonic Ionic Cloth Radio Amplifier Maser)" in her hands during an apparition. The resulting waveforms on Dr. Callahan's oscilloscope were of a sort that he had never seen "from any living creature before (plants or animals)." The eyewitness accounts of miracles on The Farm were filled with many of the stock elements that have come to be associated with Marian apparitions over the centuries. Statues winked, blinked, cried, glowed, moved, and even bled. Rosaries routinely turned gold-colored. Gold dust fell from the sky. The sun danced, spun, and changed colors. At times the accounts read like pious hagiography from another century. Nancy Fowler was said to have once fasted for forty days, taking no food except the Eucharist. In another account, someone "holding a relic containing a piece of the cross of Jesus Christ" was standing before a crucifix on the Holy Hill when the corpus began to bleed. "It looked as though there was blood on Christ's arms and legs," the woman said. "We could all see this. As we continued to pray we saw a heart form in the sky. Gosh, what a miracle for God to give such a heavenly display for just a few of us. Ann Marie took a picture, and the Blessed Mother came out on the film."

A sign I had seen at The Farm that evening noted that the apparition was scheduled for noon the next day. The only thing I felt sure of seeing was a crowd. In the weeks prior to the trip, I had heard estimates as high as two hundred thousand people. I was certain that was an exaggeration, but I did expect to encounter traffic problems. Pilgrims had been encouraged to arrive as early as possible in the morning to ensure finding a parking place. With that in mind, I hit the bed about ten, vowing to rise early and be on my way before sunrise. Eventually I fell asleep to the late-night sizzle and drone of traffic in rain on nearby I-75.

CHAPTER TWO

✤ ✤ ✤

Our Lady of Light
Cold Spring and Falmouth, Kentucky

Cold Spring

Although it is one of the most popular, Conyers is not—by a stretch—the only site in the country hosting purported apparitions of heavenly persons. In recent years visionaries all over the United States—in New Jersey, Arizona, Florida, Kentucky, Maryland, Ohio, California, Illinois, New York, Texas, Oklahoma, and Pennsylvania, to name a few—have reported visitors from heaven. Claims of other mystical phenomena have also been on the rise: an icon weeps in Brooklyn; a portrait of Jesus is discovered in a plate of spaghetti on a Pizza Hut billboard in Georgia; a soybean oil tank draws crowds in Fostoria, Ohio, thanks to a Jesus-shaped rust spot on its side; an outline of Mary appears on the glass exterior of a newly constructed building in Clearwater, Florida; a young priest in Virginia claims to bear replicas of the wounds of Christ, the stigmata. From wherever you are in the United States, you could probably reach the site of a purported miracle quicker than you could a Waffle House.

The first apparition site I ever visited was one of two regionally popular spots within a half-hour's drive of my Cincinnati home. Two months before my trip to Conyers, I joined a crowd of 8,500 in the parking lot of Saint Joseph Church in Cold Spring, Kentucky, a bedroom community six miles south of Cincinnati. The crowd was waiting for an appearance of the Virgin.

An unnamed seer living in a small town east of Cincinnati first predicted Mary's appearance at Saint Joseph Church two years prior to my visit. Crowds assembled on the night of the first predicted appearance (August 31, 1992), on the first anniversary, and again on the second, the night I attended. On the first two occasions believers claimed to have seen mysterious lights and taken photographs of heavenly beings.

Cold Spring is the kind of suburb that can escape your attention even as you drive through it, stretched out as it is in succession with several other communities of similar size along a busy corridor leading to a large city. The town parentheses—the "Welcome to Cold Spring" and the "Thank you for visiting Cold Spring" signs—are literally blocks apart. Saint Joseph Church sits uneasily on this major artery amid an inflorescence of restaurants, gas stations, and other commercial enterprises—Tan-a-Rama, Tire Discounters, Country Goose Concrete Figurines, Gold-N-Tan, Buckskin Bev's Cattle Company, Kmart.

Mary was a night owl at Cold Spring. She habitually arrived at midnight. Her coming was announced, it was said, by a brilliant display of lights and other unusual phenomena, including the scent of roses, peculiar effects in the sky, and sightings of the Virgin herself in the trees, on the side of the church, and atop the church's bell tower. Pilgrims I met early that evening predicted I would be astonished come midnight. "It's not light like you know it," one returning visitor, an elderly woman accompanied hand in hand by her even more elderly sister, told me. "It has to be from heaven. It's not man-made, there's no way. You know what flashes look like from cameras; it's not that kind of light. Stick around and you will see. I guarantee you." Her sister nodded in agreement.

This being my first experience with this kind of talk, I was optimistic. Sure, the sisters might be overstating the case, but if whatever was coming at midnight was a fraction as striking as these women remembered it, I might be in for something extraordinary, maybe even inexplicable.

It was a warm summer night. The crowd at Saint Joseph covered the large parking lot with lawn chairs, blankets, coolers, sleeping bags—looking for all the world like a fireworks crowd. Babies slept in portable playpens; teens (some with rosaries around their necks or religious jewelry dangling, one in a Nine Inch Nails T-shirt) hung out with each other or did homework; adults talked, prayed, were shriven by one of the dozen or so priests arrayed on a grassy courtyard serving as a makeshift confessional, swapped stories of miraculous experiences at other apparition sites, and looked through photo albums and stacks of snapshots.

The purportedly miraculous photos taken at apparition sites around the country and shared with great relish at these gatherings are, for many of the faithful, the proofs that establish and support the genuineness of the apparitions. Believers claim to see, in certain of these pictures, miraculous images of religious significance—saints, angels, the "golden door" to heaven, Christ, Mary, even Satan. They are pored over wonderingly and, in great measure, uncritically. All over the Saint Joseph parking lot, small knots of pilgrims gathered around others who were displaying and interpreting their photographs.

A pretty, dark-haired young woman in a bright red-and-blue-print dress shared her photo album with a circle of appreciative onlookers.

"This was taken here. I'm sure ya'll have seen this one." She showed an image photographed on this same parking lot the previous year. It was shot across the crowd after dark; a bright white streak blurred across the middle of the picture. With a little imagination, the streak could be a phantomish Mary floating from left to right, but could, with a notch less imagination, be a white handkerchief waving in front of the camera. She flipped to the next photo. "This is the light that came down off of the cross; this was taken in Conyers." Next: "The flight out of Egypt, the Blessed Mother on a donkey."

This was the first of many pictures I saw that night purportedly taken by pointing a camera into a cloudy sky. Once developed, the pictures seemed to show recognizable figures in the clouds. This particular cloud image showed Mary—in astonishingly clear silhouette—riding on a donkey with a baby in her arms. The woman ended by telling us, breathlessly, that every morning flowers fall from an otherwise clear sky, covering her backyard.

Another young woman stepped up to take over—this one short and heavy, her blond hair hanging down in long, uncombed strings, a large wooden crucifix suspended from a leather strap around her neck. She produced a photograph. This image, too, was taken in the Saint Joseph parking lot at a past apparition. It was another shot across the lot after dark, showing two streaks of yellow and red light twisting together about six feet off the ground. The effect was of the sort produced by moving lights photographed with a long exposure.

"This is here, August thirty-first, 1992. It's serpents over the crowd," she said, speaking rapidly in a Kentucky accent.

"What do you think it means?" I asked.

"That's Satan. Wherever Mary and Jesus are, Satan's also there, tryin' to, you know, distract people and that. And usually he'll appear among some of the pictures in these apparition sites and that."

I asked her if the presence of the devil himself scared her.

"No, because Jesus is more powerful than the devil, so if you cast it out in the name of Jesus, you don't have nothin' to worry about, you know, he can't harm you. He can aggravate you or taunt you, but he can't harm you." She brought out another picture. "I took this at Conyers, Georgia, in the apparition room, of a picture of Christ." It was indeed a photograph of a picture of Jesus. The image was obscured, though, by large blurred patches of red and white.

"What do you think caused those blurred colors?" I asked.

"Jesus of mercy," she explained patiently. "That's his mercy, the red and white rays."

She had more, but she had led with her big guns, and the drama of the pictures waned as she proceeded. One was a shot taken from outside the apparition room on the farm at Conyers. She pointed to a spot of glare on a window and asked if I saw an image of the pope kneeling. The glare could, I allow, be construed as a vaguely John Paul II–shaped blob of light. "OK," I said. Another had been taken of a statue inside Saint Joseph Church the previous year; a suspiciously finger-shaped white lump intruded into the left-hand side of the frame. "Hmm," was all I could think to say. The awkward denouement having petered out, she restacked her pictures and headed off in search of a fresh audience.

A string of volunteers in white T-shirts and "Hello My Name is—" stickers had stretched across one side of the parking lot and were leading the gathered faithful, at least those close enough to hear them, in praying the rosary. Those near the back of the crowd were less organized and coalesced into smaller groups to chat or pray.

The flattening sun neared the horizon; some of the pilgrims squinted at it, their eyes shaded by a handmade visor in an arrested salute. Some claimed to see a rainbow forming around the setting sun. A few took pictures of it.

"How can you do that?" I asked one woman who was staring skyward.

"Just look at it," she said. "Just go ahead and look at it. It doesn't hurt."

I tried it for a few seconds. Just before my eyes were overcome by a deep, you'd-better-stop-now pain, I had seen past the initial harsh glare and perceived the sun as a two-dimensional ovoid disk that oscillated slightly thanks to the fact that my gaze refused to settle on it fully. Nothing more.

A crowd had gathered around yet another woman showing

photographs. Probably in her late forties, her hair was blond, shoulder-length, sprayed stiff. In blue slacks and a bright orange blazer, she looked like a real estate agent. Her speech was animated and well rehearsed, and she seemed to be enjoying the attention. She began by showing the crowd a rosary that she claimed had turned to gold. Next she produced an oversize laminated photograph in which a clear image of Jesus' face could be seen in the clouds. The crowd pressed in.

A man next to the woman momentarily vexed her by producing, from his wallet, his own photo of Jesus in a cloud. Visibly ruffled but undaunted, the woman pressed on, drawing the crowd back to her portfolio, nudging her volume up.

"OK, that picture was taken into the sky in Conyers, Georgia." She moved on to the next photo, also enlarged and laminated. "This is my most awesome picture I've taken so far. This was taken on Mother's Day this past May eighth at Falmouth." It was Mary in the clouds, looking precisely like a statue floating in midair. The crowd oohed. "Mary shows up for me as little statues in the sky," she explained. "She showed up for me in *Hawaii*; everywhere I go, I take pictures, she shows up." Next she produced a copy of a photo I had already seen, the wispy white blur crossing the parking lot. "This was taken two years ago back at that grotto." A grotto with a three-quarter-size statue of Mary stands at the back of the Saint Joseph parking lot. "And today," she continued, slowing down as her listeners leaned in, "a child saw the baby Jesus in Mary's arms."

An astonished woman in the crowd: "Back there?"

"Yes. Back there. Today. This afternoon. The child said, 'Mommy, don't you see the baby Jesus?' " A chorus of ahs rose from the women gathered around.

Next was a picture of a hotdog-shaped smear of white cutting across a night scene. "Now, this is something you might see tonight. We call them laser beams. They just flop all over the place. In the trees, in the sky. Maybe it's energy, maybe it's the Holy Spirit. I really don't know what it is. We've never really determined what it is."

The phenomena of the pictures baffles me, I admit, but not for the reasons most believers would assume. Though many of the photos can probably be explained as natural effects resulting from the interaction of light and lenses, refraction and reflection, many others are filled with realistic details too obvious to be explained as unintentional tricks of lighting. I have seen photos of Jesus in the clouds—and Mary and various other saints—that were as clear as mug shots. But I have not seen any photographic evidence of purported miracles that could not have been produced by either airbrush enhancement, computer manipulation, or simple double exposure. Many of them do, in fact, look like clumsy double exposures of statues and clouds. These photos are troublesome, because barring any supernatural explanation (and I refuse to believe miracle-essence would be squandered on such ham-handed, cheesy, and inconclusive effects), the only alternative is that they are being faked and passed off to devotees as genuine. It seems unlikely that consumers accustomed to seeing age-enhanced photos of Elvis and animal heads grafted onto babies' bodies ("Birth of World's Ugliest Baby Scares Father to Death!") in grocery store tabloids would so readily ignore the possibility of photographic fakery in favor of a miraculous explanation, but they do.

A crowd had been building at the confessional courtyard all evening. Fifty or sixty people waited in a line stretching the length of the courtyard behind the church. Volunteers directed penitents to priests as slots became available. I joined the line and fell into conversation with a smallish middle-aged man who looked up at me from beneath jutting black eyebrows. In slightly manic Brooklynese, he told me of his own personal miracle.

"My mother is kind of the reason I'm here, you could say. When she died she had the stigma of the rosary around her neck. My father called me into the room where my mother was laying. He said, 'Look around your mother's neck.' I said, 'Oh, yeah, she's got her rosary around her neck.' He said, 'No, look closer.' When I got close, I could see that it wasn't her rosary. It was the shape of a rosary in little blue welts under her skin going around her neck. There were groups of ten little welts and then bigger ones for the Our Fathers. And then there was the little straight part, three Hail Marys and two Our Fathers, but there was no cross at the end."

He stopped talking and looked at me for a few seconds before continuing.

"I think that was Our Lady's way of thanking her for leading a saintly life. When my sister and I were looking at her when she was first laid out at the funeral home, the welts were still there. We stood there looking at them, and all of a sudden they got bigger and bigger and then they were [here, a splaying "poof!" gesture with both hands] gone. They just disappeared. Within about ten seconds."

My eyebrows must have jumped toward my hairline.

"Oh, yeah," he insisted. "It's true. My mother was a saint. I'm doing all this for her. She had cancer, but they didn't find it until it had almost killed her and she was in tremendous pain. The doctors said they could give her some medicine that would help with her pain, but she said no, she'd rather offer up her suffering for the poor souls in purgatory. You don't hear about anybody offering up suffering or pain anymore these days. You don't even hear about purgatory. My mother was a good woman. A saint."

I had joined the line to talk to pilgrims, not intending to stick with it all the way to a confessor, but the longer I inched forward with those waiting to air their transgressions, the less I felt like leaving the queue. I eventually found myself detailing my faults to a young, red-faced priest on the lawn and receiving absolution. Afterward, confession's typical effect, a noticeable spring in the soul's step, lightened my heart, and I sat on the stone stair of a school building at the back of the property, watching the crowd and enjoying the all-too-transient clean-scrubbed feeling. A group of children had taken to tumbling down a grassy hill next to the parking lot, near where I sat; they tucked their arms close to their sides and rolled down like logs, giggling all the way. Others bounded through knee-high weeds, chasing grasshoppers.

By eleven-fifteen the crowd had settled into a mood of quiet expectancy. Several separate groups were saying rosaries and singing Marian hymns. Sleeping children were strewn around the parking lot on blankets, in tents, in playpens. Restless toddlers were slung across weary parents' shoulders. I didn't know what I expected to see or feel come midnight. I knew I was not the same sort of Catholic as these believers, yet I was sympathetic to their hopefulness and found myself wishing very much, for their sake and for mine, that something unbelievable would happen.

At half past eleven, a priest, Father Leroy Smith, the former pastor at Saint Joseph, arrived in the side yard of the church to lead the assembly in the rosary. It was Father Smith who had first received word from the anonymous visionary that Mary had selected his parish for an earthly visit two years before. The crowd shifted in Father Smith's direction and thickened in the yard and along the edge of the parking lot beside it.

The rosary was irritatingly slow; I could not hear Father Smith as he led the prayers, but those near the front could, and the crowd followed their lead in reciting the responses to each of the prayers. They were throwing in a lot of extra petitions and songs that I was, at that point, unfamiliar with. One of the songs, a short version of "Ave Maria," was sung at the end of each set of ten Hail Marys. The acoustical context—8,500 people singing in an asphalt lot under the open sky—was unique in my experience; the sound was big and echoless and oddly moving.

As midnight and Mary's anticipated arrival approached, all eyes were on the church, the bell tower, and the trees in the yard. The rosary lasted until just before twelve, when Father Smith ended the prayers and stepped slowly backward up the slight incline of the yard toward the church. We stood, watching and waiting. An old-style Marian hymn—"Immaculate Mary"—was begun in a far-flung section of the crowd; it rolled on for a verse or two before dying out. I looked at my watch: midnight on the button. The crowd pressed forward a step, then fell silent, the rhythmic trilling of crickets emerging from the background. Camera flashes began firing out of the crowd, slowly at first and then faster, until they seemed to be flashing almost continuously, strobing the side of the church and the trees in the yard. Out of this sparkling stillness, a woman beside me spoke. "It's starting," she said.

A chorus of "Ave Maria" arose, as if spontaneously, from a section of the crowd near me. It caught on and wafted toward the rear sections. The flashes continued. I could not, and never did, see anything extraordinary beyond the rapid expenditure of what had to be thousands of flashbulbs.

I worked my way from the parking lot up into the side yard of the church through the press of believers and toward a banner of Mary that had been standing in the yard all evening. Pilgrims crowded around the banner (a life-size picture of Mary, standing on a cloud with stars around her head, on a blue background trimmed in gold), reaching out to touch it and taking pictures of the camera flashes lighting it up. As the banner was periodically illuminated, they exclaimed:

There, it's flashing, but you can never see where it's coming from. It's not coming from the sky.

The lights around the banner are just going *crazy*.

Well, that's "Our Lady of Light"! The banner's called that!

A woman who had stepped behind the banner to help brace it against the crush of devotees declared, "There's no lights attached. Mary's doin' it. We're just holdin' it up."

Another woman near me drew in a deep breath, smiled, and declared, "Mmmm, roses!"

Falmouth

Two months before the first predicted appearance of the Virgin at Saint Joseph Church (but, worth noting, after the prediction itself), another visionary, a Cold Spring housewife known only as Sandy, began hearing Mary's voice. She started dreaming of Mary and eventually received both apparitions and messages. In October 1993, according to Sandy, the Virgin led her to a farm in the middle of Kentucky tobacco country thirty miles south of Cold Spring, near a town called Falmouth. Sandy's visions occurred on the eighth of every month at the farm, which was purchased for the purpose and was supported by an organization of volunteers called the Our Lady of Light Foundation.

Eight days after spending the evening at Saint Joseph Church in Cold Spring, I drove to Falmouth on a clear, warm September morning to witness an apparition. It was the feast day of the birth of Mary, as celebrated by the Catholic Church. After thirty minutes on a four-lane highway, I turned onto a country road and drove the next five miles winding through corn and tobacco farms. The fence lines and side yards were alight with wildflowers—Queen Anne's lace, white snakeroot, goldenrod, fantastically violet tall ironweed. Some thistle was in bloom, but much of it had gone to seed and was standing tall, brown, dry, and spiky. Tobacco was still in the fields, but some had already been cut and hung in black, open-ended barns. The land is hilly, and from the tops of some rises, yellowing acres of tobacco looked like thick quilts thrown over distant hilltops.

The Falmouth farm was marked by a sign in front of a leaning gray farmhouse: "Our Lady's Farm. Our Lady of the Most Holy Rosary." Next to the farmhouse, a gravel road led into the farm, past a Dumpster, past a dozen Porta Pottis.

Behind the farmhouse new arrivals, lugging coolers and lawn chairs, stepped out of buses and walked in a line along the gravel road toward the apparition "grotto."

There had been some development of the ninety-nine-acre Falmouth farm as a devotional site. A set of stations of the cross led down one hillside, culminating in a life-size Calvary tableau. The day I was there, smiling couples posed before the crucifix to have their pictures taken by friends. The apparitions occurred on a point of high ground referred to as the grotto (strictly out of pietistic convention—there was not a cave or cavern in sight) in front of a life-size statue of Mary. As in Conyers, Mary arrived near midday and conveyed her message to Sandy, who wrote it down before relaying it to the audience.

But for the incessant prayers and Marian hymns playing over a p.a. system of sufficient wattage to serve a baseball park, the Falmouth farm would be a peaceful place. It's perched high among serene hills. Hawks occasionally appeared, scanning the fields and yards for a meal. Farmers could be seen at work on the surrounding landscape that is at once their home and their industry.

Standing near the crucifix, I overheard a conversation about a miraculous photograph and joined a small cluster of pilgrims to have a look. A young man, a probable middle manager dressed like a golfer, said he had just taken the picture with his Polaroid, that he had heard a voice telling him to. The photo was of the sky, and it was lit in the middle by a glowing rectangular doorway; an aura of light spilled out around the edges of the door. This was the first photo I had seen of the purported "golden door" to heaven, but I would see many more that day and over the next year. In these photos, and they're all similar, the door shape takes up fully a third of the area of the picture, and its top and bottom edges are slightly convex. Believers claim the golden door is the same door mentioned in Revelation 4:1—"After this I looked, and lo, in heaven an open door!" The phenomenon only occurs, according to the faithful, with Polaroid cameras. The technique for "getting doors" is to point your camera at the sun and snap away. If you don't get one on the first try, snap another one. A woman nearby showed me a golden door photo she had just taken. While I stood next to her, she shot another into the clear blue sky. When the second picture developed, there was no door. "There," she said, "that proves it. The first one was for real."

In his book *Looking for a Miracle*, Joe Nickell reports on an experiment conducted by a group of spoilsport empiricists known as the Georgia Skeptics. They achieved the "golden door" phenomenon by pointing their camera—also a Polaroid—at a bright light. Afterward, they took the camera apart and discovered that its aperture is, yes, golden-door shaped. Apparently, shooting the camera straight into a light source causes reflections to carom around inside the camera and occasionally catch the illumined outline of the aperture on film.

The man who had shown me the first door picture said there was a shape resembling Mary off to one side of the door. I looked but could not make it out. He also said that while he himself had not been in Cold Spring for the apparition at Saint Joseph Church eight days earlier, he had been told by someone who had been there that at midnight it was completely still except for one large tree thrashing around. Someone took a picture of it, and in the photo the tree had turned to gold.

I walked up the hill past the stations of the cross. Near the grotto a woman sat on the ground with her legs curled to one side, staring intently at a small crucifix lying on the grass in front of her. The cross was of brown wood, about a foot tall, with a gold-colored plastic corpus attached. I asked if she had a minute to talk. "If I can . . . I'm in shock right now," she said in a quavering voice. "This cross just turned gold." She looked to be in her late forties, and her hair was dyed platinum blond. Her moist eyes were opened wide behind thick lenses and seemed to focus somewhere beyond me when she looked in my direction. There was a skittishness in her manner that at times seemed like worry, at times like confusion. As our conversation progressed, it became obvious she had a great need to talk about her experiences, but her delivery suggested at least the possibility of creeping doubt—perhaps a fear that if she stopped talking about the miracles they might stop happening, or she might stop believing in them.

"It's an old cross," she began. "It was a wedding gift in 1966. It was totally silver, and last night I was trying to see what to bring down—I always bring something for someone else, to have blessed for them or whatever. And this was in the back of my closet, forgot I had it, don't even know how I saw it, and I had this . . . you know, *prompting* to bring it. I thought, 'OK,' and I hid it in the bottom of my bag. And I was just showing people some pictures, and I took everything out of the purse, and the whole cross . . . it's gold . . . it was totally silver. I had not taken it out of the bag yet today; it was in the bottom of the bag."

I asked if things like that had happened to her before.

"Over at Cold Spring last Wednesday night, this rosary [she pulled out a handful of dull brass-colored beads], when I walked in the church at ten after nine, was completely silver, completely silver. And it turned gold. My mom and dad just died not that long ago, and I asked for a sign. I knelt in front of the statue of grace—Our Lady of Grace—said some prayers, took some pictures, went to the Sorrowful Mother, the pietà, and I touched the statue with this rosary in my hand. I wasn't even looking at it; it was like that [she closed a fist around the rosary]. I touched the statue and I went to leave and I opened up and looked, and a totally silver rosary had turned gold."

I asked whether she had seen anything else miraculous the previous week in Cold Spring. "Oh, yeah, the lights. I mean the lights at midnight, oh yes, yes, the lights. I'm not talking about flashcubes, you know. And then the one tree, the entire tree just . . . *shimmered*; it stayed lit, it was just lit and lit the whole time. Now, last summer when I was there, the lights just went everywhere—through the crowd, into the church, they were jagged, they were zigzag, they were just everywhere. It was not like any earthly lights you've ever seen. And last summer when I was there, after the lights left, someone said, 'Look.' I looked up into a tree, and it looked just like someone had put a statue of the Blessed Mother in the tree. I was too far away to see her face or her hands, but I saw her. Then she disappeared and the lights came back. That was the summer of '93. Also, the statue in the grotto, tears ran down the left cheek. I watched the tears run down. Now, this year they said inside the church that the statue of the Sorrowful Mother was crying off and on during the day. That's where this rosary turned gold."

I asked what she thought all this supernatural activity meant, why it was happening.

"The Blessed Mother's trying to bring everybody back to God. She's trying to bring people back to Jesus. The world is in such a mess. And she says time's short, look around, look at the signs. She says, 'I'm your Heavenly Mother, I'm here to help you. I will pray for you, I will intercede. But come back to the Father, come back to God.' And she just loves us all very much and wants us to come back to Christ. Just pray, pray like she says, pray, pray, pray and fast. I know—I've got two sons, they're twenty-five and twenty-six, they're atheists, they're killin' each other, they're making suicide attempts, the one's in drugs. The world's a mess, you don't need to turn on the news to see that. Just live it."

The longer she spoke, the more the trend of the conversation seemed to agitate her, so I said I had to move on.

"Thank you for your time," I said.

"Thank *you*," she said. "I'm getting more overwhelmed by the minute. You just caught me at a bad time. Time's runnin' out . . ."

She stuck for a second, blinked, looked past me, then looked back.

". . . and I can't think. I can't talk. All I can tell you is . . ."

Instead of finishing the thought, she shook her head and began packing things back into her large handbag. I thanked her again and left her alone.

By one o'clock most of the crowd, somewhere between five and ten thousand people, had collected around the grotto. An area in front of the statue of Mary had been cordoned off, reserved for Sandy, a close circle of followers, and visiting priests and nuns. At one-thirty, Father Leroy Smith—the same Father Smith who had led the rosary at Saint Joseph the week before, but whom I had neither seen nor heard clearly that night—stood before the statue, microphone in hand, and addressed the crowd. He is of average height and build, and his face is freckled but serious-looking. A natural orator, Father Smith's voice cuts cleanly through a crowd. He speaks in a grave, loping meter—a rhythm that sounds considered and thoughtful but which may be little more than habit from years of having to sound considered and thoughtful on deadline. His voice is deeply pitched and gravelly, and his words are delivered in discrete phrasal units, like little packages.

"I'd like to welcome all of you this afternoon to Our Lady's birthday party. She definitely will be with us, as she is always. . . ."

After some introductory remarks Father Smith led the crowd through a rendition of "On This Day, O Beautiful Mother." At its completion he spoke again, filling us in on the afternoon's agenda. We were to begin by praying the rosary, during which Mary would make her appearance and impart a message to the visionary. When the prayers were completed, Sandy would write out the message and read it to the gathered faithful. A variety of litanies, prayers, and songs

would follow, capped by the singing of "Happy Birthday" to
Mary.

"As we begin our rosary," Father Smith said, "let us do
so in the name of the Father, and of the Son, and of the Holy
Spirit, amen."

Two women near me, both with white hair and alert,
ready-for-anything expressions, watched a butterfly as it
darted above the crowd in front of them.

"There's Mary's sign," said one. "A butterfly's Mary's
sign. Did you see that?"

"Take a deep breath," said the other, closing her eyes and
smiling. "Do you smell it? Roses." Her friend sniffed and
smiled too.

"Mmmm. Yeah," she said. "She's coming."

After the first section of the rosary, Father Smith handed
off the duty of leading the prayers to the visionary. Sandy is
petite, with shoulder-length, frosted hair. In her late forties,
she is trim and conventionally pretty. That day she wore a
simple purple cotton pullover shirt and pleated khaki slacks;
dark red-framed sunglasses hid her eyes. She knelt on a
wooden kneeler with her head bowed slightly as she prayed
into the microphone.

Midway through her portion of the rosary, in the middle
of a Hail Mary, Sandy suddenly stopped short. She remained
kneeling, motionless, her rosary swaying slightly in her hands
and her gaze directed upward into the harshly bright blue sky.
She smiled serenely. There was a shuffle and some squeaking
of lawn chairs as some in the crowd came to their feet—then
silence, the first real silence I had heard on the Falmouth farm
all day. From somewhere across the crowd a child whined,
probably hot and tired. Pilgrims lifted their cameras and
snapped away at the clear sky. Some without cameras made
fists and looked through the thumb end of this handmade
aperture toward the sun. One woman squinted at the sun
through the mesh weave of a cheap baseball hat. Father Smith

broke in: "Let us welcome Our Lady to her farm this afternoon, on this, her birthday."

The silence resumed and continued for three or four minutes, during which one elderly woman seated on a blanket near me grew faint from the heat, passed out, and was eventually revived, after the application of water-soaked compresses and a sweating cold can of Sprite held to her forehead, by an orange-vested member of the medical emergency team.

Suddenly, Sandy, reverberating off the neighboring hillsides via the p.a., took up her prayer where she had left off. As the rosary progressed, I walked around the perimeter of the crowd. The heat, particularly unforgiving on top of this treeless hill, had surprised most of us, and was obviously making a lot of the older folks seriously uncomfortable. Later in the rosary, I watched as another woman, probably in her seventies and looking unnaturally pale, was lowered from her chair onto the ground, laid flat by a medical volunteer, and made to rest with a cold rag on her forehead. She had been seated beneath an open-air tent set up next to the grotto and reserved for the elderly and infirm. Many under that tent were in wheelchairs, and some had been brought in on conveyances that looked like hospital gurneys. One severely handicapped young man was pitched back in a special reclining wheelchair. A woman I took to be his mother attended to him, intermittently using a green rubber tube and a handheld pump to suction something from his throat. Each time she finished, she picked up her rosary in one hand and held her boy's hand tightly in the other.

When the rosary was completed, Sandy took her seat and, with one knee crossed over the other and in no apparent hurry, wrote in a spiral-bound notebook. As she wrote, the crowd sang "Immaculate Mary." After that some prerecorded New Agey music was piped over the intercom while everyone waited to hear the message.

When Sandy had finished writing, she read calmly from her

notes, taking pains to enunciate clearly. As she progressed, though, her speech grew more halting and assumed a languorous cadence, as if she were speaking out of a dream.

"I first would like to give you a little description of what I experienced here today," she began. "I know I was in the middle of saying the decade of the rosary. I was distracted . . . I don't know if that's the word to use [short, dry laugh], but I heard a sound. I've heard this before. It's like a musical, heralding-type sound from off in space. Then I looked up, and I saw a brightness . . . and she started to appear through this brightness."

Mary had come, Sandy said, to show "an everlasting love from my Immaculate Heart and from my Son's most precious Sacred Heart" and to ask that her children unite with those two hearts in love, put aside their differences, and "allow God's love to shine through you at all times." She urged our prayers for world leaders and dispensed a general blessing before departing.

"Go with peace in your hearts," she had said. "I am Mary, the Lady of the Most Holy Rosary."

Sandy finished reading and sat back in her chair. After a quiet moment Father Smith picked up the microphone and again broke the silence with his low croak: "Thank you, dear Mary, for that beautiful message of hope, of love, and of concern for one another. It is so important for us to unite, to unite with Christ, to be ever close to him and recognize that in our unity we will bring others close to you. Let us offer now Our Lady's litany for the consecration of all hearts to the Immaculate Heart of Mary and for the reparation and elimination of the terrible evil in our society of abortion. 'Lord, have mercy on us. . . .' "

Here, Father Smith began a prayer which, in its present form, dates from the sixteenth century but which had its beginnings in the Dark Ages. It is an invocation of the Holy Trinity followed by a series of petitions enumerated by the priest and answered by the crowd. In the Litany of the Blessed

Virgin Mary, the petitions consist of fifty names or honorific titles given to Mary, to each of which the crowd responds, "Pray for us." The names of Mary in the litany include Mother of divine grace, Mother undefiled, Virgin most venerable, Virgin most renowned, Queen of angels, Mirror of justice, Vessel of honor, Mystical rose, Tower of David, Gate of heaven, and Ark of the covenant.

By the time the litany was complete and Father Smith struck up "Happy Birthday," many devotees were already back in their cars, their air conditioners switched to high and sucking for wind like jet engines.

I stuck around for the end of "Happy Birthday," then got back in my car and joined the line of traffic snaking slowly out of the parking area. On my way down the gravel drive leaving the farm, I had a semi-mystical experience of my own. The visionary, Sandy, was emerging from beneath the tent sheltering the elderly and handicapped. As I watched her step from the shadow of the tent into the light, one of the most powerful apprehensions of déjà vu I have ever experienced surged up from my subconscious and shimmered over my memory like heat lightning. Something about Sandy's emergence—the transition from dark to light—turned over in my mind a fragment of a dream, a dream in which I was at an apparition event and someone was pointing the seer out to me as she stepped from some sort of shelter into daylight. "There's the visionary . . ." someone in my dream had said.

CHAPTER THREE

❖ ❖ ❖

A Date with a Virgin

Conyers, Georgia, Day Two

On Wednesday, March 26, 1399, the Virgin appeared to a Spanish shepherd named Pedro, conveying to him her desire that a Benedictine monastery be built on the spot. She left him with a list of messages, instructing him to pass them along to the authorities in his village, threatening punishment if he dare disobey. Fearing he would not be believed, Pedro told no one. Four nights later, Mary returned and appeared at Pedro's bedside with two men dressed as monks. At the Virgin's direction, one of the monks yanked Pedro from his bed while the other beat him with a belt.

Early on apparition morning in Conyers, I left my motel bed only slightly less reluctantly than Pedro. It was dark and I could hear the rain still falling; the traffic on I-75 heading toward Atlanta sounded thick. Soon enough I was out in it, chewing on a cold bagel, car stereo throbbing. The forty-minute drive from my motel to The Farm took me first north toward Atlanta, then east along the loop, then shot me out again to the southeast. On every side grim-faced commuters clutched their steering wheels, cars pointed into the city, lurching toward work. The red taillights ahead, bleary from the rain on my windshield, rippled back to me, on again, off again, in waves. I spied a lone man walking along the berm, umbrella-less in the rain with a suitcase in his hand, heading away from Atlanta.

Five miles from The Farm, I pulled off at a McDonald's for coffee. In a lot behind the restaurant, several tour buses idled noisily. Inside, a small throng of pilgrims had invaded, mainly, it appeared, to use the rest rooms. The line to the women's room stretched from the back of the restaurant to the front counter. The men's room was running at full capacity too, but with a quicker turnover. Inside the rest room, several rumpled middle-aged men, most of whom looked as though they had spent the night in their cars, crowded around the sink—brushing teeth, combing hair, and washing faces.

Outside, the sky was beginning to lighten, but with a hundred percent chance of rain, it would not progress much beyond a pearly gray. Coffee in hand, I drove the rest of the way to The Farm. With a mile or two left, traffic began to thicken and drift into the left turn lane, where it was a very slow stop and go. A sign on the side of the road read "Pilgrim info, tune to 99.9 FM." I tried but could not find the station. At the corner of the road leading up to The Farm, a brown Rockdale sheriff squad car was parked in typical cop fashion, angled with pointed nonchalance out into the highway, its blue lights pulsing. Deputies directed us into a field across the road from Nancy Fowler's farm, where volunteers in orange mesh vests pointed us to our final parking destination, the far edge of a horse pasture. I gathered my things, threw another bagel and a soft drink into my pack, opened my umbrella, and headed off across the pasture. I passed a muddy corral holding the five horses our cars had displaced for the day; they were milling around in the muck, backing up nervously, shoving into each other.

Before I had made it out of the pasture and across the street to The Farm, I passed a half-dozen slotted wooden boxes set on poles and marked for donations. Also out in the middle of the pasture was a booth set up and staffed by members of

Our Loving Mother's Children (the organization of Conyers volunteers) selling copies of *To Bear Witness That I Am the Living Son of God*, which, in two volumes, offered transcripts of many of the messages Nancy Fowler had received from heaven over the past four years. A sign in front of the booth advertised, "BOOKS, LIBROS, BOOKS."

I fell into a slow-moving line heading down a mud path and across the road to The Farm. Along the path we passed a large wood and wire cage holding one white dove. A little farther along was a grotto set on the edge of a small wood. Within the grotto a life-size statue of Mary, identified as "Our Lady Queen of Peace," was surrounded by flowers, and a rosary and a scapular had been draped over her hands. Two signs were stuck in the ground at the statue's feet: "Whoever dies wearing this scapular shall not suffer eternal fire" and "The soul which recommends itself to me in the recitation of the rosary shall not perish." After a left turn at the grotto, the path shortly deposited us in Nancy Fowler's backyard, known to the faithful as the Holy Hill.

The Holy Hill was distinguished by three primary features: another life-size statue of Mary, a well offering purportedly miraculous water, and a larger-than-life crucifix bearing a giant wooden Christ. At the foot of the crucifix was a stone altar in the shape of a cross lying flat on the ground. A group was gathered around the foot of the crucifix, reciting the rosary and pressing forward to get near the feet of the corpus, reaching up and over each other to touch it with hands, rosaries, crosses. The triangular space between Jesus' crossed ankles and the cross had been stuffed full of letters and petitions.

The stone altar beneath the cross was overflowing with devotional items and envelopes and folded papers left by pilgrims. Many photographs had been laid on the altar—a couple at the beach, a boy on a pony, graduation pictures. There were also gallon jugs of water drawn from the well, crucifixes, candles, rosaries, brown and green scapulars, medals, chaplets, baskets of flowers, a statue of Jesus knocking at a door, many small statues of angels and of Mary, lit votive candles, stone doves, wildflowers, cut flowers wrapped in newspaper, a Spanish edition of *The Imitation of Christ*, a gray bust of Jesus, a thirty-inch white statue of Jesus pointing to his heart on the outside of his chest, money (I counted about fifty dollars in ones and fives), a jar of Pompeiian Extra Light Olive Oil, an umbrella, a baseball cap, and a pack of low-tar cigarettes. Many of the faithful were kneeling around the edge of the altar, their faces tight with prayer.

On the other side of the yard, a crowd of umbrella-clutching and plastic-covered believers surrounded the statue of Mary. This statue represented the Virgin as she is believed to have appeared to the shepherd children in Fatima, Portugal. Her hands were folded in front of her chest as if in prayer, fingertips pointing heavenward, her head inclined slightly to the left and downward. An oversize wooden rosary was draped over the statue's folded hands, and a garland of pink flowers had been placed on her head. The crowd around her prayed the rosary quietly. Some moved forward to touch the statue with their hands and rosaries; some stroked the statue, crying, their expressions screwed into pink, sorrowing grimaces. The literature on the Conyers phenomenon suggests that miracles have been associated with most of the statues and other trappings here on Holy Hill. This statue of Mary, according to believers, sometimes assumes a lifelike quality, the white plaster skin becoming pinkish, the facial features becoming more defined and realistic.

Many people walked around toting two or more plastic milk jugs filled with well water. The well is said to have been blessed by Christ, and many claim to have experienced the healing properties of the water. This sign was posted near the well:

BLESSED WELL WATER. Jesus said, "Let all who come drink of my water."—1/5/93. Jesus said, "Draw the Holy Water

from the well to bless your families and homes."—1/15/91.
If there is a line, one gallon limit please.

The line waiting to draw from the well remained constant at
about fifty people all day long. The well itself was capped, and
water was being drawn from spigots placed around its perimeter and from a drinking fountain attached at one end.

The Farm was crawling with volunteers in Day-Glo orange
mesh vests, most of them directing foot traffic around particularly viscid mud holes. I stopped to talk to one volunteer as
he manned his post and handed out "miraculous" medals.
His name was Bob. In his mid-forties, with gray eyes and
a closely trimmed mustache, he was tall and aggressively
healthy-looking; he wore jeans and a brown bomber jacket
beneath his orange vest. Before telling me his story, which he
did affably and easily, he handed me a Miraculous Medal. I
asked him if he had been there before and whether he had
seen miracles.

"This is my third visit; I was here in November and March.
When I first came in November, the moment when they said
Our Lady was coming, everybody looked up at the sun; you
could look right into it. And it was just a whirling mass of
reddish orange, gold, and yellow, just swirling around." His
hands came up, making a swirling movement. "And a gray
area started to come out from it, a light gray area, concentric.
It spread out just like an umbrella. And then a rainbow started
to appear. Not an arc—the rainbow was all the way around
the outside of the gray area. The sky stayed like that for thirty-
five minutes, roughly, while the whole apparition took place.
When it was announced that the Blessed Mother was leaving,
the rainbow started to fade and the whole thing started to
come back in, and the moment they said she was gone, you
couldn't look at the sun again; it was very bright. When I was
here in March, they announced that Nancy saw a red light
coming across the ceiling of the apparition room, she saw a
red glow, and so everybody was looking for things to happen

because if she sees anything like that, the Blessed Mother's coming. And there was a red streak coming right down from the sun, right down to the house. When they announced that she was leaving, that the red light was going up onto the ceiling and was dissipating, the red light was back in the sky going back up toward the sun."

I asked Bob why he thought these things were happening.

"Well," he said after a moment's thought, "it's happening everywhere. People are dividing, people are fighting, and heaven's trying to give us a last chance for salvation. Nancy has seen maps that show the Second Coming, and the geographical shape of the United States totally changes. For example, Phoenix becomes a port, a seaport. You know, that's kind of a scary thought. It's very much a warning, to come back to Jesus, come back to being good. God's all merciful, he's all forgiving, but we need to be reminded that you can't just go to church on Sunday, then go out and drive across your neighbor's lawn because you don't like the way he looked at you that morning. You have to be forgiving too. And if somebody needs help, you gotta lend a helping hand. If you're walking down the path here and you see an elderly woman slipping, well, you take her hand and help her along. A lot of people don't, and that's what's happened to this world. Everybody's out robbing, injuring, hurting, raping, everything. . . ."

I was just about to concur with Bob on the state of the world when a friend of his, another volunteer, approached. He was holding a Sony Video-8 camera. The friend said to Bob, "Have you told him about my wink?"

"Show him the wink," Bob said. Then to me: "This video is from Falmouth, Kentucky."

The friend, introduced to me as Michael, cued up the videotape, and I put my eye to the eyepiece. It was a shot of a statue, Mary's head, white plaster. The camera zoomed in on one of the statue's eyes, and then, sure enough, it appeared to blink.

"Whoa," I said, stepping back from the camera. Bob and Michael laughed. It was not until later that I thought to wonder how the cameraman had known to zoom in on the eye *before* it blinked.

I told Michael I was from Cincinnati, near the Falmouth farm. He said that Sandy, the Falmouth visionary, was in Conyers for the apparition.

Bob said, "I heard there was an apparition last night, at nine-thirty, an apparition of Jesus. Jesus was so pleased with people going through all this that he was sending out special graces and blessings to everybody here."

I asked Bob if his faith had always been this strong. "Not always, but my faith has gotten very strong. I find if I start to talk about it, just mention a word, somebody will show a hunger to learn something about it, and I find myself just opening up. And I don't even think it's me talking; sometimes I think it's the Holy Spirit. One of the things I'll say—for example, in a bar scene—somebody will say, 'You're going to Atlanta? What are you going to Atlanta for?' I'll say, 'I've got a date with a virgin.' That always sparks their interest, starts a conversation. You'd be surprised how many of these medals I've handed out in bars. Everybody hungers for peace. It's really peace everybody's looking for."

I left Bob and Michael and headed toward the other end of The Farm, to work my way closer to the farmhouse, where the apparition was to occur, before the crowd got too thick around it.

There were plenty of teens and children here with their parents. They did not appear uncomfortable, nor did they seem distressed to be at large on a school day. The younger children were frenzied by being outdoors and amid so many people—and, I imagine, a little dismayed to find it so much like church. Outlets for youthful fidgeting (for those kids whose parents would tolerate it) were limited to running up and down wet, grassy hills and stomping through mud.

As I neared the farmhouse, I overheard a woman near me

talking about miracles occurring in her church, and I introduced myself. Margaret was from Louisville. She was middle-
aged, unsmiling, and her eyes looked red from crying. Her
adult daughter tagged along beside her in silence. I could not
gauge the daughter's reaction to her mother's monologue,
which was hammered out in the tortured vowels of the northern Kentucky accent. Many of her declarative sentences curled
at the end like questions.

"It's at an Episcopalian church. The Blessed Mother revealed that the more rosaries we said, the more miracles
would happen? And we just had us a small group, started
saying the rosary, and on Wednesday night we had a healing
service? And the scent of roses was so strong that it would
have knocked you over. Then, Thursday morning—usually
on Wednesday nights we have the rosary, but that night it
was so late we couldn't, so Father told us to come in at nine-
thirty on Thursday—when we went in there, we were standing there a while and Father said, 'Oh, look, Our Lady's
shedding tears.' Well, the tears were just pouring out of the
statue of the Rosa Mystica, and before the night was over
with, all the statues in the church, except for the crucifix, was
crying. And he had an icon that's got salt, like there's a skim
of salt going down it? From the tears? There's a picture of
Jesus in his office was shedding tears. Our Lady of Medjugorje's picture was shedding tears. He had a statue in his office that was shedding tears. And now we're expecting the
crucifix to start bleeding, because it just is lookin' more and
more that way. It's getting around all over, everybody's
findin' out about it. 32 News wanted to interview Father, but
he wasn't prepared for it at that time, and he took off for
Falmouth with a bunch of us."

I asked Margaret if she expected to see anything miraculous
in Conyers.

"Nope. No, because I don't need to see, I already have
it." She paused while we took five or ten more squishy steps
through the mud. "Our Lady speaks to me. I get messages."

"How do you receive them?" I asked.

"A locution. Inner locutions. A voice, just as though I were talking to you. It's been happening ever since I went back to the Church. I've been out of my church for nine years, and I'm in the process of divorcing, and this is the way I'm being led." Margaret invited me to visit her church and see the weeping statues for myself if I was ever in Louisville. I promised her I would.

Standing to one side of the mud path, a group had gathered around a woman displaying a large, laminated photograph of a pregnant woman kneeling near the cross on the Holy Hill. In the photograph a translucent Mary appeared to be encircling the kneeling pilgrim with her mantle in a protective gesture. People pressed in toward the woman holding the photograph, taking pictures of the picture. A question came from the crowd: "Have they sent a copy of that to the Vatican?" The woman answered: "I don't know. I don't know where-all they've gone. They're going around the world, I can tell you that." For newcomers she recounted the story behind the picture.

"The woman in the picture is not Catholic; she wanted her sister-in-law to bring her up here to Conyers. She's pregnant with her second child, and she was praying for protection for her baby when her sister-in-law took this picture. It was taken September thirteenth, the last day of the Cairo conference to try to control world population through abortion. This baby is due December eighth, the Feast of the Immaculate Conception. . . ." She paused to let the crowd make all the necessary connections. "And you see," she continued, "the mantle covers the baby. Is that a powerful message?" The crowd made appreciative oohing noises. One woman said this: "Awesome, awesome, awesome. Beautiful."

A male voice came over the loudspeaker from the direction of the farmhouse: "We are now ready to start our prayer portion. We would like you to take the sheets that were given to you and refer to the consecration. . . ." Three helicopters, news crews, thumped the air loudly overhead. "After Nancy arrives in the apparition room, we will say all fifteen mysteries of the rosary. When we sing the 'Ave,' take out your white handkerchiefs and wave them up toward the sky so all of the newspeople in the helicopters will see doves of peace flying up." Everyone looked up at the helicopters, which were trying to stand still but couldn't help inching backward, like hovering dragonflies. The man on the p.a. continued: "If this is not shown on TV, something is wrong with our media."

The crowd that gathered in the fields surrounding the farmhouse eventually reached a total of around thirty thousand—far less than the predicted two hundred thousand but enough to cover a lot of ground and make a fairly impressive sight when one of the helicopter crews' film ran on CNN later that night. Except for the absence of drunk bikers, the combination of rain, mud, and crowd reminded me of the infield on a wet day at the Indianapolis 500. Many had come the night before and staked out plots of ground near the farmhouse with their lawn chairs and today carried in coolers, setting up camp and holding it through the cold, wet morning hours. Some were spread out on blankets under large beach umbrellas. Many people carried in religious statues— Christs, Marys, one plaster angel easily four feet tall—hoping to have them blessed by Mary during her visit.

I had my first glimpse of the visionary, Nancy Fowler, on a television screen. Volunteers were selling videos (correction: giving them away with a suggested donation of fifteen dollars, and no, they couldn't make change for a twenty) out of a barn near the farmhouse. Two videos, *Why Do You Test Me?* and *Miracle at Conyers*, were available, and one of them was playing on a television in the sales booth. On the tape Nancy Fowler was addressing a crowd somewhere, exhorting them to a closer examination of the state of their souls: "Look at the world today. You are given a free will, and you have a choice to make. You can either follow after Christ or you can live in sin. If you're choosing to live in sin, your soul is not living in light, not living with Christ." Nancy had straight, dark hair just above shoulder length. The arrangement of features on her face made her appear tired; her eyes were deep-set, the corners of her mouth inclined downward. She was overweight, and the fullness of her face and rubbery double chin had capitulated to the effects of gravity. "I've seen my father's soul," she continued. "I've momentarily seen a vision of my father in purgatory. And it's very horrible."

At noon, the man's voice returned to the loudspeaker: "Nancy has just arrived. We will start singing the Fatima 'Ave'; we will sing fifteen verses. So again we will glorify our Blessed Mother by raising our voices." He began the hymn. During the choruses everyone waved white hankies and Kleenexes above their heads.

The song ended, and the crowd became quiet. With Nancy in the apparition room, it was just a matter of time now. The rain had stopped, and a cool breeze was blowing. Half a dozen sparrows soared and dipped above the crowd (the presence of birds before an apparition has been said to herald the Virgin's imminent arrival). Mesmerized by the intensity of the prayerful, anxious silence of the crowd, I found myself staring expectantly, along with the others, at the roof of the farmhouse. Shortly, from within the apparition room, Nancy, sounding far away and small, described what she was seeing. The man with the microphone reported her vision: "A light has descended. There are people appearing." Silence again.

At ten after noon, Mary arrived. The man's voice came over the p.a. again, flatly, evenly, slowly: "Our Blessed Mother says that she will give the message at the end of the Glorious mysteries." He paused, passing the baton to a Spanish translator, who was off like a shot.

All eyes were locked on the roof of the house. "Our

Blessed Mother says, 'I am praying with you now, dear children.' We should begin to pray.''

Most rosaries consist of a few introductory prayers and five
sets of ten beads (called decades) representing Hail Marys set
off by larger beads representing Our Fathers. A complete cycle
of the rosary, however, is accomplished by working your way
around the five decades three times, for a total of one hundred fifty Hail Marys. Each of the fifteen decades is accompanied by a prescribed meditation on one of the "mysteries"
of salvation history. There are five "Joyful" mysteries (the
Annunciation, the Visitation, the Nativity, the Presentation of
Jesus in the Temple, and the Finding of Jesus in the Temple);
five "Sorrowful" mysteries (the Agony in the Garden, the
Scourging at the Pillar, the Crowning with Thorns, the Carrying of the Cross, and the Crucifixion); and five "Glorious"
mysteries (the Resurrection, the Ascension, the Descent of the
Holy Spirit, the Assumption of Mary into Heaven, and the
Crowning of Mary as Queen of Heaven). Various traditions
place additional prayers or short songs at the end of each
decade of Hail Marys.

A smoky, broadcast-quality male voice came over the p.a.
to begin the rosary. Suddenly, like a surprised guest on *This
Is Your Life* cocking his head at a familiar voice from the
wings, I recognized the golden tones of none other than Father Leroy Smith, former pastor of Saint Joseph Church in
Cold Spring, Kentucky, and master of ceremonies at the Falmouth, Kentucky, farm. He began in his slow, satiny rumble:
"During this first rosary we will meditate upon the five Joyful
mysteries." He introduced the first mystery, the Annunciation, which recalls the appearance of the angel to Mary and
his request for her to be the mother of Jesus. "She gives her
fiat, and at that moment the Word became flesh in the
womb of our Blessed Lady." By the cadence of his speech,
Father Smith invested the key words—*fiat*, flesh, womb—
with an otherworldly weight. If words can be made to sound

pious by the way they are spoken, Father Smith has the knack.

The plan was to pray all fifteen decades. With extra prayers and songs included, it would take nearly an hour and a half to complete the rosary. Most pilgrims were sitting, but many remained standing throughout the prayers. Some knelt on the muddy ground; a few of the kneelers pressed their foreheads to the ground in front of them as they prayed, giving their meditation a peculiarly Eastern look.

The rosary was led, in call-and-response fashion, by various guest leaders who took turns at the microphone. Much of it was led in foreign languages, from French to Urdu, with the crowd answering in English. In the foreign versions, especially the non-European ones, the droning, chantlike quality of the rosary prayer cycle was even more pronounced than usual. It was peaceful and soothing. I sat on a low concrete wall and enjoyed the lulling, somnolent rhythm of this centuries-old plea for heavenly mercy, forgiveness, attention.

After about an hour, with the end of the rosary in sight, people crowded the Porta Pottis, hoping to relieve themselves and be back in their spots before Mary delivered her message. As the last decade of the Glorious mysteries drew to a close, the crowd came to its feet. The rosary ended, but a few extra prayers were tacked on at the end—the Hail Holy Queen, the prayer to Saint Michael, a prayer for Pope John Paul II. Then, after ninety minutes of unceasing prayer, silence again.

Eventually, the male voice from inside the apparition room came back on the p.a., relaying the message as dictated to him by Nancy Fowler, whom we could hear faintly in the background, her voice high-pitched and sleepy-sounding. Nancy's words were reported by the spokesman in short phrases, which were then repeated by the Spanish translator.

" 'My dear children, in the peace of my Son Jesus, I greet you. Peace. Peace will not come upon the world unless you return to God. I have come to deliver an urgent plea. . . .' "

We had provoked heaven, and Mary had come to ask for reparation.

Nancy continued: " 'Please, dear children, you must stop offending God.' A dark substance is coming out of her eye. 'I have warned you of wars, of natural disasters—' The substance is coming down her nose again, on the side of her nose, from her eye."

Mary's eye continued to leak the "dark substance" as she detailed the natural disasters (including floods and epidemics) set to be loosed on mankind should we not acknowledge these warnings. The prescribed response? "Pray as you've never prayed before."

According to Nancy, Mary imparted a blessing to the crowd as she left. "My hands will be outstretched to all my children as graces fall."

Everyone was standing by that point; video cameras were trained on the farmhouse; 35mm cameras, Instamatics, and Polaroids clicked like castanets.

"In the name of the Father and the Son and the Holy Spirit. Amen. The image of Our Lady is on the ceiling . . . still on the ceiling . . . still there . . . She's disappeared."

And that was it. Though I couldn't imagine what else I had been expecting, I felt cheated somehow. There was nothing in the message that had not been stated dozens of times before in past messages. I had witnessed no miracles. Pilgrims—many of whom had traveled thousands of miles and had spent the last twenty-four hours slogging gamely through this Old Testament weather to see Mary make good on her promise to appear "in a special way"—had been told once again that (1) almost nobody's praying enough and (2) punishments are coming. I looked around, expecting to see my own slightly embarrassed resentment reflected on the faces of those around me. But they looked no different than they had all day—blissed out just to be here, no matter what.

The crowd broke into a Marian hymn known as "The Fatima Song." At the end, another man came on the p.a. and suggested we all sing "Happy Birthday" to Mary, as it was the fourth anniversary of her first appearance at Conyers. The crowd did just that. Afterward, the man said wistfully, "Hurry back." A foil balloon in the shape of a red heart with an arrow through it rose out of the crowd toward the clouds.

The spell had broken. A spokesman came on and said Nancy would be out on the front porch of the farmhouse in a few minutes to answer questions. Waiting for Nancy to appear, the crowd started to shift, move, come back to itself, shaking off the torpor of the afternoon's enchantment. People were up and about, talking, smoking, eating. Near me, two toddlers shared Fruit Rollups in the middle of a muddy path. A smiling old man in a hat with a feather in it cut slices of cheese from a stash in a cooler, put them on crackers, and handed them to a small girl.

I was trying to figure out how to think about all this. As in Cold Spring and Falmouth, I had seen nothing out of the ordinary in Conyers. When pressed about the lack of substantiating evidence (at least of the sort that would stand up to mildly rigorous scrutiny from an impartial observer), supporters argue in one of two ways. The evidence, they say, is necessarily just a shade less than irrefutable. That way, wishing to leave room for the possibility of faith, God respects our choice in the matter. An obvious miracle would amount to his riding roughshod over one of his own key axioms—man's free will. How believers reconcile this fundamental, God-given freedom with Jesus' and Mary's threats that we accept these messages *or else* is a question that's generally not touched on. The second argument is drawn from Jesus' own claim that prophets can be judged "by their fruits," and it amounts to this: Thousands of people are having their spiritual lives turned around for the better as a result of these apparitions and messages, so how could they possibly not be genuine? It's an argument that defines speciousness, but one that the faithful play like a trump card for skeptics who discount the "miraculous" evidence.

Before long Nancy appeared on her front porch, wearing a blue raincoat and trailing an entourage like a prizefighter's. With her were priests and nuns (in spite of the local bishop's position on the Conyers phenomenon) and laypeople. Her face was round and pale and ghosty-looking under straight gray-black hair. She stepped to a microphone. Her voice was lilting and little-girlish and sometimes hard to understand. She slurred some words; "sisters and brothers," for instance, sounded like "sers 'n' brers." At points in the narrative, as she got excited and her voice rose, she sounded like Rocky the flying squirrel. "God bless all of you for your journey of faith," she said breathlessly. "I want to tell you that Our Lady was radiant. She wore a white veil and dress, and she's *beautiful*!"

Nancy repeated Mary's message; the crowd still seemed satisfied with it. She then segued into a matter of local politics that was threatening to topple The Farm's future as a pilgrimage site. Her voice tightened up: "You know Our Lady talked about freedom. There has been a situation that has developed here in Rockdale County I'm very sad about. Some Rockdale County officials have imposed a new law. They did this on October eleventh, to be implemented November first. I've asked a friend who is an attorney to explain a little bit to you. It's very important that you hear what he has to say for a couple moments."

The lawyer took the microphone and proceeded to lay out for us—in a profoundly Southern accent—just what the local officials had been up to.

"The county of Rockdale, Georgia, has passed a law that will affect any gathering of five hundred or more people, to be effective November first," he said.

The county's point was that gatherings such as those at The Farm placed too great a burden on local resources by snarling the highways, polluting the air and the environment, and denigrating the local surroundings with excessive signage.

"They say we threaten the integrity of the county's wetlands," the lawyer said, drawing chuckles from the faithful. The county was also asking for the installation of proper waste-management systems, drinking facilities, improved lighting, standard parking facilities, and "effective control to minimize the presence of rats, arthropods, flies, roaches, and other vermin." Moans and laughter from the crowd.

The lawyer wrapped by stating that the legislation was "ridiculous" and that "necessary things will be done in order to prevent it."

Nancy returned to the microphone as the crowd buzzed.

"On the way going down Highway 138," Nancy said, "I noticed that there is a Catholic bookstore there, and oftentimes I have read their sign, and the words are 'Pray for the freedom to pray.' Nowhere in the history of mankind has it been easy to follow Christ, but I want to go on record and tell you that I want to be a great warrior of Jesus and Mary.

"We must pray, my dear sisters and brothers [sers 'n' brers], for peace. Our Lady's message today tells us again that suffering of every kind is about to befall us and will, and more if we do not turn back to God. . . . The time is now to ask for the gift of greater faith. I would like to remind you of the words of Our Lady: 'Do not let a single day go by that you do not pray for the grace of a greater faith.' Is our faith not being tested this very day when we live in a country that is imposing more and more restrictions upon us?"

After her monologue Nancy fielded questions from the crowd. The front yard of the farmhouse, a large hill sloping away from the porch on which Nancy stood, was covered with thousands of devotees, all looking up at her. The questions and answers covered a variety of topics, including the local archbishop ("I am very grateful to have such a holy bishop"); the charge that the Conyers gatherings are cultish ("We have simply come together of all faiths to honor the Mother of

God. People are totally free to come and to go"); and heavenly chastisements ("I think there are warnings from heaven coming").

When the last of the questions had been answered, Nancy left the farmhouse with her immediate circle of supporters, and the crowd began to thin. With a slow-moving pack of pilgrims, walking behind a man wearing an evening-gown-length plastic garbage bag and mukluks made from multiple layers of plastic grocery bags, I headed back down a mud path toward the Holy Hill, on my way to the neighboring farm where my car was parked. Everyone seemed tired, perhaps worn out from two days of slogging through rain and mud, perhaps dispirited by the prospect of this being the last large gathering here on The Farm, thanks to the county's new regulations. I still didn't hear any grumbling, though, about the lackluster, pretty-much-the-same-as-always message.

Back on the Holy Hill, the rain had begun to fall steadily again. A group of dancers in native costumes from Juarez, Mexico, had begun a dance in front of the statue of Mary. A young man beat time loudly on a bass drum while a dozen others in red fringed costumes stepped rhythmically in a large circle before the statue. The group's guide, an overweight man in a too-small white T-shirt and umbrella hat, told me the group had ridden forty hours on a bus from Juarez to be there. He said they danced "for Our Lady" and that the group's patron saint is Juan Diego, the sixteenth-century native Mexican on whose cloak Our Lady of Guadalupe left her image.

I stood beneath my umbrella and a tree in Nancy Fowler's backyard, watching the dancers. The longer they danced, the harder the rain fell. In spite of all things meteorological mitigating against even being outdoors, much less dancing, this group seemed happy. They were oblivious to the downpour. At the end of their dance, a solid ten minutes later, the Mexicans' bright red costumes clung to their bodies and their hair hung down in wet streams. They were all smiling.

I walked across the road and through the horse pasture to my car. Again, I laid my shoes on a plastic bag on the passenger-side floor. Traffic heading out of the pasture was at a standstill, so I sat with my engine idling, waiting for the heater to crank up, to warm me, to dry me. It felt good to sit down. I was tired of being on my feet all day, tired of being wet.

Eventually, the traffic leaving the pasture cleared up, and I found my way through the field back to Route 138 and Interstate 20. The rain had become a torrent. Semitrailers on I-20 were kicking up sheets of water; passing them required an adrenaline surge and a blind stab of the accelerator. I turned up the stereo, moved to the passing lane, and headed north without looking back.

After living for two days under rain and roiling gray skies that had clamped down over Atlanta like a lid on a pot, I drove out toward Chattanooga—past pine woods, past misshapen kudzu-covered trees looking like giant shrub-carving attempts gone horribly wrong, past blown shreds of semi retreads curled on the side of the road (when I was a kid we called them alligator tails). Forty miles north of Atlanta, I edged out from under the low-pressure system and finally turned my wipers off. The clouds were breaking up, and for the first time in two days I saw blue sky.

CHAPTER FOUR

✤ ✤ ✤

Discernment

Private Revelation and the Catholic Church

*P*sychology confidently places apparitions and other claims of private revelation within the category of delusion, whether hallucinatory (seeing/hearing something that is not there) or illusory (misinterpreting a genuine external stimulus of some kind). The Christian religion, on the other hand (and it is mostly within the Roman Catholic tradition that the phenomena discussed here have developed), while respecting and often embracing the psychological explanation, posits a second possibility: that God, being God, can choose to communicate with his creatures in any way he sees fit. Historically, according to the Church, one of those ways has been through private revelation.

The Church has all along considered yet a third possible explanation for the genesis of ecstatic visions, in addition to both the psychological and the divine (and always admitting, of course, the potential for cases of outright fraud), and that is the possibility of diabolic intervention and influence. The devil's work. This is not a viewpoint that gets much play from Church officials these days—Satan having become nearly as great an anachronism as the hair shirt—but it is an explanation held in reserve for those cases that seem to the Church to have a genuine, if tainted, supernatural component.

Visions

Over the centuries the Catholic Church has devoted a good deal of energy to dealing with the question of apparitions. As it has done so determinedly with most other areas of human experience, the Church has codified and categorized these phenomena with the result that they are at least easy to discuss in theory.

According to the Church, the ways in which visions can manifest themselves fall naturally into three categories: corporeal, imaginative, and intellectual.

Corporeal visions are those in which the eyes of the seer actually perceive an object. Whether that object exists as a separate entity in the real world is another matter. A corporeal vision could also be the result of some higher power conveying an image directly to the visionary's sense of sight. For a vision to qualify as corporeal, then, the seer's physical eye has to be involved, either because it is responding to a real object or because it is being made to perceive something that is not there.

Imaginative visions, as the name implies, are triggered directly in the imagination, without the involvement of the physical sense of sight. Much of the church's understanding and articulation of the details of imaginative visions are drawn from the writings of the great sixteenth-century mystics Saint Teresa of Avila and her friend Saint John of the Cross. The imaginative vision, according to Teresa, is imparted to the recipient in an instant.

"And so quickly does God reveal it to us," says Teresa, "that even if we needed to open our eyes in order to see it, there would not be time for us to do so. But it is all the same whether they are open or closed: if the Lord is pleased for us to see it, we shall do so even against our will."

John of the Cross concurs: "It is as if a door were opened into a most marvelous light, whereby the soul sees, as men do when the lightning suddenly flashes in a dark night. The lightning makes surrounding objects visible for an instant, and then leaves them in obscurity, though the forms of them remain in the imagination."

Despite the fleeting nature of imaginative visions, they can be as richly detailed as the corporeal, as the following passage from Saint Teresa's *Life* amply demonstrates:

> It pleased the Lord that I should sometimes see the following vision. I would see beside me, on my left hand, an angel. . . . He was not tall, but short, and very beautiful, his face so aflame that he appeared to be one of the highest types of angel who seem to be all afire. In his hands I saw a long golden spear and at the end of the iron tip I seemed to see a point of fire. With this he seemed to pierce my heart several times so that it penetrated to my entrails. When he drew it out, I thought he was drawing them out with it and he left me completely afire with a great love for God. The pain was so sharp that it made me utter several moans; and so excessive was the sweetness caused me by this intense pain that one can never wish to lose it, nor will one's soul be content with anything less than God. It is not bodily pain, but spiritual, though the body has a share in it—indeed, a great share. So sweet are the colloquies of love which pass between the soul and God that if anyone thinks I am lying I beseech God, in His goodness, to give him the same experience.

Before the reader is too hastily tempted to make sport (Freudian or otherwise) of Saint Teresa's impassioned encounter with the angel, consider this passage from Herbert Thurston's *The Physical Phenomena of Mysticism* (a book best read in the broadest of daylight, preferably with a light on): "Teresa's heart was extracted after death and in that heart was found a wide horizontal fissure, as those may see to this day who visit the relic in its shrine at Alba de Tormes, or who procure one of the many photographs of it which are in circulation."

Intellectual visions, the third classification, in contrast to the corporeal and the imaginative, produce neither visual impressions nor imaginative pictures. They simply fill the mind with a new knowledge of some truth or mystery without the aid of images, symbols, or even the faculty of reason.

"It is as if," Saint Teresa writes, "food has been introduced into the stomach without our having eaten it or knowing how it got there. . . . We see nothing, either interiorly or exteriorly. . . . But without seeing anything the soul conceives the object and feels whence it is more clearly than if it saw it. It is like feeling one near in a dark place." One of Teresa's first intellectual visions was of Christ:

> I was at prayer on a festival of the glorious Saint Peter when I saw Christ at my side—or, to put it better, I was conscious of Him, for neither with the eyes of the body nor with the eyes of the soul did I see anything. Being completely ignorant that visions of this kind could occur, I was at first very much afraid, and did nothing but weep, though, as soon as He addressed a single word to me to reassure me, I became quiet again, as I had been before, and was quite happy and free from fear.

Locutions

Locutions (Latin, "to speak") are the aural equivalent of visions. Instead of seeing things, locutionists hear them (many mystics do both). As it has done with visions, the Church carefully delineates its understanding of the various classes of locutions. These include auricular locutions (those actually heard with the physical ear—thought to be rare), imaginative locutions (words perceived directly within the imagination, without the aid of the ear), and intellectual locutions (the direct perception of concepts or ideas by the intellect, without filtering by either the ear or the imagination). Some locution- ists speak the words as they are being received; others write the words either as they hear them or immediately after a message has ended.

Again, Saint Teresa is the source of much of the Church's teaching on the subject of locutions. Of imaginative locutions, she writes, "Though perfectly formed, the words are not heard with the bodily ear; yet they are understood much more clearly than if they were so heard, and, however determined one's resistance, it is impossible to fail to hear them."

The Church and Private Revelation

Visions and locutions usually come to the seer or locutionist for the purpose of conveying a message. Messages received in this way—divine disclosures of hidden truths to an indi- vidual—are known as private revelations. They are called private by way of contrast with what the Church defines as "public" revelation—that revelation of the truths of Christian history and salvation that dates from the time of (and in- cludes) the Gospels and is considered by the Church to have ended with the death of the last apostle.

When it comes to judging the authenticity of private rev- elation, the Catholic Church's course can, I think, genuinely be called a conservative one. In the first place, it is generally assumed that as long as a natural explanation suffices to cover the facts of the phenomenon under consideration, that phe- nomenon should not be adjudged of supernatural origin. And as the Church admits the possibility of diabolical mimicry of visions and locutions, abundant precautions along those lines have always been deemed prudent. Before they were con- vinced of the authenticity of her visions, Saint Teresa's spiri- tual advisers counseled her to greet her apparitions with "the fig," a contemptuous gesture produced by holding up a closed fist with the thumb thrust between the first and second fingers—the sixteenth-century equivalent of flipping someone off.

Private revelations—even those "approved" for belief by the faithful (more on this shortly)—can in no way take precedence over the accepted canon of public revelation. They may never contradict or alter the facts of Christian history and salvation; any indication that a revelation opposed official doctrine would in itself signal the vision's falseness. The *Catechism of the Catholic Church* makes clear the Church's position on the subject of private vs. public revelation: "Christ, the Son of God made man, is the Father's one, perfect and unsurpassable Word. In him he has said everything, there will be no other word than this." The *Catechism* continues, quoting Saint John of the Cross, offering this admonition for those tempted to throw too much faith into the corner of private revelation:

> Any person questioning God or desiring some vision or revelation would be guilty not only of foolish behavior but also of offending him, by not fixing his eyes entirely upon Christ and by living with the desire for some other novelty.

Even when the Church "approves" a particular revelation —as it has done in the cases of Lourdes, Fatima, and a handful of other, less well-known apparitions—that approval extends only so far as to say that the particular revelation under consideration is "worthy of belief." It does not make such belief mandatory; it is not incumbent on the Catholic faithful to accept the revelations as gospel or to live according to any directives set down in the "approved" messages. Pope Benedict XIV, writing in the eighteenth century, formulated the standard language by which the laity's obligations in regard to private revelation have been described ever since:

The assent of Catholic faith ought not and indeed cannot be accorded to these revelations even when they have been thus approved. The assent of human faith is owed to them in keeping with the norms of prudence when these indicate that such revelations are probable and religiously credible.

Catholic faith, in the distinction drawn by Pope Benedict, is the sort of faith church members reserve for the elements of public revelation (faith in the Gospels, in the Incarnation, and in the Trinity, for example). Human faith is simply the kind of faith we would have in the word of another human being. What Benedict proposed, and what the Church has taught ever since, is that it's OK to believe in approved revelations, but you don't have to—they are not a necessary component of salvation. What Catholics must not reject is the *possibility* of private revelation. Such an attitude, a fundamental disbelief in supernatural revelation, would reveal a flawed understanding of the Christian faith, which, after all, is itself a supernatural, revealed religion.

After going to such pains to assure the Catholic faithful that private revelations are superfluous to the question of salvation, the Church, by the very fact that it has paid so much attention to seers and revelations over the centuries and has devoted so much energy to discernment and analysis of these phenomena, still invests private revelations with considerable weight. Present-day bishops and priests, many of whom would just as soon see this throwback to medievalism left behind with self-flagellation and the sale of indulgences, recognize that new claims of apparitions and locutions must not simply be dismissed out of hand. If the Church admits the possibility of divine revelation at all, it must entertain the possibility that such revelations are being given to seers and locutionists even down to the present day. And, the thinking goes, if God (or a representative) is truly communicating with us, can whatever it is he wants to tell us be unimportant? Even if most claims of private revelation are eventually disapproved or, as is more common (particularly as such claims proliferate), are never ruled on at all, the Church must appear to remain open to the theoretical possibility of this sort of divine intervention.

Perhaps more important, today's bishops and pastors recognize that for many Catholics, active participation in events surrounding claimed private revelations—whether it be attending a rosary service or searching the sky for Mary-shaped clouds—fulfills a particular kind of spiritual hunger, one that is not being fed in modern churches. It's a common enough sentiment, almost an axiom, among apparition enthusiasts that the Catholic Church in America has been overmodernized, has relinquished its claim to moral and spiritual authority, has demystified this ancient "mystery" religion, and has thus diluted itself nearly to the point of insignificance. Most apparition supporters are careful to define themselves as *Roman* Catholics, and by this declaration profess an allegiance to a brand of Catholicism that has largely disappeared, even in Rome. In maintaining or reviving age-old devotional practices, these Catholics fashion for themselves the kind of religious experience they find meaningful. And in this age of dwindling church attendance and significant defection of Catholics to other denominations, the hierarchy is loath to alienate thousands of churchgoers by holding too tightly to a modernist line. The upshot is that most bishops within whose dioceses alleged apparitions occur (those bishops on whom the onus of judgment rests) treat the matter gingerly, being careful to toe the Church line and, at the same time, avoid drawing fire from the visionaries and their supporters.

Assessing Private Revelation

Given that the Church is expected to rule on matters of this sort, it has over the years fashioned a set of more or less official guidelines for deciding which apparitions, which private revelations, are likely of divine origin and which are not. Several standard texts are useful to this end. One of the most often quoted is Father Augustin Poulain's *The Graces of Interior Prayer*, a tome on the mystical life, first published in 1901. Modern books aiming to make clear the Church's method of discernment of private revelations—most notably Father Benedict Groeschel's concise and helpful *A Still, Small Voice*—draw in large part on the work of Father Poulain, as I will here.

The discernment of the true character of purported private revelations is, as Father Poulain states, based on a thorough review of the person alleging the divine favors and the actual facts of the revelations themselves, including the content of the messages and their attendant "fruits" or effects in the lives of believers.

Poulain's questions about the seer are the ones you or I would probably pose if given the chance. Is the visionary mentally stable? Is she known as a person of at least moderate virtue? If she wasn't virtuous before the apparitions began, have the experiences inclined her in that direction? As Father Poulain puts it, "Have these states created a centre of moral energy?" Does the seer submit to the direction of a spiritual advisor? Is she open to questions and a thorough investigation of the phenomena? Does the seer display an attitude of proper humility regarding the events? Any visionary who enjoys talking about her mystical experiences a little too much should probably be ruled out. "It is a sign of pride, and therefore of illusion," Poulain says, "to have a craving to divulge the graces that we believe ourselves to have received. . . . Humble souls avoid publicity as much as possible." In fact, any seer who so much as actively *desires* the revelations she receives is probably not a true visionary, according to Poulain. A longing for such experiences opens the door too easily to deception, he says, and is a strong indicator of their probable falseness.

It is assumed that persons granted private revelations will normally be those who have already made some considerable progress in the matter of a prayer life. It is also assumed that persons claiming revelations will have been—whether before, during, or after the events in question—put through some of life's harsher trials. Often the seer's toughest challenge is merely in standing up to the public's reception of the claimed revelations, which usually falls somewhere between lukewarm and absolute zero. Bernadette Soubirous, the visionary of Lourdes, faced harsh criticism and disbelief from local citizens and clergy. The three shepherd children of Fatima were harangued mercilessly by neighbors, priests, and local government officials. The principal Fatima seer, Lucia dos Santos, was more than once beaten by her mother in an attempt to draw a confession. Poulain says that both graces and crosses are signs of God's friendship, and the existence of the former without the latter would be cause for doubt in a case of purported private revelations.

It is accepted by most Church authorities that simply by the fact that revelations are received via a human instrument, they are bound to be colored by the mind and imagination of the person receiving them. It's sort of the Heisenburg principle of mystical phenomena. Some "approved" visionaries, even many who went on to be canonized as saints by the Catholic Church, are recognized to have occasionally introduced personal bias or errors of the imagination into the substance of their visions. German theologian Karl Rahner, in *Visions and Prophecies*, enumerates an instructive list of such errors found in the visions of well-known saints and holy persons:

St. Norbert of Xanten [died 1134] was absolutely certain that Anti-Christ would appear in his generation. . . . St. Vincent Ferrer [died 1419] declared on the authority of his visions that the end of the world was imminent. . . . Blessed Margaret Ebner was instructed by the child Jesus "how his holy circumcision was performed," and believed she heard the voice of the Lord bidding her give suck to the wooden statue of the child Jesus which she kept in a crib. . . . St. Mary Magdalene of Pazzi watched Jesus write his name on her heart with the milk of the Blessed Virgin. . . . Sister Maria Anna from Cuba mystically experienced in herself the conception, pregnancy and on August 15, 1901, about midnight, the birth of the child Jesus. When she afterwards nursed him she was soothed by Our Lady.

In part because of such absurdities, the Church is careful to keep separate the question of a person's saintliness and any proclivity that person may have had for mystical experiences such as visions. It recognizes that genuine saints may have flawed visions and that receiving visions, even genuine ones, is by no means an irrefutable indicator of saintliness. "When a servant of God is canonized," says Father Poulain, "it is his virtue that is canonized, and not his visions."

In judging the revelations themselves, the Church's primary concern is the conformity of the messages with existing dogma as well as questions of propriety and overall sense. First and foremost, is there anything in the revelations that contradicts the dogmas and doctrine of the Church? For that matter, is there anything that contradicts established facts of science or history? Do the visions violate the unwritten laws of decency or morals? "If, as sometimes happened," Poulain offers by way of example, "an apparition professing to be Jesus Christ were to appear without clothing, we might be sure that it was not divine." Is the information conveyed through the revelation useful and not merely sensational? Seers who open the floor for questions about the afterlife or future events or who aim, with heaven's help, to assist pilgrims in the finding of lost objects are, in Poulain's view, simply playing the part of fortune-tellers. "God," he asserts, "does not stoop to run an Inquiry Office."

More relevant to today's apparitions are Poulain's warnings against revelations that consist of little more than "truism[s], occurring in all ascetic writings." He says, "God would not employ such great means for such a small result." He suggests that seers who purvey such messages probably are unwittingly repeating things they have read or heard elsewhere. Today's popular apparition series, most of which have been active every week or every month for years, have been the cause of the printing and dissemination of thousands of pages of "messages" from the Virgin. A striking characteristic of most of those messages is their lack of anything new or surprising or even truly substantial. Many modern-day "revelations"—excepting those that spend more time dwelling on end-time cataclysms than offering inspirational advice—could properly be described as spiritual "truisms." The necessity of prayer and conversion and repentance has been preached to the point of cliché since the days of Saint Paul, and yet it seems that those three points are primarily what the Virgin wants to talk about, again and again. She has come to Medjugorje, for instance, *every day* since June 24, 1981, to convey what is, essentially, an unchanging message: the above-mentioned admonition to pray, convert, and repent. Received in such quantities, can each of the messages be said to be unique and indispensable? Believers defend the Virgin's redundant rhetoric as an unfortunate necessity due to humankind's hardheadedness. If we would only listen and obey, she wouldn't have to keep repeating herself. Supporters usually don't stop to consider that such constant hammering can quickly fade into background.

Finally, the Church watches to see if the revelations and the devotions they inspire will stand the test of time and whether, in Poulain's words, they produce "great fruits of grace."

Taken together, the case-by-case scrutinizing of the visionary, her messages, and the revelation's effects on the lives of believers constitute the Church's tripartite standard of assessment in cases of purported private revelation. Failure along any one of the three lines of investigation means an end to the investigation.

None of the cases of private revelation reported in this book has received the unqualified approval of the local bishop. A few have received more or less explicit disapproval. Some have not drawn comment from the local Church at all, and likely never will.

Again, Karl Rahner: "The principle always remains valid that supernatural agency is not to be presupposed but must be proved. The history of mysticism justifies Poulain's judgment that even with pious and 'normal' people, in three cases out of four visions are well intentioned, harmless, genuine illusions. With such occurrences, therefore, there is more danger in credulity than in scepticism, especially in unsettled times."

Chapter Five

✦ ✦ ✦

Let It Be Done

Belleville, Illinois

Ray Doiron stood, listing slightly toward a rubber-tipped aluminum cane, in a nearly empty amphitheater on an early February morning. He wore brown mechanic's coveralls, a navy winter coat, dark glasses, and a black baseball cap with MAUI spelled on it in tropical pinks and yellows. It was colder than anyone had expected. Squadrons of clouds passed overhead; some slowed and congregated, eventually neutralizing the already meager warming effects of the sun. The wind was picking up.

The amphitheater is really an outdoor church. The stage is a sanctuary; on it are a black marble altar, a silver tabernacle, and a larger-than-life stylized statue of the Virgin and Child. The roof over the stage describes a low arc under a bell-shaped steeple of swooping concrete buttresses. The architecture is of the sort that was probably meant to appear futuristic when it was built and so looks outdated these thirty-some years later. Twenty-four hundred permanent seats fan out from the stage and up a slight rise; a terraced hillside behind the seats provides additional room for blankets and lawn chairs when crowds exceed the seating capacity—a frequent circumstance when Ray Doiron is in the vicinity.

We were near St. Louis, at the National Shrine of Our Lady of Snows, in Belleville, Illinois, a sprawling religious attraction founded by the Missionary Oblates of Mary Immaculate in 1958. In addition to the amphitheater, the shrine includes a church, a replica of the grotto of Lourdes, an outdoor Way of the Cross, a hotel, and a visitors center with a restaurant and gift shop, all in a closely trimmed, gently rolling wooded setting. Not mentioned in the shrine's literature is the fact that crowds of thousands have gathered here regularly since 1994 to witness apparitions of the Virgin Mary to Ray Doiron.

At the time of my visit Ray was sixty years old, the survivor of three heart attacks. He was also plagued by leg and back problems, hence the cane. "In 1989 I was hurt real bad on the job; I had my legs and my spine crushed," he told me. And though he moved confidently and without obvious distress, he complained of being easily winded.

I helped Ray carry four metal folding chairs from his car to a position directly in front of the stage and near the stairs leading up to it. It was ten o'clock. The apparition would not come for three more hours, but Ray had been on the grounds since nine forty-five to greet the early arrivals, the people who had slowly begun to trickle into the broad, shallow bowl of the amphitheater, toting blankets, sleeping bags, coolers, and thermoses of steaming coffee. Ray told me he felt an obligation to be at the shrine early on apparition days, to answer pilgrims' questions and to pray with them if that's what they wanted.

"People ask me about things they want to know," Ray said. "They talk about the experiences they had if they were here before. They share a lot of stuff with me. I think I'm the only apparitioner that does this—comes out to meet the crowd. It's not that I think I'm some gift or anything, but I figure if people come this far, I should say hi to 'em, at least."

Shortly after we got the chairs set up, a small group of women gravitated over to Ray. One young mother asked if it'd be all right to take a picture of Ray and her daughter together.

"Sure," Ray said, giving the probable kindergartner a warm smile and bending over to speak to her. "How are you, bright eyes? You got pretty eyes." Despite Ray's convincingly grandpaternal delivery, the girl remained silent and unsmiling. Ray asked the mom how she was doing. "Are you gonna stay warm enough?"

"Yeah, we brought sleeping bags."

Ray stood beside the girl with his arm around her while the mother took the picture.

An older woman nearby looked at Ray admiringly and said, "Do you know how fortunate you are?" Ray, avowedly uncomfortable with this particular sort of attention, answered, "The thing is, we're all here together. That's the whole thing. She loves us all."

"How did she start appearing to you?" the woman asked.

"Well," said Ray, "it started three years ago today."

"What'd she do? She just appear to you? Didja hear a voice, or what? At your house?"

"On January the thirteenth, 1993, around three o'clock in the morning, I was laying on the couch in my living room and I was awakened by this soft voice that kept saying, 'Ray . . . Ray . . .' I woke up, and there at the end of the living room, right in front of the TV, there was a brilliant light—"

"Can I get a picture with you?" the woman interrupted, looking at him wonderingly.

"Sure," said Ray. "Anyway . . . I kept looking at it, and from that light Our Lady came forth. And she told me to come here—"

"Sandra, I want a picture of me with Ray," the woman blared to a companion. It turned out Sandra wanted to be in the picture too, though, and a brief hubbub arose concerning who would pose, who would work the camera, etc. Within seconds a bystander, in that amicable spirit of photographic volunteerism seen at many public attractions, stepped forward and snapped the picture for them.

"She told me to come here to pray," Ray continued. "And that's what I did, and she said, 'They'll come,' so that's what happened. The one thing I'd like to tell you—"

"Would you ask her if my mother's with her in heaven?" the woman interposed again. "She died fifteen years ago. On April twenty-seventh."

"You just asked her," Ray said.

"Just *ask* her?" The woman's forehead wrinkled.

"*You* just *asked* her," he repeated. "You know there are so many people who ask me to ask questions to Our Lady when I'm with her. I don't ask her hardly anything. The whole thing of it is, you just asked her yourself."

The questioner smiled dimly, trying, I think, to work up some measure of satisfaction with this enigmatic response from the visionary. In the interval another woman, with short mouse brown hair and bulging eyes, said what she had pressed forward to say.

"Well, I've seen Jesus in a dream, and we just looked at one another; we didn't say anything, you know." She sped up, as if worried about the possibility of being interrupted. "He had a white robe on, a gown, and he just looked at me. All I said was 'Jesus, I love you.' And that was it, the dream ended."

Ray looked at her kindly and nodded. "That's all you needed. All you needed."

More people were arriving, and many were staking out their seats by draping blankets and sleeping bags over them. A white-haired man was busy unrolling and tearing lengths of masking tape, X-ing off a row of five or six seats, reserving them for him and his companions. People ascended the stairs next to us at the front of the stage and left religious articles on and around the marble altar. One woman carried a two-foot-tall bloody crucifix up the stairs, beaming happily at Ray

as she passed. Ray smiled back. A fat man up on stage un-
loaded several cardboard boxes of statues, framed pictures,
and other paraphernalia, arranging them carefully on the altar.

The wind was now coming in shattering icy gusts down
the sides of the wok-shaped amphitheater, and I was having
a hard time taking notes. My fingers kept stiffening up. Ray
seemed undaunted, though, by the weather. He retained his
good humor, listening patiently to anyone who cared to approach him.

Another elderly woman spoke up. "I got a *lot* to be thank-
ful for this year. I got two feet." Unsure whether that was
the extent of her testimonial, a couple of the others snickered
tentatively, thinking she was making some kind of joke. She
quickly corrected them.

"No, see, something bit me, and my foot got this big."
She indicated with her hands a foot the size of a slightly
smaller than average watermelon. "It got real big. I went to
the hospital and they opened it up and they thought I was
gonna hafta lose my leg. The doctor said, 'You wouldn't of
got that sick if God was on your side.' "

Some of the women nearby, seemingly eager to amend
their earlier snickering faux pas, made sympathetic clicking
noises with their tongues. The woman then hastily related the
history of her personal miracle: the ballooning foot, a targeted
campaign of prayer by her and her friends, a medically un-
expected and inexplicable recovery, and a properly astonished
and humbled physician. The bystanders were impressed.

Ray seemed happy to hear about the healing, but really not
all that surprised. What's one more miracle when your world
teems with them?

The day before the apparition, I spoke with Ray in a small
chapel behind the amphitheater's stage. We sat facing each
other on a wooden pew. Light streamed in the clear windows
at the front of the chapel and glowed through fist-size chunks
of red, blue, and yellow stained glass in windows around the

room's perimeter. Ray's face is jowly and friendly and full. His eyes are hooded but occasionally open wide to punctuate his narrative. The first time he looked at me straight on with his eyes opened wide, I was startled by his sudden resemblance to Rod Steiger. He wore a white shirt with a chalice-shaped brooch pinned to it and a black leather coat that squeaked sumptuously when he gestured with his arms.

Before he was injured on the job and had to quit working, he was a retail store manager and a bread truck driver. "I been off of work since then, and I been trying to do pastoral care in the hospital, just praying with people. That's what I was doing when all this started."

He told me about the first time Mary had appeared to him. He had indeed been awakened from a sound sleep on his living room couch. The glowing light had appeared in front of his television, and Mary had stepped out of it and told Ray to go to the shrine on February 11, 1993, to pray.

Ray went on the appointed day and, as promised, received his vision while praying at the shrine's Lourdes grotto, a life-size replica of the famous grotto in France at which Saint Bernadette received her visions.

"I thought at first it was only supposed to be for four months, but then in June, the fifth month, I came back here to pray anyway. And Our Lady appeared to me and asked me, 'What are you doing here after the fourth apparition?' And I thought, 'Well, I'm here out of love for God and Jesus and you, so I can give your messages to the people.' Our Lady said then that I had made my *fiat* with her. I didn't know what she meant. I thought a Fiat was an automobile. But *fiat*, I found out later, means 'Let it be done according to your will.'"

At first Ray was instructed to keep the apparitions a secret. He was relatively successful at this for most of 1993, although a small circle of supporters had caught wind of it and gathered with him during his monthly vigils at the grotto. Finally, on October 13, 1993, Mary gave Ray permission to spread the word. "Today, Ray," she told him, "make it known to the world."

In subsequent months, crowds grew exponentially. By early 1994 the group had outgrown the facilities of the grotto, and the apparitions were moved to the shrine's more spacious amphitheater. Up to eight thousand people gathered at each of the monthly events through October 1994, at which time Mary indicated to Ray that the apparitions would be slowing down. The next was in February 1995. There were two more in 1995, in May and October, and then again in February 1996, the apparition I attended and the third anniversary of Mary's first appearance at the shrine.

I asked Ray about his religious background. How had he come to be someone chosen to receive messages from heaven?

"I was about a one hour a week Catholic like everybody else is," he said, "and I've had a lot of sickness in my life, yes. The first encounter I had with Jesus was during the sickness, in 1968. I was praying—I was going to have some pretty extensive surgery done—and I asked Jesus to give me a sign. I said, 'Give me a sign. Give me a will to live.' There was a small statue of Jesus there where I was in the hospital, and the hands moved like this." Ray held his hands up in front of him, palms facing forward, and waved them from side to side in a sort of warding off or don't-come-any-closer gesture.

"I said to myself, 'Well, Ray, you got your sign.' So I had the surgery, and out of four of us that had the same operation, I was the only one that made it. After that I thought Jesus would follow up with something. I got involved with youth baseball. I taught kids, trying to keep them off the street, and I thought, 'Well, maybe that's what he called me to do.' But after I worked with them for a while, I began to think, 'Where you at? Why aren't you comin' back?'

"But I had to realize that heaven does not move in seconds or minutes or hours or days or years. It's forever, you know, so you have to have patience. Then, through the seventies, I began to think that maybe the statue moving was just something I thought happened but didn't happen, you know?"

In 1983, following a heart attack, Ray had a near-death experience that convinced him his original vision of Jesus had been genuine. He had two more heart attacks and two more near-death experiences, one in 1983 and one in 1989 while vacationing in Florida with his wife. According to Ray, his near-death experiences have been identical to those he has seen described in books and on television.

"After my heart attack in 1989, my heart didn't beat for five minutes. That's when I had my third near-death experience. Each time I've had one I've got further into it. And all the books and everything that you read about it—it's exactly like what they say."

Ray had some concern that his visions of Jesus might have a diabolical origin. A priest friend allayed those fears by asking Ray whether when he saw Jesus, he saw the exposed Sacred Heart. The traditional iconography of the Sacred Heart is based on an apparition to Saint Margaret Mary Alacoque in the seventeenth century and is usually depicted as a glowing heart with a wound in it, a circlet of thorns around it, and a small cross on top. Some portraits of Jesus picture this heart floating outside his body, in front of his chest. Ray told the priest that he had seen the exposed Sacred Heart.

"Well, then," the priest assured him, "that wasn't Satan trying to trick you, because when you see the exposed Sacred Heart, that is truly Jesus. Only Jesus can do that."

"So that made me feel good," said Ray.

Back outside on apparition day, it was almost noon. Though the crowd would eventually fill the available seating, many sat in their running, warmed cars, waiting until the last possible minute. Ray was still holding court at the foot of the amphitheater's stage. He listened patiently as a woman, tapping her sternum ruefully, described in superabundant detail the symptoms of her diverticulitis.

A slight elderly woman with paper-white hair approached

Ray next and said, "I used to be a Eucharistic minister until I heard that John Paul II does not approve of Communion in the hand. So I resigned my ministership. What do you think?"

"Well," said Ray, after considering for a moment, "the only thing I can go back to is in the Gospels, at the Last Supper, when Jesus broke the bread and gave it to the apostles. He handed them the bread. He did not put it in their mouths. It's the banquet of the Lord. It's the feast of the Lord. If I come to your house for dinner, you don't sit down and put the peas in my mouth, put meat in my mouth, put bread in my mouth. If we take it in our hands, are we respecting Jesus the same as we did when we took it on the tongue? It's in the person's heart, that's where it's at. That's what we're gonna be judged on. Years ago, if the host fell on the floor, you was not allowed to pick it up. Now you pick it up, see? But that was all man-made laws, and man-made laws are subject to change over a period of years as the Church progresses. The main thing is how we respect the body of Christ that's in our presence, and even when it isn't in our presence, how we respect Jesus or God. That's the whole thing."

I think the woman had expected less of a lecture and more in the way of support for her position. She looked disappointed and said to herself, "It's difficult to know. Difficult to discern."

Ray's wife, June, passed away in July 1995 after a bout with cancer and heart problems. The next woman who stepped up asked, incredibly, "Ray, are you missing your wife?"

Ray's smile slackened. "Yeah, I miss her a lot, there's no question about it. I cry a lot. And when the day comes that I don't shed a tear over her, I'll stop loving her, which I'll never do. Maybe I'll remarry again; I don't know. I don't know what Our Lady's plans are for me. I was thinking about going into a monastery. But that's running away from you people if I do."

Several women within earshot chorused, "Don't do that!"

"See what I mean?" said Ray. "That'd be runnin' away, wouldn't it?"

Ray told the women that he hoped the group would continue to meet at the shrine for prayer on the thirteenth of every month even after the apparitions stopped. They seemed relieved and converged on him for a multi-pilgrim hug.

One of the few males to approach Ray prior to the apparition was a tall, solemn teenage boy pulled up front by his mother. "I want to show you something," she said to Ray. "This is my son's medal." She produced a medal on a chain that had evidently been hanging around the boy's neck. "He's thinking about studying as a priest. And the medal has started to turn gold over the past three or four weeks. The words on the back—'I am a Catholic. In case of accident, please call a priest'—those words changed first. And I asked one of the priests about it, I thought maybe it was from rubbing against him, that the finish on the back of the medal was rubbing off. He said no."

"No," said Ray decisively, "that's your sign, son." He leaned forward enthusiastically, gripping the teen's right hand in both of his own. The boy was startled but remained silent. "Be that priest, because we need you, OK? Take care." Ray pumped the hand once and released. "You go be that priest." Expressionless, the boy nodded in agreement while his mother beamed at both of them. They turned without another word and returned to their seats.

The altar and the sanctuary around it had been filled with a collection of religious articles, flowers, and framed photographs. A universe of devotional styles was represented. There were statues of favorite saints, Sacred Heart and Immaculate Heart of Mary figurines, photographs of the pope, crucifixes, photographs of crucifixes, dozens of rosaries, Baggies filled with medals, several dozen red roses. There were a couple of framed pictures of clouds. One of the cloud pictures featured a hundreds-of-feet-high hazy outline of Mary in the sky on a mostly sunny day. A paper taped to it stated, "This picture was taken by a couple that was traveling through Wyoming." Another photograph showed Mary, a twenty-foot-tall semi-transparent phantom, clear in every important detail, hovering over the very stage steps I'd been standing beside all morning.

There were three Infant of Prague statues (copies of the famous figure depicting Christ as a child king, globe in his left hand, the right raised in a two-fingered gesture of blessing) on the altar. One was over a foot tall and had been meticulously robed in yellow and red satin and lace.

As at other apparition sites, visitors had placed photographs of loved ones on and around the altar, hoping in that way to secure special blessings for the people in the pictures—beaming newlyweds, small children, high school and college graduates in cap and gown, whole families gathered around visibly proud grandparents. I couldn't help wondering about all the reasons the pictures had been laid at the feet of the Virgin. I felt sure, though, that most of them were there because something had gone wrong—a career, a marriage, a family—and healing was needed. Existing in direct proportion to photography's power to arrest time is its effectiveness as a poignant reminder of life's relentless ratcheting forward. To me the photographs, representative as they were of better days gone by, seemed sad and dully pathetic.

Behind the altar, leaning against the back wall of the stage, was a large framed photograph of a statue of Jesus. The statue was bleeding and appeared to have been crying tears of blood. The blood had painted the entire front of the statue, and a cloth that had been laid beneath the statue to collect the excess was stained dark red and black. In the same vein, near this photo was a framed "Meditation on the Sorrowful Mysteries" taken from the diary of Blessed Faustina, a Polish nun who had received visions of and messages from Jesus in the 1930s. Someone had highlighted, with a fluorescent green marker, Faustina's account of the second Sorrowful mystery:

I saw how the Lord suffered as he was being scourged. Oh, such an inconceivable agony. How terribly Jesus suffered during the scourging. Oh, poor sinners, on the day of Judgment, how will you face the Jesus whom you are now torturing so cruelly? His blood flowed to the ground, and in some places his flesh started to fall off. I saw a few bare bones on his back. The meek Jesus moaned softly and sighed.

As I was reading this, a woman standing nearby, assuming I was tuned in, devotionally speaking, to the physical aspects of Jesus' suffering, produced a Polaroid picture of another statue of Jesus and held it out for my consideration.

"This is at the convent where my aunt's at," she said. In the photograph a life-size statue of Jesus stood in what appeared to be someone's living room. It depicted Jesus after his scourging at the hands of the Roman soldiers; a purple robe was draped over his shoulders, and he looked badly used.

"There's only two statues like this," she continued. "There's one in the Holy Land and one in the convent where my aunt's at. The statue's about as tall as I am, and it's so real; the eyes are brown marble and he looks so sad. It's got the meat and everything just peeled off of him. The meat just hangs on him."

The macabre tendency to dwell on the physical aspects of Christ's suffering, according to sociologist Michael P. Carroll, springs from the same source as does Marian devotion. Both, he argues, result from a son's strong but strongly repressed desire for sexual intimacy with his own mother. Basing his arguments on Freudian notions of Oedipal desire and subsequent repression of that desire, Carroll, in his book *The Cult of the Virgin Mary: Psychological Origins*, suggests that Marian devotion allows men to "dissipate in an acceptable manner the excess sexual energy that is built up as a result of this desire." The emphasis on the grislier aspects of Christ's passion, says Carroll, is a variety of masochism whose subconscious aim is to assuage the son's felt need for punishment for his misplaced sexual desires. And while women may not share the same psychological motivators (they apparently have their own Oedipal kinks to work out), the cult took hold somewhere around the fourth century and thrived with both sexes, primarily on the strength of male psychology.

I didn't mention Michael Carroll to the lady with the meat picture.

"I remember one thing," Ray told me, "and it sticks out very, very vividly. I was about eight years old. We didn't have no money, we didn't have no car or nothing. Well, there was a movie that came out, and my grandmother said, 'I'm gonna take you kids to see it.' So me and my older brother and older sister, we went to this movie, and it was something that I think has been a bell ringer in my life ever since. The movie was *The Song of Bernadette*, and it's stayed in my mind all this time. Once, when I was studying for the lay ministry, they asked me about anything that stood out for me as a moving, religious memory from a younger age. That's the thing I put down."

The Song of Bernadette tells the story of Bernadette Soubirous, the fourteen-year-old visionary of Lourdes. Bernadette experienced eighteen apparitions of the Virgin in the first half of 1858 near her impoverished home in the French Pyrenees. Though initially vilified and grilled by local church and civic officials, Bernadette was eventually taken at her word, and Lourdes became—and remains—one of the most popular Catholic shrines in the world. Bernadette described the Virgin as a girl of about her own age:

> She was not quite as tall as me. She wore a white dress and a blue sash. She had a white veil, which fell to her feet. I saw a yellow rose on each foot. She kept her hands slightly apart and held a rosary. She was young. Her face and clothes reminded me of a statue of the Blessed Virgin before which I

used to pray, but she was alive and surrounded with light.
(*We Saw Her*, by Charles Henry Green)

Ray, too, sees Mary as a young woman, between eighteen and twenty-five years old. "She's got blue eyes and dark brown hair. Sort of an oval face with a thinner chin. She's very beautiful. She's petite, maybe five foot, five one, something like that. She holds a glowing rosary that looks like it's made out of pearl. Usually she's dressed all in white with a blue sash, and she gives off a golden glow. I've also seen her with a white gown and a blue mantle. I've only seen her with a crown one time, but it was not a crown on her head, it was a crown of twelve stars. I've also seen her with a rainbow around her, a rainbow-colored halo." He says the golden glow Mary radiates lit up the grotto where he originally saw her.

"Her gown is made of a material that I can't describe; it looks like there's diamonds and jewelry all over it, but there's not really. It just sparkles, but I don't see actual jewels, you know. And her gown moves in the wind; I can hear it rustling. It whispers in the breeze. It looks to me like it would be heavy, but it floats in the breeze almost like a negligee. I don't know how else to describe it; I don't mean a negligee, but you know that kind of material. Yet it rustles, so it has to have some weight in order to make it rustle, you know. It's material that we don't know of. And colors that we don't know of.

"We talk back and forth. I always thought it was some kind of telepathic communication, but some people say they can hear me speak. But they don't know what I'm saying. Someone said maybe I'm speaking in tongues. I have a hard enough time with English; if I'm speaking in tongues I'm not aware of it. It seems like she knows everything that I think, and I know what she's gonna tell me. She can look right down into my heart and my soul and know exactly what I'm gonna say. And when she's here, I don't hear anything else.

There's a lot of trains go past here, and apparently last October there was a helicopter they said was almost right above us. I didn't hear that. All I heard was music—like a drumroll and music. It's beautiful music. I've heard a lot of songs, and it's nothing I've ever heard. Whether it's a horn or stringed instrument, I couldn't even tell you that. It's just beautiful, beautiful music."

The Virgin typically appears, according to Ray, while the crowd is praying the mystery of the Visitation, the second set of ten Hail Mary beads on the rosary. While she's there, she joins in on the other prayers of the rosary but doesn't recite the Hail Marys "since they are a prayer to her," Ray says. "That's when she talks to me, during the Hail Marys." Saint Bernadette too claimed that the Virgin had not prayed the Hail Marys, but only passed the beads through her fingers as Bernadette prayed.

I asked Ray to describe the sound of Mary's voice.

"For one thing," he said, "you can't tell if it's a male or female voice—it also sounds like Jesus too—but I know from hearing it before that it's her voice. It's a very loving, tender voice; it's got discipline in it, yet it's very tender. I've never heard anyone on this planet with a voice like it."

On apparition days in the amphitheater, Ray kneels behind a railing in front of the stage-sanctuary, facing the altar. The Virgin appears somewhere between Ray and the statue at the back of the sanctuary.

"Some people have said, 'You're just mesmerizing yourself to thinking that the statue moves.' The truth is, I don't even see the statue; it's blocked out. It's a totally different being." The statue is a good eighty to a hundred feet away from Ray when he's kneeling, but he says that when he sees Mary, there is no appreciable distance between them.

"She's so close that anytime I would want to, I could reach out and touch her."

"Have you ever?" I asked.

"Well, I wouldn't until she gives me permission to do so,"

he replied. "I've never just reached out to touch her, but I was permitted, last October, to kiss her foot."

"So you felt her foot?"

"Oh, yeah."

"What did it feel like?"

"It felt just like kissing a human foot. She did have a yellow or golden rose on her left foot—I kissed her left foot. And no more than I kissed it, I think I passed out, or fell down, I don't know—it was just from relief or something."

One of the women praying near Ray that day said her first thought was that he had had another heart attack.

"I just fell forward," Ray continued. "I think the anxiety of being able to do that—to kiss her foot—was just overwhelming. I think I was just in awe about it. I don't know."

The day we met, Ray was carrying some Polaroid photographs from a recent apparition. It was a series of three shots of the altar and sanctuary taken by a young girl at roughly ten-second intervals. When Ray sees the Virgin arriving, he raises his rosary above his head as a signal to the crowd. The first photograph was snapped at the moment Ray raised his rosary. There was nothing remarkable in the picture. The second, though, was marred by a multi-particulate flood of glare shooting down from skyward into the middle of the stage, obliterating the altar and the statue behind it.

Ray pointed to a spot in the middle of the glare and said, "You can kind of see—some people say they can see—her coming. I don't know."

The third picture was similar, but the glare was brighter and covered a wider area.

"The light is so brilliant. When they showed me these pictures for the first time, I almost fainted, because this light is exactly like I had been describing it to people. If it's not from heaven, then what caused all of this? And what causes us to get sunburned when we're up there close? And women's earrings and everything to get red-hot? And what's all these lights flyin' across the floor? The heat's there. We feel the heat. I feel it. Someone said that in Conyers they put a Geiger counter out there, and when she comes, it goes up like there's radiation."

"Is the light hard to look at?" I asked.

"It's not hard," Ray says. "It's like, when you see the miracle of the sun, you know when it's OK to look at it. You don't just get out here and start staring at the sun, 'cause it'll hurt your eyes. But something tells you, 'Look at the sun.' And all of a sudden you'll see the sun start spinning. But it looks like an eclipse. You know how the sun gets in an eclipse? You know, that eeriness? That's what it looks like." His remarks echo Saint Teresa's description of the light accompanying many of her visions: "It is not a radiance which dazzles, but a soft whiteness and an infused radiance which, without wearying the eyes, causes them the greatest delight."

Ray says Mary seems to stand on something like a cloud. "It don't look like her feet touch the ground, no. She's on something," he said. "My eyes lock onto hers and I never take 'em off. One time, though, I was almost level with her, and we were eye to eye. Her eyes were open more that time, it seemed like. And while she was talking to me, her eyes were going from side to side like this [Ray's eyes ticked slowly back and forth, as if tracking a hypnotist's pocket watch], like she was takin' in the count of the people. It gives me goose bumps to talk about it. She didn't move her head much, but she kept rolling her eyes like she was counting everybody or blessing them or something, I don't know."

Ray explains Mary's youthful appearance as typical of a glorified body. "There's no way you can capture this beauty and the beauty of the way our life will be in eternal life, in a glorified body. One time I asked Jesus what age we will be in heaven and what a glorified body meant, and he said, 'Whatever age that you were the most beautiful on earth, that's the way you'll be in heaven, but you'll be so much more beautiful.' That's why Mary Magdalene didn't recognize Jesus in the garden. She took him for a young gardener, because

she was looking for a thirty-three-year-old man all beat up
and everything. Until you see a glorified body you don't
know the beauty of what that is. It's just like the inner light
or your inner self comes out and shines."

Again, Ray has succeeded in uncannily recalling the words
of Saint Teresa: "There is such beauty about glorified bodies
that the glory which illumines them throws all who look upon
such supernatural loveliness into confusion. . . . If I were to
spend years and years imagining how to invent anything so
beautiful, I could not do it, and I do not even know how I
should try, for, even in its whiteness and radiance alone, it
exceeds all that we can imagine."

It was 12:30 P.M. Almost everyone had left their cars and
filtered into the amphitheater. Those who had come prepared
with blankets and sleeping bags sat, clustered together for
warmth. Others, me included, were up and moving, trying to
keep the blood flowing.

Petitions—scraps of paper with prayer requests written on
them—were being collected in a slotted cardboard box at
stage right. Mary, the faithful believe, will pay special attention to these written requests, conveying them back to
heaven, where she will present them to God the Father. Another petition box rested on a card table near the back of the
amphitheater. People bent over the table, writing.

Halfway up the permanent seating and off to one side a
greatly overweight man sat beside two boxes filled with photographs. Curious pilgrims stood near him, looking through
his photographs and listening as he talked. As I approached,
he was being questioned by an elderly woman.

"Will you pray for my family?" she asked.

"Oh, yeah," he said. "Just give me your name—your first
name. See, God goes by your first name. Your last name
means nothing to him. Just your first name."

The woman asked me for a piece of paper. I tore one from
my notebook, and she stepped aside to write.

"Did you take all these pictures yourself?" I asked the man, indicating the two overflowing cardboard boxes at his side.

"Yeah. But it's stuff that was given to me, shown to me by God, to show the people," he said in answer to my question. "It doesn't belong to me; it belongs to God.

"Most of these pictures were taken right here, except for a few, like this one that was taken in front of my house on Christmas. I was told to get out of my car by an angel and start takin' pictures. I was invited to Christ's birthday party." At that point he laughed suddenly and uproariously, amusing himself into a wracking, tubercular coughing fit. I waited it out.

"Hell," he continued, after settling his lungs, "I was going around the driveway just taking pictures. I said, 'Aw, man, am I glad the neighbors ain't out here!' They probably woulda thought I was crazy."

The woman who had asked him to pray for her family finished writing her name and those of her nine children and handed the paper to him. "Is that all you need?" she asked.

"That's it," he said. "I'll take care of you. I'll put it in."

The woman said, quietly, "We've got a . . . dysfunctional family."

"It's OK," he said. "You're as good as in. I've got your name and everything, it's all I need."

He turned from her and lifted from one of the boxes a stack of two-foot by two-foot sheets of poster board. Onto each sheet, of which there were dozens, he had laminated six or eight Polaroid photographs. Between the photographs he had drawn on the poster board, in crayon and colored pencil, geometric designs composed of pyramids, circles, boxes, wavy lines, and triangles. Each set of photos was accompanied by its own unique design. He explained the drawings to me as "insignias" and said that they somehow "go with" the pictures they accompany, though he doesn't always know what they represent. He had simply rendered them as they had been transmitted to him from heaven.

As I watched, he flipped through the stack for my benefit, offering rapid thumbnail interpretations of the photographs as he went. Each picture was of sky and clouds. Some were smeared with bits of glare and lens flare, but mostly they just looked like clouds. His chubby index finger jumped from picture to picture, almost too rapidly for me to follow, pointing out cloud features that I could make nothing of. It was like watching a self-administered Rorschach test with a time limit.

"OK. This here, that's Mary right there. And that's her right there again. That's her right there with a soul right there. That's the angel Gabriel. That's her again right there. There's an angel being blessed by Christ. There's another angel right there. There's Christ right there, smiling. There's Christ hanging on the cross. Mary. And these are angels singing right here. That's Christ right there. There's Mary right there. I think that's Christ right there. And this here is an alien angel."

"A what?"

"An alien angel."

"Now, what's that?"

"Well, see, we're not the only creatures in the universe— the *vast* universe is what they call it. God has other planets, other universes, other solar systems where he has people. And these alien angels take care of the other people in other worlds."

"I see."

"That's Mary right there. And right there. And there she is right there. Just before Christ was crucified, he went to pray to his father, and there he is right there, like he's kneeling down, looking up. There's his father right there. This here is judgment hall. And there's Christ on the cross. Do you see Christ hanging on the cross there?"

"Well, maybe . . . ." I looked harder.

"Arms out? Head down? That's him. There's an angel wavin'. There's Christ again right there. The angel of death.

Your guardian angel. If you confess to God that his son came to die for you and just for you, you won't have to be judged by Christ; you will go on and your angel, your guardian angel, will take you into the gates of paradise.

"OK, this here, this is the first time you're ever gonna get to see God. This is God right here, and this is Christ right here that sits on the right-hand side of him. I always wondered what this was." He pointed to a fluff of cloud near the clump he had just identified as Christ. "It took me six months to figure this out—he's hauling our petitions in his hand!" He burst into a wheeze of graveling laughter, and I braced for another calamitous lung clearing, which didn't come. "When Mary picks 'em up, she gives 'em to God, and then God gives 'em to his Son, and whatever his Son decides is what is going to be."

The last thing he pointed to was a cloud that seemed a paradigm of cloudness—fluffy, white, amorphous. "There's Mary right there," he said, then checked himself. "No, wait, that's Christ. Sorry. *No*—it's Mary! It's Mary."

It was almost one o'clock, and something was wrong with the p.a. system—two Bose loudspeakers up on spindly stands. Ray bustled around with a technician, checking wires and connections, and soon it was up and running again. The stairway to the stage and altar was now blocked by a volunteer, and the faithful were being urged to return to their seats.

Ray and a group of close friends knelt at the marble rail that wraps around the front of the stage. The rosary began. The prayers were led via the p.a. by a woman kneeling near Ray. The crowd responded in unison—a loud, collective chant that for some reason reminded me of one of those over-the-top Old Testament movies, the kind nobody seems interested in making anymore.

After the first decade, the mystery of the Annunciation, came the mystery of the Visitation, when Mary was expected to arrive. I moved into a position from which to observe Ray's face better. Still in his tinted glasses and baseball cap, he stared straight ahead, working the rosary beads slowly with his bare fingers. At the start of the third Hail Mary, both of Ray's arms shot straight up over his head, the rosary stretched between them. He lowered his arms, and cameras began flashing from the crowd. His face was expressionless and his lips moved, but not in sync with the prayers that continued around him.

I asked Ray if he ever had visions of persons other than the Virgin Mary.

"People have asked me that before. I think I have seen little cherubims, or something like that. One time I noticed that there was something on the side of Mary that looked like babies that had larger heads, you know, than their bodies. I can't say if I saw wings, but there was something on the side of her like little angels. I have seen—not in the vision with her—I have seen Raphael, the angel, and a few other angels down there at the grotto.

"Of course, I've seen Jesus. Seen Jesus here. He talks to me and gives me messages. One time, in June of 1993, Mary came and asked me what I was doing there. She kind of floored me a little bit, and then she disappeared and Jesus came. And Jesus took me through hell. I got to see hell."

Ray shares the privilege of having seen the inferno with many other visionaries. Lucia dos Santos, one of the young seers of Fatima, described a famous vision of hell shown to the children by the Virgin:

[It was] a sea of fire; and plunged in this fire the demons and the souls, as if they were red-hot coals, transparent and black or bronze-colored, with human forms, which floated about in the conflagration, borne by the flames which issued from it with clouds of smoke, falling on all sides as sparks fall in great conflagrations—without weight or equilibrium, among shrieks and groans of sorrow and despair which horrify and cause to shudder with fear. The devils were distinguished by

horrible and loathsome forms of animals frightful and unknown, but transparent like black coals that have turned red-
hot.

According to devotional accounts, the vision of hell instilled
in the children a sober respect for the reality of divine
judgment and the finality of eternal damnation. The soul-
consuming fires, as hell supporters like to point out, are the
instruments of God's perfect justice, a necessary corollary to
his perfect mercy.

Ray described his vision of the abyss: "It was in June of
'93 when Jesus came and took me through hell," he said. "It
was like standing on a bridge—a big bridge—and you're
looking down into a lake of clear water. You see big fish swimming. The only difference of it is that the lake is a lake of fire,
and the fish you see swimming are people. And that's about
all I can say. Can you imagine being burned by a flame like
we know it? Can you imagine how excruciating it would be
to be burned at the stake? That kind of flame can kill this
body, but it can't kill the soul. The flame in hell is a different
kind of flame, and it's much more excruciating than a flame
that could kill this body, this flesh. The flame in hell burns
up the soul, and it is more painful. That's about all I can say."
Like the Fatima seers, Ray thinks visionaries are shown the
fiery pit in order that they might speak more persuasively on
the subject.

Though reluctant to talk about it, Ray told me that he had
also had experiences with Satan. I told Ray that I had heard
that where Mary is appearing, Satan is also thought to be in
the vicinity (he had shouted "Get out! Get out!" at Saint
Bernadette as she prayed before the Virgin—until the apparition of Mary had turned to regard him).

"You'd better believe it!" Ray said. "Our Lady told me,
she warned me, she said, 'Where my son and I manifest ourselves, so will Satan.' And I've seen him, yes. When my wife
died, he was in the room trying to tell me to drop all this

stuff and walk away from it, just get away from all of it. And I told Jesus to get him out of there."

"Do you see him as a physical being?" I asked.

"It's not as clear as I see Our Lady, but it is like an image there, yes. And I told him, 'Get out of here. You're nothing but lies and promises; just be out of my sight.' And I asked Jesus to get him out of there."

Sometimes, according to Ray, though the devil might not make an appearance, his influence can be felt all the same.

"I have had bad dreams," he said. "And one time I was trying to get here—for the last prayer meeting we had here—and I thought I'd wash my car on the way. Well, I think the lady that was in the car wash in front of me used a whole water tower before she got out of there. And I was in line with people behind me, I couldn't back up, couldn't get out or nothing, I had to wait until she got out. She was washing it out underneath and everything. I think I sat there for about forty-five minutes, waiting for her to get out of that bay so I could wash my car and get out here. Then, afterward, it seemed like every light I hit was red. It seemed like everything that could possibly happen that day was thrown in my way. Like the devil was saying, 'I'm gonna fix it so you don't get there,' you know. It happens. The closer you get to God, the more Satan is active."

Mary stayed at the amphitheater for nearly forty-five minutes, during which time the crowd completed all fifteen decades of the rosary. Afterward, they tacked on a few extra prayers, including the petition to Saint Michael, in which petitioners seek protection from the "wickedness and snares of the devil" and ask Michael to cast into hell "Satan, and all evil spirits who wander now throughout the world seeking the ruin of souls." Ray then requested that pilgrims raise their rosaries for a blessing from Mary.

Shortly after, Ray held a microphone and, in a quavering voice, addressed the crowd over the p.a.

"My dear friends in Christ. Our Heavenly Mother was here with us again today. She was dressed all in white and had a blue . . . band around her waist. She appeared to me as Our Lady of Lourdes, which is fitting for today, since it is the feast day of Our Lady of Lourdes. I will try to repeat the message she gave to me and say that, in case I make mistakes, I am human and I know she will forgive me. Do not judge me on how I give you this message, but judge yourselves on how you receive it in your hearts, because it is from Our Heavenly Father, given to us by the Blessed Mother.

" 'My dear children. Three years ago I came down from heaven to be with you, my children, my humble servants. My heart is happy the way you are gathering here in this great cenacle of prayer. . . .' "

In a somewhat wandering oration, Mary exhorted her followers to live the messages received at Belleville and at other apparition sites around the world, to love God, to have faith, to pray more fervently. She also warned of Satan's ascendancy. "God is sad," she told them frankly, "because his people still follow the path of Satan's sin just as in the days of Noah. . . . A time is near when Satan's power will seem to rule the whole world and everything in it. . . . God has permitted sin to work in your life so that you can choose between the good and evil, but the world must pay for these sins. You will see how the prince of darkness, temptation, and lies will lead you on the path of total destruction." With some urgency Mary invited everyone to turn to the Spirit *today*, "because the time is coming when a famine of this Spirit will sweep over all the world and you will hunger and thirst for this Spirit of God for your soul, for without it your soul will wither and die. Pray, pray, pray, for yourselves and for your loved ones, so they will not witness these things and be put to the test." She ended with a promise to return the following June and a reminder that she had already presented the crowd's petitions to God. "Go in peace," she said, "and love God."

Most in the crowd rose to their feet at the end of the

message. Many had already packed up and were waiting to go—having taken all the cold they could stand. A line formed up the steps and onto the stage, where people began retrieving their "blessed" objects. Plenty of others made their way down toward the foot of the stage, where Ray stood, waiting to greet them one by one, for as long as they cared to stay.

"My dear friends," Ray spoke again, "I will stay here, and I will talk to anyone who wishes to talk to me for as long as it takes. I know it's cold, but you've come here for the word of God, and I hope I give it to you so that your heart is opened up to his words. Amen." He put the microphone down and greeted his public.

A crowd quickly coalesced around Ray, and everyone seemed to be talking at once. The cold had us all with our hands in our coat pockets, arms close to our sides, shoulders tensed. Some of the faithful cried. From the stage just behind, someone dangled a baby down to Ray.

"Ray, this man here said you were going to pray over a baby, and he has to leave," someone said from behind Ray.

"He's in a lot of pain," said the man handing down the baby.

"Oh, sure," said Ray, taking the toddler under the armpits and hugging him close.

The little boy looked healthy enough, but you never know. He was in jeans, a stocking cap, and a thick winter coat. As soon as Ray took him, he began to cry and craned his neck to see his mom.

"Just a second," said Mom. "Mommy's right here."

Ray bowed his head and prayed for the child.

"In the name of the Father and of the Son and of the Holy Spirit. Amen. Our heavenly Father, I ask you to look down with favors on this small child of yours that loves you very much in his heart. Be with him and protect him. And heal him of whatever is wrong with him. Always stand with him as you did your own beloved son. I ask this in the name of our beloved Christ Jesus." Ray raised his head and looked at the child in his arms before handing him back to his father.

"Peace be with you, my friend," he said to the child. "God bless you, little buddy."

A white-haired priest with a pale face and a black hat, a friend of Ray's, stood beside him. After his prayer over the child, Ray turned to the priest and asked, "That sound OK?"

"Yeah, you're doing great."

"I'm really shaky," Ray confided to the priest. I wasn't sure if he meant from nerves or from the cold.

Everyone crowded closer to Ray, each wanting to be heard, to have Ray's attention if only for a few seconds. Ray tried his best to attend to them all.

One woman, speaking through gritted teeth and sounding like a bad ventriloquist, said, "I didn't get my mouth opened today, but I'm not giving up. I'm gonna go ahead and have the surgery." Ray gave her a hug.

Another woman pressed forward to give Ray a hug. She had nothing to say.

Someone handed Ray a steaming Styrofoam cup of coffee. Several people in succession assailed him with questions: "Do you remember? . . ." "How come Our Lady? . . ." "Why doesn't Jesus? . . ."

Ray explained to one questioner that he had had trouble remembering the word *sash* when describing Mary's appearance to the crowd earlier. "That shows how Satan interferes with me trying to give the message," he said. "That's what happens, you totally lose it."

"The Blessed Mother can fix Satan," someone nearby offered.

"Yeah," Ray agreed. "She's *going* to. You can hear, I think, what she said in the message. We must come to the table of the Lord. Without it there will be a famine, a shortage of priests."

A woman: "Did you see sparks around the altar?"

Ray: "There's heat up there that you can see."

Another woman: "Where does she appear?"

"She comes with a brilliant light," Ray answered, "right there where the statue is. And a lot of people think that maybe it's just the statue, but it's not. There is a light that completely engulfs the statue that I don't even see it anymore. And there's no depth. I could reach out and touch her right here." Ray stretched an arm out to show how close the Virgin appears to him.

"Mmmm-mmmm," the woman moaned, as if she'd just tasted something good.

"It's just like she's right here, right in front of me," Ray continued. "We have a picture that was taken here on October the thirteenth that proves what I said. Our Lady tells me, 'My sign to you is my presence in you,' but these pictures are given then, and the turning of the rosaries, which mine do, are signs for you people, all of you." He fished out the three pictures I had seen the day before and showed them around. "You can see it blots out the whole statue; you can see that there's no depth there in that light."

"Yes. I kind of understand that," said the priest.

"Mmmm. Oh, my heavens," one woman responded.

Ray said, "That is how she comes. When I seen these pictures for the first time, I turned white."

"Did you?" asked the priest rhetorically.

An elderly woman in front of Ray said, "If I seen her, I wouldn't tell nobody I did." No response.

Ray turned to the priest, who was still standing near Ray's left elbow. "I don't know what she has planned for me yet, or how long the apparitions will keep coming here. She wants us to keep coming here in prayer, even if the apparitions stop. But I want her to keep trying to give me locutions so I can pass them on to the people."

The priest nodded. "Sure. That's what she wants, I'm sure."

"I'm so glad to have been so blessed," Ray told the priest.

A young woman with a look of amazement on her

face came forward and asked, "Today it was the Lady of Lourdes?"

"Yeah," Ray answered. "She appeared as Our Lady of Lourdes, yeah. I couldn't even think of the words 'blue sash.' That shows you how Satan's trying to stop me from giving this message."

"Oh, believe me," the woman concurred, "he is working worse and worse."

"It's a fight like you can't believe," Ray assured her.

"Oh, I bet it is."

"It's a fight to try to keep with this. The temptations and stuff that comes in my life . . ." Ray fell silent.

"Yes," the woman continued, "like when Satan tries to get at you through flashes in the mind. You know, that drives me crazy, and I worry about that. And I think, 'God, *please*, you know, I'm really not thinking that!' But yet he's there, and he makes it very difficult."

Someone poked a head up over the outer ring of the crowd and shouted to Ray, "The mad monk needs your car keys!"

"In the trunk," Ray shouted back. "You push that trunk button and it will open."

The woman continued, "How can we hear more of your messages?"

"Just write to the address that's on the bottom of the sheet you got today," Ray answered. "I gotta talk to others, so could you just keep filing through?"

"God bless you," said the woman as she left.

"God bless you," Ray agreed.

Ray handed his coffee cup to someone nearby, asking her to hold it. He said to the priest, "I'm still shaking. I'm not only shaking because it's cold. I'm shaking because you have to realize what goes through a person. I'm shaking because of the battle that we have with Satan. Whenever Our Lady and Jesus manifest themselves in a place, Satan's right behind her. Right behind her."

With some urgency the priest suggested we all stop for a

moment to recite again the prayer to Saint Michael. Everyone nearby reached toward Ray and asked once again for protection from the "wickedness and snares of the devil."

"Thank you, Father," Ray said with some relief when the prayer had ended.

"You're welcome."

A very old Asian woman stood in front of Ray. She was crying freely, unable to speak.

Ray extended his arms to her. "Come here. Come here, come here. Come here," he said, and wrapped her in a hug. As soon as she got control of herself, she posed next to Ray long enough for a friend to snap a picture.

"Could you pray for my daughter, who's falling away?" someone shouted from the crowd.

"If you put a petition in the box, it's in the right hands," Ray assured the shouter.

Next, Ray was hugged by a small group of crying women. Immediately after, a middle-aged woman clutching a wooden rosary fell into Ray's arms, sobbing loudly. She was bawling. Bawling and talking, but I couldn't make out anything she was saying. I don't think Ray could either. "God bless you," he said. "God bless you."

The priest reached over to reassure Ray. "You're doing very well, Ray," he said. "The Blessed Mother's pleased with you."

"I hope so. I hope so," Ray said. "I shed many tears after this here. I go home and I think about this, I think about all the people that asked me to pray. And there's another thing I found out that whenever I pray with people—the reason why I'm shaking—whenever I pray for something for a person, I feel something come out of me. And it makes me weak. It does make me weak."

"That's divine energy," suggested another elderly Asian woman. Ray hugged her as her husband took a picture. She started to cry and spoke quietly to Ray.

"I love you too," Ray replied. "I love you the way Jesus

loves you." This last sentiment sparked a thought, and Ray lifted his head to address the crowd. "I love you all the way Jesus loves you," he said, "and that's the deepest love that we can have." Here Ray began a desultory, stream-of-consciousness monologue that touched on, among other things, the quality of a parent's love for a child; the humility of Jesus; the fact that Jesus laughed and cried; the fact that Ray himself sheds many tears ("I didn't cry as much today as I did October thirteenth. That day, when I got up, my whole chest was wet"); the nature of spiritual "craving" illustrated with a story about a chocolate bar; Ray's assurance from Mary that his wife is "in a safe place"; his past experiences with Satan ("At my wife's deathbed I had to really kick Satan in the butt. I'm sorry, but I can't put it any better way than that"); and his belief that he is "in good company because they called Jesus crazy too."

Ray continued talking as the crowd began to thin; eventually the group around him shrank to a small circle of hangers-on. As he spoke, they looked at him in silence, listening intently. One woman stood with a yellow-checked blanket wrapped around herself and her little girl of five or six. The girl's head poked out of the V of the blanket, and she too stared at Ray in silence.

His address wound down and eventually rolled to a stop. For a moment we all stood looking at one another. Finally a nice-looking dark-haired man of about twenty-five stepped forward and said to Ray, "I want to take a hug back home." Ray hugged him, and the man turned in the opposite direction and ran to his car. The others seemed to take that as their cue, and they dispersed happily in a flurry of hugs and good wishes and "God bless you's."

In spite of the fact that Mary's appearances had been coming less frequently, at the time we spoke, Ray was still coming to the shrine to pray on the thirteenth of every month.

"And I want the people to keep coming here, long after

these apparitions are over," he told me. "I don't know how much longer the apparitions are gonna come. A lot of the places that I hear of, Our Lady has stopped coming. So a lot of this must be coming to a close. I look for this to come to an end, but she has never told me yet when. I think she'll wait and tell me on that day, 'This is my last apparition to you,' because if she would tell me tomorrow that the next time she comes will be my last one, I would be in mourning something like you can't believe. It's like saying good-bye to someone very, very special in your life, knowing you'll never seem 'em again; it's gonna be very hard. But we're gonna keep coming here on the thirteenth as long as I've got breath in my body. So I hope the people keep coming. I hope that's what they do.

"I think there will eventually be a sign given. That's just my opinion. The sign could be in Medjugorje or in Garabandal, Spain, I don't know. That'd be her last, final thing, I think, that she'd do on the earth. But when will this happen? I have no idea.

"Everybody thinks because you've seen the Blessed Mother that you have all the answers. You don't. You don't. That's the first thing I try to get across to people. I don't know much more than what the average person knows."

He amended that last statement, explaining that there have been some messages that he simply has not been allowed to pass on—secrets imparted by the Virgin: "I am told some things that I'm not permitted to speak on. When I try to speak on them, something blocks out my ability to get the message to people. People say, 'Well, what do you mean by that?' I say, 'Well, if Sister Lucy could give us the third secret of Fatima, she would have. If the kids at Medjugorje could tell us the ten secrets, they would have. But they can't because they're not allowed to speak on them.' "

It seemed to me as we talked that the one thing weighing heavily on Ray was his perceived responsibility to those who come to be with him at the Belleville Shrine. He made a point of explaining that he was not trying to pass himself off as somehow better or more deserving than his followers. His humility seemed genuine, and by his own admission he is as astonished by heaven's insistence on speaking through Ray Doiron as anyone else might be.

"People come up and say, 'Let me touch you,' " he told me with a pained expression. "I say to them, 'Let me touch *you*, because the same God that created my hand created yours; there's no difference.' They say, 'Well, you're touched by certain things.' That's true, but I don't think that. They've got the same thing—they've been touched the same way. All you gotta do is have God in your heart and open your heart up to him. People may never see what I see, but I try to describe it to them, and I draw pictures of what I see; I try to do everything that I can—I try to be their eyes, you know?

"There was a blind lady here one day, and this nun brought her up and said, 'She's got something to tell you.' The lady walked up to me and she said, 'I'm blind.' I said, 'Yes. And I know what you have to tell me. You seen Our Lady, didn't you?' She said yes. I said describe her to me. She described her exactly. She's blind, but she seen it. And I've noticed a similar thing; if I close my eyes, the vision is still just as bright with my eyes closed. So that shows you I'm meant to see it. I can try to close it out, but it's there. I'm the first visioner I know of that ever said they could witness it with their eyes closed. I'm supposed to see it. I cannot get away from it."

As the crowd dissipated, I walked back to my car, started it up to get the heat going, and ate a sandwich from my cooler. From where I sat, I could see Ray still standing in the bowl of the amphitheater, leaning heavily now on his cane, speaking patiently with one remaining pilgrim.

I recognized a feeling in myself that I had first noticed at the end of my second day in Conyers, melancholy colored by a vague glaze of uncleanliness. Melancholy over the universal human difficulties that compel people to cling to this kind of solace, and unclean as a consequence of peeping into other people's cosmic struggles. Nobody likes a voyeur.

Whatever the actual facts of Ray Doiron's situation, he seemed sincere. He seemed dedicated and compassionate. And what can you say against compassion? Again, though, I had seen nothing miraculous. All I had seen, again, was more people than you would probably expect standing out under the open sky awaiting a visitor from heaven.

On my way out of the Shrine of Our Lady of Snows, I stopped at the gift shop. It was wall to wall with Doiron pilgrims. I poked around for a while in the book section, then looked through bins of medals dedicated to particular saints. In a section of brooches and necklaces and other nonsacramental tchotchkes, I spotted a small gold pin attached to a little white card. Affixed to the pin was a blue stone about the size of a lima bean. On the card were these words: "Glorious Visions of Mary. Warm the blue stone in your hand and watch the image of Our Lady appear." The lima bean looked like it was made of the same stuff mood rings are made of, and I figured it probably worked on the same principle. I picked up the stone and warmed it for a few seconds in my hand. No Mary. I cupped it in my hands and breathed on it, then held it between my palms for a full half minute before opening my hands to look again. Nothing.

CHAPTER SIX

✤ ✤ ✤

Mercy and Motions of the Spirit
Scottsdale and Phoenix, Arizona

Scottsdale

The gene pool in Scottsdale, Arizona, is a healthful soup indeed. Aided by favorable environmental factors, including wealth and almost cloying yearly amounts of sunshine, the citizens, as a class, simply look better than Midwesterners, which is what I am. Even Scottsdale's homely people (there are a handful) are lifted beyond their natural attractive capacities by association. Their plainness doesn't seem as complete or as debilitating as it might in Indianapolis. Perhaps it's a matter of the background. Scottsdale is a seriously well-kept city, particularly from a floral point of view, and the sky is a solid, keen-edged blue 314 days out of every year. Towering palms and flaming Mexican bird of paradise fill most available vistas. To an Ohioan less than eight hours out from under an endlessly cold and rainy spring, Scottsdale can feel like an answer to some kind of prayer.

On my first afternoon in Scottsdale—a bright, dry day in early May—I drove up Scottsdale Road, a main north-south thoroughfare, past art galleries, rug shops, jewelry and craft shops, and restaurants. Blondes in sunglasses and German cars were ubiquitous—gunning past me through green lights, idling beside me at red ones, looking straight ahead, smoking languidly. College-age male valets lingered outside restaurants, all polo shirts and khaki shorts. Inside a fast-food chicken restaurant where I stopped for lunch, the counter help all looked collegiate and natty—deeply tanned, hair sunbleached and gleaming from swim team. They were polite in a way that seemed to owe far more to breeding than to any kind of corporate coaching the chicken franchise might have come up with.

I was on my way to Saint Maria Goretti Church, a wealthy parish on the northern side of this wealthy community. A popular series of purportedly supernatural events had begun at Saint Maria Goretti in 1988 that were, by the time of my visit, drawing to a close. The events involved Jesus and Mary, nine young adults, and the pastor of Saint Maria Goretti, Father Jack Spaulding.

In 1987 Father Spaulding and a group of parishioners made a pilgrimage to Medjugorje, in the former Yugoslavia, to visit the site of Mary's alleged appearances to the young seers at the parish of Saint James. Upon their return to Scottsdale, the parishioners formed prayer groups at Saint Maria Goretti (similar Medjugorje–inspired prayer groups were springing up in Catholic parishes all around the United States).

Also in 1987 Gianna Talone, a Saint Maria Goretti parishioner and, at the time, a thirty-year-old doctor of pharmacology, had a series of what she at first thought were dreams about the Virgin Mary. Over three successive nights Mary appeared near Gianna's bed and seemed to be praying over her but did not speak. By the third night Gianna had determined, based on the lucidity of the experiences, that she was not dreaming. Nothing else miraculous happened for a while, but Gianna noticed that she now had an overwhelming desire to attend Mass, to receive the Eucharist, and to pray the rosary.

One day in November of that same year, Gianna stopped in to pray at Saint Maria Goretti during her lunch hour. When she had finished praying, she began to rise from the kneeler and found she couldn't get up. She has said that she felt as though a force on her left shoulder was holding her down. Then she heard an interior male voice say, "The Lord seeks favor upon you, for you have cried for the Lord. You will do great things." Gianna later understood the voice to have been that of the Archangel Gabriel.

In June of the next year, 1988, Father Spaulding returned to Medjugorje for another pilgrimage. This time the group included Gianna Talone. It was in Medjugorje that Gianna first heard the Virgin Mary speak to her, asking her to pray for peace in the world and in the family. During this pilgrimage Gianna had a private meeting with Vicka Ivankovic, one of the Medjugorje visionaries, who gave her what she perceived to be an encouraging word concerning the supernatural experiences she reported. "Keep your heart open," Vicka told her. Just before returning to the States, Gianna was praying before a statue of the Virgin at Saint James Church in Medjugorje when Mary spoke to her and told her it was time for her mission to begin. "You will do great things, and many will come to you," Gianna heard Mary say. "I will guide and protect you."

Not long after their return to Scottsdale, Gianna reported to Father Spaulding that she was receiving what she believed to be messages from heaven—from both Mary and Christ—that were meant to be shared with the parish. Father Spaulding began reading the messages aloud to the weekly prayer group. Shortly thereafter, Gianna told Father Spaulding that she had received a "prophetic" vision, in which she saw herself and a group of young-adult parishioners praying before a statue of the Virgin in church. This was to be the group of nine young adults that, with the addition of Father Spaulding, would constitute the circle of Scottsdale seers and locutionists. Over the course of the next few years, thousands of pilgrims would travel to Saint Maria Goretti to be near them.

In August 1988 Father Spaulding made yet another trip to Medjugorje. This time it was his turn to experience an "interior locution," the internal apprehension of a supernatural voice speaking to him. The voice told him, "You are to walk by faith, not by sight." Later during that same trip, he heard the voice of Mary telling him, "I am here, and I'm going home with you."

Back in Scottsdale, from fall 1987 to spring 1989, the young adults revealed in Gianna's vision, so the story goes, presented themselves to Father Spaulding, most claiming varying degrees of inexplicable spiritual phenomena. Typical of them was one of the first to approach Father Spaulding, Susan Evans, a twenty-nine-year-old in ill health. She had heard a voice she identified as that of Jesus asking her, first, "Would you suffer for me?" Then, "Would you suffer for others?" Others claimed that Mary or Jesus was speaking to them and wished the messages to be written down and shared with the parish. Still others were said to be receiving messages, but primarily for guidance in their personal lives. Eventually at least three others besides Gianna would claim to have had visions of supernatural persons—of Mary, Jesus, and Satan. It is said that the nine did not know each other, at least not beyond a passing acquaintance, before sensing the call to come forward. The group ranged in age from sixteen to thirty and included among their ranks a teacher, a musician, a florist, and a rodeo rider.

The prayer group met every Thursday night, and over the next few years the popularity of that gathering grew until eventually crowds overflowed the church, spilling out onto the manicured lawns of Saint Maria Goretti. Pilgrims came to be near people whom they believed were near Mary and her son. The Thursday night service consisted of the prayers of the rosary, some additional prayers for healings and blessings of various kinds, and a Mass. During the rosary Gianna, sitting in the front row, would receive her vision of the Virgin, who would impart a message that would be read later that evening to those gathered and waiting. A videotape about the events at Saint Maria Goretti, entitled *I Am Your Jesus of Mercy,* shows Gianna, a petite brunette with doe eyes and an incandescent grin, at the moment of her ecstasy. She bounds from her pew to the kneeler at the arrival of the Virgin, her eyes locked forward and raised. She smiles intensely and seems to be carrying on a conversation with the apparition.

Things went on in this vein for some time, with Gianna as the primary visionary and message bearer. Then one night during Mass, in November 1988, after the reading of the Gospel, Father Spaulding walked to a spot in front of the altar to deliver his homily but found he had gone blank. As he stood there struggling to recall what it was he had intended to say, he suddenly heard himself speaking. The voice was his own, but the words were not. It was, according to Father Spaulding, Mary speaking through him. Gianna told Father Spaulding that the Virgin would continue to make use of him in this way from time to time, as long as he was willing. Father Spaulding assented, and messages continued to come through him during the Thursday night prayer group on a more or less weekly basis for the next eight years. Although the first message through Father Spaulding had been from Mary, the majority of subsequent messages were said to be from Jesus himself.

The Scottsdale messages were, generally, sunnier and less threatening than messages from many other popular apparition sites. They stressed a critical reassessment of our fast-paced lives, and offered as antidote a return to the spiritual life, a recognition that the Kingdom of God is within, and an invitation to respond to the love and mercy offered us by Christ.

At the time of my visit to Saint Maria Goretti, in May 1996, most of the young people from the original circle of nine had dispersed. Gianna had moved to Maryland and continued to receive messages and draw weekly crowds at Saint Joseph's church in the city of Emmitsburg. Father Spaulding remained and still presided over the Thursday night prayer group. He was also still receiving messages from Jesus.

I arrived at the church on a Thursday evening to attend the weekly prayer meeting. The parish takes up nearly an entire block in the midst of a meticulously kept suburban neighborhood. The ranch-style homes around the parish—mostly in muted pinks, tans, and creams—are surrounded by palms, prickly pear, yucca plants, and the swollen, impudent fingers of saguaro cacti. Some of the lawns had been watered to lushness, but many homeowners had forgone grass in favor of reddish pea gravel and sand. Some lawns sported tall trees, unknown to me, that rose twenty feet in the air but were no bigger around than my forearm; they had small orange tufts at the top and looked like something out of Dr. Seuss. The sun was low, casting a dusky golden light on the sides of the taller palms.

A series of connected buildings, all off-white, make up the parish complex. They include a parish center, offices, a preschool, several meeting halls and community rooms, and a gift shop. A small building made of white masonry and floor-to-ceiling walls of smoked glass stands between the parish offices and the church itself. This is "The Tabernacle," a building specifically constructed for display and veneration of the Blessed Sacrament—the consecrated Communion wafer. The Tabernacle is open for quiet prayer and meditation every hour of the day.

Seen from above, Saint Maria Goretti Church would appear as a stubby cross—a fat, white X. From ground level it is four vaulted sections of cream-colored stucco joined in the center and overarched by a white, parabolic exoskeleton surmounted by a white cross. It was built in 1967 and makes architectural allusions to the Sydney Opera House, Los Angeles International Airport, and most of the buildings on *The Jetsons.*

Inside, the church is modern but tasteful. The interior walls are off-white stucco. The vaulted arches rise toward the center of the roof, culminating in a stained glass cross of rich pinks, purples, and blues inlaid at the apex—an ecclesial skylight. The sanctuary and altar occupy one of the four main sections of the cross-shaped interior; the other three are filled with pews fanning out from the direction of the sanctuary. Above the altar hangs an etched-glass rendering of Salvador Dali's *Christ of St. John of the Cross*. The altar is flanked by life-size bronze statues of Jesus and Mary. Mary's right knee is bent slightly, as though she is in mid-stride, and her veil billows out behind her, enhancing the illusion of movement. Her right hand extends forward, and an arc of stars floats above her head.

Organ pipes fill one wall of the church. On the opposite wall is a large stained-glass image of Our Lady of Guadalupe done in an array of deep and deeper blues.

I took a seat near the back of the church and settled in as the faithful began filling the pews. The crowd was a mix of old and young adults, with the majority on the far side of forty. A few women were in the cry room with infants and toddlers. At seven o'clock, Father Spaulding and another man, a deacon, came into the sanctuary. In his mid-fifties, Father Spaulding is a slight man, short and thin. His face is serious, with a small, downward-turned mouth, a thin nose, and large, seemingly unblinking eyes. His hair is thick and dark and looks carefully shaped.

Father greeted the crowd and invited Mary to pray with us and lead us closer to Jesus. We began by singing the "Ave Maria," after which the rosary was begun. By seven-ten the church was full and we were well into the first decade of the Joyful mysteries: the Annunciation. The prayer was peaceful and soothing, and it began to have the effect on me which, under the best of conditions, I have known it to have in the past. On those occasions it passes from mere rote recital of a laundry list of praise and petition into the resonant, transcendent instrument it is meant to be, delivering me to a mental space in which the traditional ends of Catholic devotion seem inevitable, desirable, and attainable. It is no small thing to feel, if only for a moment, the warming effect of a God who cares and to realize that the search for holiness really might be the only thing that matters. No doubt this is the common experience of those who pray the rosary with undimmed faith and fervor, but it is a regrettably rare experience for me. For the next twenty minutes or so, I had no trouble curbing the critical faculties and entering into and enjoying the spirit of what was going on.

Saint Maria Goretti Church is as far from Nancy Fowler's Georgia farm aesthetically as it is geographically. Everything about the church was contributing to my prayer-favorable frame of mind. The decor was subtly stylish. The upholstered pews were comfortable, and the air temperature was perfectly controlled. Our mingled prayers rolled around in the arched ceiling high above our heads and fell lightly back to us like a bright, celestial dividend. The blue stained-glass Guadalupe Virgin glowed imperially, lit from behind by the setting sun, her hues dimming in all but imperceptible increments as the day's light faded: cerulean, cobalt, indigo, navy, black. I began to think, and immediately to regret having thought, that perhaps the positive effects of the evening's rosary—as opposed to rosaries I had sat through or maybe tried to pray along with at other apparition sites—were more or less a conditioned response to my surroundings. This church had a lot in common with churches I had grown up and been happy in, churches in which an excess of emotionalism would have seemed out of place, churches in which quiet, respectful, dignified recitation of this age-old devotion would have been common. I began to suspect that the cause of my positive response to the prayers at Saint Maria Goretti might be nothing more than some portion of my brain resonating contentedly at an aesthetic frequency to which it had been tuned as a child. And of course, once you start thinking about things in that way, you can kiss the fragile experience of the numinous good-bye.

After the rosary, the crowd started in on the Chaplet of Divine Mercy, a prayer cycle also recited using the rosary beads. I had first heard this prayer on the farm in Falmouth, Kentucky, and it consists in large part of a seemingly endless repetition of this plea: "For the sake of his sorrowful passion, have mercy on us and on the whole world." After a further series of songs and shorter prayers, Father asked us each to turn to our neighbors and introduce ourselves "so you'll know who is praying the Mass with you tonight." I made the acquaintance of an elderly woman beside me who looked like my mother. I forgot her name immediately, but she pulled mine out effortlessly about twenty minutes later during the sign of peace. At one point in the middle of Mass, we were all standing, singing the "Lamb of God" prayer. I could see out of the corner of my eye that my neighbor was swaying back and forth. Her hands were clasped over her chest, her eyes were closed, and her features were smooth and relaxed —it was a look of pure contentment, of pure prayer.

The musical accompaniment was lush and full—a grand piano and synthesized strings. The keyboardist was busy during most of the Mass, tinkling and noodling around in a sort of Windham Hill-ish way at what seemed to me to be the most inappropriate times—while the Gospel was being read, for instance, and later during the consecration of the bread and wine.

Shortly before eight o'clock, and immediately after the Gospel, it was time for the homily, that portion of the Mass in which the priest addresses the assembly, presenting his gloss on the day's reading and typically extracting a useful lesson for the benefit of those of us in the pews. It is what's commonly known as the sermon, and it was the time at which Father Spaulding, on occasion, instead of discussing the Gospel reading, simultaneously received and delivered his prophecy from Jesus. Father walked down front and center before the altar, facing the congregation. He stood still for a moment, then bowed his head. His arms hung limp at his sides;

I couldn't tell whether his eyes were open or shut. An air of quiet anticipation hung over the assembled faithful, some of whom stood. Suddenly, without looking up, Father began to speak: "My dear ones. I come this night to remind you of the care that God, my Father and your Father, has for you. . . ."

The message, slightly over one hundred fifty words, took nearly three and a half minutes to deliver. The words came slowly, with long pauses between phrases. The gist of the communiqué was that God would guide us on the right path and use us as his instruments of peace and mercy if only we would answer yes to his call. As the message ended, Father Spaulding's arms rose, and Jesus imparted a final blessing, leaving us with the gift of his peace. Father Spaulding then lowered his arms, turned, and walked back to his seat beside the deacon.

The rest of the service passed uneventfully. Father Spaulding offered the Mass with extreme reverence. At the raising of the host and wine during the consecration, he held each species high over his head for what began to seem an uncomfortably long time before lowering it to his lips for a kiss and then back to the altar. After Mass rosaries were brought out again, this time for the Glorious mysteries. Then more prayers and a litany that included Our Lady of Fatima, Our Lady of Lourdes, and Our Lady of Medjugorje. At the end Father Spaulding offered a general blessing of any religious articles we might have brought with us. We then knelt as he prayed for the healing of our minds, our bodies, our hearts, our souls, our wills, our spirits, our intellects, and that God would break down the barriers keeping us from a closer relationship with him. Then he asked for that same healing for our loved ones. When the service was over, we moved slowly and quietly up the aisles and through the double doors at the back of the church.

Outside, the sun was down and the air was warm. The moon was full, a white plate suspended amid glittering blackness. Crickets trilled in the short grass. Small knots of prayer-group members lingered on the parish grounds, talking quietly among themselves. I didn't feel like talking to any of them, though. Of all the prayer groups and apparition events I had attended, this one—aside from the "prophecy," which in its bland obviousness had not done much for me—had come closest to satisfying something in my heart. Even if it was, in the final analysis, mainly a matter of a conditioned response to religio-aesthetic imprinting in my youth, it was still a hard effect to shake. I was enjoying the afterglow too much to risk having it blown by listening to someone go on about some supposed miracle or other.

I took a walk around the grounds and ended up being drawn into The Tabernacle by the promising glow of candle-light from within. Inside there was seating for thirty or forty people. In the center of the room stood a burbling fountain. At the center of the fountain an upright, cross-shaped metal framework held a glass bowl filled with consecrated hosts. An angel knelt at each of the four corners of the square fountain, holding a votive candle sunk deep in a translucent red glass vessel. The angels—bronze-colored with big bronze wings and dressed in green robes—stared up at the bowl of hosts. People who had gone in just before me were dipping a hand in the fountain, crossing themselves, and kneeling to pray. I dipped and crossed, then sat on one of the seats arranged around the room's perimeter, expecting to collect my thoughts and enjoy just a little more of the serenity of this place before driving back to my hotel.

It was then that I noticed a woman lying on the purple-carpeted floor, weeping in soft gasps. Her head rested in the lap of a man sitting cross-legged on the floor beside her. He stroked her hairline softly with one finger and looked around the room with surprising nonchalance. I was afraid she was in some kind of distress and was considering asking if there was something I could do when I noticed that no one else in the room was taking the slightest notice of her. Even the man cradling her head seemed utterly unconcerned.

As it turned out, she was in a condition I would later come to understand as being "slain in the Spirit," her emotions overcome to the point at which her legs had simply buckled beneath her, refusing to go on until this urgent spiritual wallop had been acknowledged and allowed to work its way through her system. This is purportedly a service performed by the Holy Spirit, and the experience is considered a spiritual boon by those who undergo it. At one point the woman rose to her knees, but swooned back down again a second or two later. At this the man looked at a nearby woman, smiled, and shrugged his shoulders. A few short minutes later, the weeping woman stood up abruptly, wiped her eyes, dipped a finger into the fountain, and crossed herself. I followed them out of The Tabernacle and into the parking lot. By the time they had arrived at their car, she had recovered completely. She chatted happily to her companion as he fished his keys out of his pocket; they climbed into a car and left. I did the same.

The next day, I was back at Saint Maria Goretti for a mid-morning meeting with Father Spaulding. I parked my car and walked toward the cluster of parish buildings. A grounds crew worked quietly under a squintingly bright sky. Lawn sprinklers ticked in the distance. Two blue signs in the middle of the main sidewalk between the parish center and the church advertised "Gift Shop Open." As I was early for my appointment, I took a detour into the gift shop. It's a cramped space—two rooms filled with books, tapes, and devotional bric-a-brac. Cassettes of Father Spaulding speaking on various subjects—titles included *Mercy*, *The Eucharist*, and *Don't Be Nice, Be Catholic*—were available. His book *Hope for the Journey* was nearby. There were medals and rosaries, T-shirts ("Proud to Be Catholic"), sun catchers, and statuary. I was not the only customer in the shop that morning; several tanned, moneyed-looking middle-aged women were browsing enthusiastically. I bought a book about C. S. Lewis and left for my appointment.

At the parish offices, my arrival was announced, and I was asked to wait in the reception area. As church offices go, these were opulent, looking more like the offices of a suburban OB-GYN than those of any Catholic parish I'd ever seen. The walls were cream stucco; the furniture was Southwestern style—lots of light beige wood, Native American patterns on the seat cushions. Mozart wafted through the waiting area from a CD player behind the receptionist's desk. I picked up a copy of the parish bulletin; the ads in its back pages—a car service "Specializing in Mercedes-Benz Automobiles," a golf shop ("In Celebration of Golf"), an electronics company advertising home theater and home security systems, a pool-maintenance company—were revelatory of the class of parish in which I found myself.

The receptionist gave me a cup of coffee and a thumbnail biography of the church's patron saint to peruse while I waited for Father Spaulding. Maria Goretti, it seems, was a young Italian girl murdered in 1902 by a young man whose sexual advances she had successfully resisted. She was canonized in 1950. Interestingly, her murderer, who had experienced a conversion of heart after having a vision of the young saint, attended her canonization ceremony.

Father Spaulding eventually appeared and invited me into his office, where we began by discussing the local diocese's reaction to the events. In 1989 the bishop, Thomas J. O'Brien, had appointed a commission to study the alleged apparitions and locutions at Saint Maria Goretti. The commission had concluded, in October of that year, that the events were "explainable within the range of ordinary human experience" and that "because the events seem to us to be explained as human experiences and by ordinary human dynamics, we are constrained to conclude that they are within the order of nature and are not miraculous." The commission made it clear that the diocese was casting no aspersions on

Father Spaulding's or the young adults' faith, devotion, or sincerity. The bishop ruled that the prayer meetings could continue at the parish, but that there could be no "unequivocal claim of miraculous intervention."

Father Spaulding was adamant that he had never forced anyone to accept, or even pay attention to, these messages. "These are private revelations; they don't have to be believed. I've always maintained that. I never told anybody that they had to believe this or that they had to come to the prayer group."

He was also sensitive to the atypical circumstances surrounding the spiritual events at Saint Maria Goretti—particularly the fact that they had occurred to privileged parishioners and their pastor at an unusually well-off parish. These sorts of heavenly "favors" have historically been granted to the poor and the dispossessed, not the comfortably well off and well placed. He said, "The fact that it happened here is proof that it can happen anywhere."

I wasn't sure I got his meaning, so I asked for clarification.

"The reason this happened here," he explained, "is that if *we* can be converted, no one else has an excuse not to be except 'I don't want to be.' This is a wealthy parish. We've got kids that were into everything. I was on the fast track— I was a good priest, but I was very busy, and I think Our Lord and Our Lady did it here to prove that if it could happen here, it could happen anywhere."

Father Spaulding had held a strong line from the beginning concerning the public nature of these events. He was determined that they would go forward in a dignified and prayerful atmosphere and not devolve into a mere spectacle drawing miracle hobbyists from all corners of the country. He claims to have had little trouble enforcing that line. "We were simply asked to pray, and that's what we've been about. This is not a circus. We're trying to do just what the Lord is asking of us. It's centered on the Eucharist. The truth is spoken here; people know that. There's joy here and there's peace here."

I noted that the subject of the end-times and heavenly chastisements had not received a great deal of play in the Scottsdale messages, and that those elements seem to be the ones that often draw a more excitable, less contemplative, crowd. Father Spaulding said he didn't subscribe to any of the common predictions concerning a heavenly warning or coming chastisement.

"It may come," he said. "Jesus may come tomorrow. But we don't know; we have not been asked to focus on that." Father Spaulding here alluded to a well-known passage from Matthew's Gospel, chapter 24: "But of that day and hour no one knows, neither the angels of heaven, nor the Son but the Father alone."

My last question to Father Spaulding concerned the future of the Scottsdale events, which appeared to be on the wane. The young adults were no longer involved, and the crowds had peaked a few years earlier.

"What's next for this series?" I asked.

He turned the corners of his mouth down and shrugged his shoulders. "It's Our Lord and Our Lady," he eventually answered. "We do what they ask us to do, and we go where they ask us to go. I don't know what's next."

As it turned out, within two months of our meeting, Father Spaulding had moved from Scottsdale to a parish in Phoenix. As of this writing, the weekly prayer meetings continue at Saint Maria Goretti, but they do so without the presence or prophetic contributions of Father Jack Spaulding.

Phoenix

The day after my conversation with Father Spaulding, I was on my way to another prayer meeting at an apparition site in the Phoenix area, at the home of Estella Ruiz. Ms. Ruiz is a wife and mother of seven children. She receives monthly visits and messages from the Virgin Mary at her home on Phoenix's south side. Crowds congregate in the Ruizes' backyard on

those days to pray the rosary, sing hymns, and hear Mary's latest message, via Estella. Estella's husband, Reyes, also plays an active part in the operation of the Ruiz ministry, which has been dubbed "Mary's Ministries."

The Ruiz apparitions began at roughly the same time as the events in Scottsdale, around December 1988, and even though the Ruiz home is a mere thirty-minute drive from Saint Maria Goretti, the setting and the events I witnessed in the Ruizes' backyard would prove to be a world away from the calm, measured disposition of the pristine Scottsdale parish.

Anyone traveling from Scottsdale to south Phoenix cannot help but be struck by the stark contrast between the two. For one thing, the flora takes a decided plunge toward the ordinary, if not the downright scrubby. There are far fewer palm trees, and what flowers there are somehow seem dirty in comparison to their counterparts a little farther north. The land is flat, although a nearby range of mountains delineates the southern horizon. Rows of small concrete-block houses are punctuated by spent-looking businesses—a scrap-metal yard, an upholstery shop, liquor stores, a pool hall, Miguel's Buy-Sell-Trade, and the occasional church. In more than one parking lot near the edge of the road, men stood beside large black oil drums that had been laid on their sides, split, hinged, and pressed into service as grills. The sharp aroma of wood smoke and barbecue sauce from these portable rib joints made its way into my car as I passed.

Nearer the Ruizes' home large, empty lots, some of dirt, some of cracked, weed-sprung asphalt, were interspersed with smallish, run-down stucco bungalows. Many of the front yards were bare dirt. A fat man in a white cowboy hat sold "Sweet Watermelon" from the back of a green van parked in an abandoned lot. Another entrepreneur, also white-hatted, pedaled an old-time ice cream vending cart with "Delicias de Michoacan" stenciled on the side. A sign in one front yard offered the services of Sister Gail: "Palm and Card Reader—

PAST PRESENT FUTURE, LOVE MARRIAGE BUSINESS." Children
were everywhere. In one front yard a young father wielding
a garden hose turned from watering his hedges to spray his
two small children; they squealed, frantic with pleasure, and
ran around the corner of their house, out of his reach.

After circling the neighborhood a half-dozen times, each
time but the last missing their short street, I finally found the
Ruiz home. It was small, one story, of brownish pink stucco,
and looked just as used up as every other home in the area.
The grassless front yard—the size of a Ping-Pong table and
covered with crushed red rock—sported a short, shaggy tree,
a yucca plant, a cactus, a collection of terra-cotta pots, and an
empty cardboard box. The front-porch light was a bare bulb.
Tufts of insulation poked through holes in the side wall of
the house where chunks of stucco were missing. A wooden
sign the size of a door turned sideways was posted beside the
Ruizes' driveway. The letters looked as though they had been
etched into the sign with a wood-burning tool: "Our Lady
of the Americas Shrine. Rosary, Saturday, 7:00. Tueusday
[sic], 7:00 p.m. Bible study, Sunday eve. Please enter and visit
the shrine. The Ruiz family meets with pilgrims after the
rosary."

Cars were parked in an empty cinders-and-sand lot across
the street. From the Ruizes' front yard there was an unob-
structed view south to the mountains, the tallest of which
bristled with radio and television towers.

The backyard was surrounded by a high stucco wall. There
were homemade stations of the cross—small wooden plaques
on short posts, portraying the scenes of Christ's passion—that
looked as though they had been engraved with a sixteen-
penny nail; many of the carvings had faded so badly it was
hard to tell just which scenes they were meant to depict. The
ground itself was raked dirt; grass would never survive the
kind of foot traffic the Ruizes' backyard endures.

There were probably three hundred people in the backyard

when I arrived. No organized prayer was under way yet, but many were reciting the rosary by themselves. Others milled around, greeting friends and chatting or praying together. Some sat on lawn chairs facing in the direction of a shrine that had been constructed in the back corner of the spacious yard. The shrine was protected by a trapezoidal wooden roof held up by posts. Beneath the roof a stone altar held a variety of statues and candles. On the back wall, above the altar, hung a picture of Mary, framed on either side by blue curtains. Dangling from a string tied to a nail at the front of the shrine's roof was a fake white dove. A p.a. system played some kind of Christian pop music.

To the right of the shrine stood a rough crucifix, slightly larger than life-size. The body of Jesus, hanging on the cross, wearing only a loincloth and bleeding from the chest, hands, and knees, looked deformed. He was skinny and appeared to be made from fiberglass or poorly executed papier-mâché. His body sagged and his head hung far below the cross beam so that his torso and arms formed a Y rather than a T. The hair on his head looked real—it was either a wig or genuine hair—and hung down to cling around his face and neck, matted and uncombed. The facial features, poorly rendered by the sculptor, were blurry and indistinct. He looked like a wild man, and I was sure this crucifix had to be the number one bugaboo among the children of the neighborhood. A sign at the top of the cross read "I love you this much."

At the foot of the crucifix, a fountain flowed steadily down a miniature fall of rocks and collected in a small reservoir. People gathered around the fountain to gaze on the crucified Christ and fill plastic Coke bottles with the fountain's water. Some carried the water back to their seats; others guzzled it on the spot.

Near the cross, on the interior surface of the yard's stucco wall, a bas-relief version of Our Lady of Guadalupe had been rendered in what looked again to be papier-mâché. It was surrounded by candles. Some of the pilgrims prayed before it, reaching forward occasionally to brush it with their rosaries or stroke it with their open hands.

I wasn't sure what the flow of events that evening was supposed to be. I did know that Estella Ruiz would receive her visitation from Mary inside the house—out of view of most of the attending faithful. I had requested and been denied permission to be inside the house during the vision.

I had arrived about a half hour before sunset. Near seven o'clock, as the sun waned, the loud pop music was replaced by a calmer, simpler piano melody. Sparrows suddenly seemed to be everywhere in the surrounding trees, twittering as if their lives depended on it. A young, thin man with a thin mustache stood up front, beneath the shrine's roof, with a microphone in his hand. He wore a white T-shirt airbrushed with a portrait of Mary and the words "I am your mother." That same T-shirt was, as it turned out, worn by many of the people in attendance that night. The back of the shirts read: "Project America. Mary's Ministries. Evangelize the World." The man spoke to the crowd.

"Good evening. Let's find a seat. We've got a big night ahead of us, so if we could get started as soon as possible. My name is Ron, and I'll be leading the rosary tonight. First of all, I'd like to say it's nice to see everybody here tonight. And tonight is a very special night. This month [May] is the month of our Blessed Mother, and we'll be honoring that and celebrating that. We'll have a little procession starting over here [he pointed to the front of the property, out near the sidewalk]; we'll have some new candidates and old candidates coming up here, and they'll be putting flowers all along here, on the altar. We'll begin with that first. So tonight we'd like you to just relax and be at peace, and just listen to what Our Lord and our Blessed Mother are telling us, because they are here tonight and they will be with us always. So with that, we'll go ahead and get started with the procession."

As Ron spoke, another worker wended his way through

the crowd, handing out white napkins for a reason that was not immediately obvious. The soft piano gave way to a doleful solo violin rendition of Schubert's *Ave Maria*.

The "candidates" Ron had mentioned were a group of young people who had recently completed an evangelization course sponsored by Mary's Ministries. They formed the bulk of the procession that moments later wound its way into the backyard from the direction of the street. The snaking line was led by a dark-skinned, heavy man in a wheelchair, who turned out to be Reyes Ruiz. He looked to be in his sixties. Reyes was being pushed by a volunteer in a Mary T-shirt, and he held in his lap a framed portrait of Mary. Estella Ruiz was not a part of the procession, and I figured she was sequestered somewhere in the house, preparing to receive the Virgin. The crowd in the yard welcomed the procession by waving the napkins in its direction. Behind Reyes came twenty or thirty children of various ages, from elementary-schoolers through late teenagers. Each of the young people was holding a carnation. Some of the kids, notably the older ones, seemed less than delighted to be taking part in the procession. One surly-looking teenager had let her arm droop and her carnation pointed to the ground. Another teen walked with his flower pointing down too and the end of his rosary in his mouth, looking as though he'd rather be just about anywhere else on earth. When the procession reached the shrine, the kids laid their flowers on the altar and Reyes was helped out of his wheelchair and up to the microphone. Some of the people in the audience were crying. The children wound out from the shrine and rejoined the rest of the crowd facing the altar. Reyes, in gray slacks and a knit white shirt, stood before the crowd, which continued waving the napkins in his direction. The plaintive violin continued over the p.a. The sparrows' chirping had reached a frantic pitch. Reyes was silent for a while, standing, smiling, looking over the assembly. Eventually someone up front motioned to the sound man to kill the violin. He did, and Reyes addressed the crowd.

"Do we have anybody here older than eighty-two?" he asked.

Someone in the back shouted, "Back here."

"OK," Reyes said. "Come up here, sister. Come on, sister." The elderly woman was helped up to the altar to stand beside Reyes.

"Do we have anybody that's eighty years?" Reyes continued. "Come forward, please. Everybody who is eighty or over, please come forward. We want to see you; we want the people to see you. Come forward."

Eventually he collected around himself a small band of the oldest pilgrims in attendance. He smiled at them and again addressed the crowd.

"I've always had a great love for people that are older. And I've never stopped giving thanks to Our Lord for those that kept the rosary alive—and these are the people who kept the rosary alive." Reyes swept his arm to indicate the old folks he had gathered around him. "They learned to pray it at a very young age, and they continued to pray it while nobody else was praying. So I want all of you here to extend your hands, and I'll ask Our Lord to bless them for keeping the rosary alive for so many years." Everyone in the crowd raised a hand. Reyes seemed on the verge of tears; his voice trembled with emotion. "Bless these individuals before me. Thank you for keeping the rosary going for all those years." He smiled at them broadly. They smiled back.

"And to you, my beautiful lady . . ." Reyes's volume climbed and he prompted the crowd, "Wave your handkerchiefs, tell her! Wave your handkerchiefs, tell her! Tell her you love her!"

The crowd responded, feebly at first, "I love you." Hankies and napkins fluttered.

"Tell it to her!" Reyes insisted, louder.

"I love you," the crowd complied, this time with a little more feeling.

"SHE CAN'T HEAR YOU!" Reyes barked, à la Sergeant Carter.

"I LOVE YOU!" the crowd shouted back.

"I love you, Blessed Mother," Reyes said, winding down now. "We love you, *mujer bonita*! Thank you. Thank you. Thank you. Put the music up." Hankies continued waving. Pilgrims cried.

The sound man took the cue, and the violin returned. Reyes resumed his seat in the wheelchair and was pushed toward the back door of the house, followed by the young "candidates," all of whom had been invited to accompany him into the house for the purpose of witnessing his wife's ecstasy. The long line piled into the small house through the back door. It took a solid fifteen minutes to fit them all in, but eventually they disappeared, like a troupe of clowns into a subcompact car.

Those of us left in the backyard now waited for Estella Ruiz to receive her message from Mary and come outside to relay it to us. While we waited, Ron returned to the microphone and read some scripture and led the crowd in prayers. At Ron's direction, the crowd prayed the rosary together and recited a variety of litanies and hymns. I wandered around the perimeter of the crowd and just watched. I felt no inclination to join in the prayers here, as I had, at least for a while, the night before at Saint Maria Goretti. It was the aesthetic thing. The Ruiz style of Catholicism was too emotional, too melodramatic, too torrid and fervent to appeal to my imagination. Or so I thought.

After the sun had set completely, the sparrows quieted. A number of spotlights came on in the yard. The shrine and altar glowed like a stage. The crucifix was lit from underneath, increasing its eeriness by about four hundred percent. Its varnish glistened like sweat.

A number of people, many with small children, had dropped back to the front of the property, away from the shrine, in order to tend to their youngsters. I watched, to my shame, as a fat, angry father furiously dragged his boy, who couldn't have been more than four years old, to the front sidewalk, whispering hotly in his ear. They had made it as far as the Ruizes' front yard when the father grabbed the back of the boy's shirt and pressed his face into the chain-link fence. The boy reacted with an "Ow!" but no tears. The father yanked the boy off the fence and pulled him to the parking lot across the street; they disappeared behind a van. I saw the pair about thirty minutes later, back in the Ruizes' yard. The boy sat on his father's lap without motion or expression.

The Schubert *Ave Maria* waxed and waned throughout the prayers; sometimes the sound man let it play long enough for the recording's solo violin to be joined by a languorous soprano, singing the Virgin's praises in carefully paced Latin. The voice and melody rose, slowly permeating the warm night air. Time began to drag, slowed to viscosity by the wait, the warmth, the hushed prayers, the single singing voice. To the north, aircraft glided into and out of Phoenix's Sky Harbor International Airport along east-west flight paths, rising and falling as soundlessly as they might in a dream, their running lights blinking portentously.

At eight-thirty, the young candidates piled out of the Ruizes' back door and found seats in the yard. A moment later, they were followed by Reyes and Estella. Reyes, clutching a large red flashlight, was helped to his wheelchair. Estella walked beside a worker, holding on to his elbow. This was my first glimpse of the visionary. She was short and wide and wore big white pants, a pink shortsleeve shirt, and black sandals. She wore glasses under a full head of permed white hair, and her face was full and grandmotherly, though she is not elderly. As the couple made their way across the backyard to the shrine, Estella stopped every three or four feet to greet visitors, hugging them or taking their hands in hers.

At the shrine, Reyes remained in his wheelchair while his

wife stood behind a podium at the center of the stage. She held a sheet of paper in her hand. Before reading the message she had received, Estella said that the Blessed Mother had given her something to do, that the Virgin wished to share with us a miracle.

"Reyes called up the ones that kept the rosary alive so that great miracles could occur in 1996, and now the Blessed Mother wants you to see the great miracle," she said.

Estella's miracle consisted of calling all the young "candidates" and others who had completed the ministry's evangelization course to come join her beneath the shrine's roof. She coaxed from the podium until eventually there were twenty or thirty kids crowded around her at the altar—from beaming little ones to embarrassed, slightly bored-looking teens.

"Is this a miracle or what?" she asked the audience. "Come on." The audience responded with a splatter of applause.

She stage-chatted with the kids for a couple of minutes before getting down to business. Reading from the paper in her hand, she addressed the crowd again.

"This is the message that our Lady gives: 'I have come into the world to call my children all over the earth to unite in my son's heart of love and to tell you about that heart of love that yearns for all souls to return to him. . . .' "

There was more, much more. The world must be immersed in the love of God. The world was facing a "holocaust brought upon humanity by the evil one, Satan." Satan was destroying souls through hate and violence, but God's love could restore love and peace to the world. The key lay in the spreading of God's love through the evangelizing efforts of believers.

"Through each soul that has allowed him in, he will reach many more, until all men and women who desire to change through his power can do so and receive his light. As his flame of love is received by each soul, it will burn throughout the world in a blaze of fire of his love that cannot be stopped, and the darkness of the evil will be eradicated from this earth, and joy, peace, and love will reign."

It was up to us, the faithful assembled here in this yard, to accomplish this conversion of the world, and we were to do so thanks to the courage and strength of the Holy Spirit with which we had been filled.

"Even now," Mary said, "as we gather to pray together, the fire of God's love is ignited into a flame of conversion. . . . Join me, full of courage and hope, as we move together to win this world and return it to sanity and to our God."

After reading the message, Estella first repeated it in Spanish, then adjured the gathered faithful not to give up the fight. Mary was urging them to evangelize, and they must not lose the fervor for that calling.

"Listen to what our Blessed Mother says. Who is going to do it? *You* are going to do it. Don't give up," Estella pleaded, her voice dropping dramatically to a whisper. "Don't give up. Don't give up."

As a transition to the next, and final, phase of the evening's events, Estella invited a deacon to join her beneath the shrine's roof and offer a prayer for the crowd. He came forward, a short, bald man in a white shortsleeve shirt buttoned to the neck, and, raising his hands toward the crowd, fingers splayed, offered a blessing.

"Heavenly Father, we ask you, with all our heart, to bless the beautiful gifts you have given us, especially Our Lady of the Americas. For her love for us. And for all those who are still searching, and we cannot find what our heart desires, I ask you to bless people, your people, your children, in a very special way and for all those that are working so hard to make your plan come alive here on this earth. In the name of the Father, and of the Son, and of the Holy Spirit."

"Now," said Estella, her voice rising with excitement, "now the new evangelizers get to evangelize. So we're gonna sing!" She shouted, "You guys need to *sing*!"

The crowd was getting whipped up, if not to a full-blown

frenzy, at least to enough of a froth for some to make "whoop, whoop" noises from the back row. Most everyone was standing now.

"That's right!" Estella agreed, acknowledging the whoops excitedly. She shouted a cue to the sound man: "*Hit it, maestro!*"

Nobody hit anything. Another man came to the microphone: "After we sing a few songs and praise our God in song, these evangelizers here are on fire for Jesus right now!—"

"*Amen!*" from the crowd—some whistling, applauding, more whooping.

"—and they want to pass it on to you," the man continued. "They are full of the *Holy Spirit*, and they want to pass it on to you—because they have been taught not to keep their faith but to pass it on. *Amen?*"

"*AMEN!*" from the crowd.

"*HIT IT, LOUIE!*"

For the second time Louie ignored the cue. Finally, a minute or so later, someone must have nudged him hard enough, for over the p.a. came an acoustic guitar and piano version of "I Am the Bread of Life." The crowd began clapping en masse to the music. Many waved their arms in the air. In a minute it would become clear just how the evangelizers meant to pass on the fire of the Holy Spirit. Small groups of them, four or five each, young and old, coalesced in front of the shrine.

A voice came over the p.a.: "If you would like prayer from these people on fire with Jesus, come up and they will pray over you."

The music continued as lines of pilgrims formed in the direction of the shrine. One at a time, believers stepped into the midst of one of the small circles of evangelizers, who then laid hands on them in prayer.

In a matter of minutes, one of the believers being prayed for—the first of many who would be affected similarly that night—had dropped to the ground in a seeming dead faint, "slain in the Spirit." She was an older woman with white hair and a purple smock, and she lay supine and motionless as a rag doll. Thirty seconds later, another woman was out; the evangelizers bore her down gently, gently, gently. She lay flat on her back, eyes closed, her forearms convulsing rigidly. A third went down, a heavy woman in a blue dress, moaning and twisting, her eyes shut tight. Again, the Schubert *Ave Maria* swelled from the p.a., sounding more surreal than ever as a backdrop to the ecstatics writhing in the dirt. Many of the faithful still standing wept freely. A few of the evangelizers took to their knees beside those who had been overcome and stretched their hands out over them, palms down, as if warming themselves at a fire. Their hands began to quiver rapidly, an effect that I imagined had something to do with either reflection or absorption of the unleashed energies of the Spirit they had called down. More people dropped, and more evangelizers fell to their knees to attend the fallen. After a few minutes the ones who had gone down first rolled to their knees, one by one, and stood up groggily, blinking and rubbing their heads. Some of the larger and older devotees had to be helped to their feet by pairs of evangelizers.

When you see Ernest Angley doing this sort of stuff on television, it just looks stupid. But in spite of the scene's garish and, up to this point, unappealing emotionalism, I had to admit that the prospect of experiencing the sort of epiphanic thunderbolt that could literally knock someone to the dirt offered a certain appeal. Seeing them all there, dropping and twitching like Holy Rollers, it was hard not to wonder what it felt like, how it happened, whether it was possible. . . . I decided I had to at least give it a try, my nagging rationalism notwithstanding.

I found myself in line in front of a preteen boy who told me he had been through the experience before.

"It's called being slain by the Spirit," he explained.

"What's it feel like?"

"It feels like you're being rocked back and forth, and all of a sudden something feels like it's shoving you in the chest and you just get laid down. When you wake up, you have tears in your eyes and it's hard to walk and you feel real sleepy."

It sounded a little like a hangover or the flu, but I had made up my mind. When my turn came, I stepped into the middle of a circle of six evangelizers, all older than me. An elderly man, his shirt unbuttoned halfway down his chest, bald head glistening with perspiration, grasped my hands tightly in his. He smelled of cigarette butts. The others, all women, placed their palms on my head and shoulders. Not by nature a hugger or big fan of close personal contact with strangers, I felt myself tense. The disingenuousness of putting these sincere believers through their paces for my admittedly selfish, rubberneck purposes also weighed on my mind. What exactly might be the Spirit's view of such a ruse? Still, though, I told myself, I really was trying to open myself to the experience, if indeed there was an objective experience to be had. I wanted to feel something.

The man holding my hands asked me what I wished the group to pray for. This was a question I had not anticipated, and so I impulsively named the one subject I spend the most time praying about when I pray myself.

"Uh . . . my family."

"A family?" the man asked, not sure he'd heard me right.

"*My* family," I repeated, afraid he was on to me, that my fraudulence had revealed itself in some obvious way I was unaware of. I tried my best to drop my guard and surrender to the experience. It was like trying not to think of an elephant.

The old man released my hands and put his rough palms to my forehead. He was silent for nearly half a minute, then: "Heavenly Father, we ask you to help our brother and his family to have love for you. Lord Jesus and our Blessed Mother, send the Holy Spirit over them so that they may have your love, so they can unite with you in the Mass, the holy sacrifice of the Mass, and have the strength to continue in your love. We ask this through Christ our Lord. Amen."

The prayer was short and sweet, and when it was over, I felt absolutely nothing. Regrettably, I was not sinking limply to the Arizona soil, wafted there by the kind hands of these gentle, elderly strangers. We stood for another half minute in silence, until I thanked them awkwardly and began backing away. One of the women grabbed my hand.

"We love you," she said, looking straight at me. "Jesus loves you too." She stepped forward and hugged me vigorously. I hugged back as best I could. I was feeling like a bit of an ass by this point, though, and to be honest I was just hoping to get out of their circle without hurting their feelings, get to my car, and drive back to my hotel. I suddenly felt as if I might have taken this whole voyeuristic enterprise one step too far. The others offered various blessings as I extricated myself.

"Praise God."

"God bless you."

"We love you. God bless you."

"Christ loves you."

"Thank you," I said, meaning it, but at the same time feeling that I had just done something wrong. "Thank you. God bless you too."

CHAPTER SEVEN

❖ ❖ ❖

Veronica of the Cross

Bayside, Queens, New York

Veronica Lueken is dead. A claimed visionary and "victim soul" (a proxy fingered by heaven to suffer physical pain in a gesture of atonement for the sins of the world), she succumbed to congestive heart failure on August 3, 1995, at the age of seventy-two, after decades of physical ailments ranging from gallstones and diabetes to heart attack and stroke. She left behind a husband, children, grandchildren, and thousands of followers who believed that she had been in direct, near-daily, communication with Jesus and his mother throughout the last twenty-five years of her life. Her faithful followers still gather to honor her memory and to take Mary up on her promise, through Veronica, that Mary would continue to visit them, effect cures, and shower graces upon them even after the seer's death. They look for the day when, on the site of Mary's early appearances to Lueken—at a parish in Queens, New York—a shrine and basilica will be erected. The shrine is to be called Our Lady of the Roses, Mary Help of Mothers. Believers also look forward to the prophesied discovery, near the shrine, of a spring of miraculous healing waters. And they await the day when the Catholic Church declares Veronica

Lueken, whom they now refer to as Veronica of the Cross, a saint.

Fat chance. Few purported apparitions in the United States are less likely to receive official sanction from the Catholic Church than those claimed by Veronica Lueken. The series of visions that began in Bayside, Queens, in 1970 has been one of the most controversial such series on record.

Lueken's visions of Mary were preceded, in 1968, by visits from Saint Thérèse of Lisieux, the beloved French Carmelite nun who died in 1897 at the age of twenty-four. Thérèse dictated poems and "sacred writings" to Lueken. On April 7, 1970, Mary appeared to the visionary in her home, advising her that she would appear again, regularly and often, on the grounds of Saint Robert Bellarmine Church, in Bayside, beginning on June 18, 1970. Mary requested that prayer vigils be held on the eves of major feast days of the Catholic Church—some twenty-eight times each year—and that a shrine and basilica be erected on the grounds of Saint Robert Bellarmine parish. Lueken did as she was told: The vigils were organized and crowds of believers began to gather on the parish grounds near a life-size statue of the Virgin Mary.

It didn't take long for area residents to tire of the throngs that assembled twice weekly, clogging the streets and disrupting the neighborhood. In December 1973, in an effort to stem the growth of the cult, diocesan officials ordered the removal of the statue of the Virgin in the churchyard that had marked the central gathering point of the group. The faithful were undeterred. They continued to meet at the church—around a statue of the Virgin they brought with them. Earlier that same year a diocesan committee had reported its conclusion concerning the purported apparitions: "No supernatural significance could be attached to these assemblies and the reports of miracles."

The pastor of Saint Robert Bellarmine parish and a member of the investigating committee, Monsignor Emmett McDonald, speaking to the *New York Times* on the occasion of the removal of the statue, reiterated, "There is nothing supernatural about the claimed apparitions." He continued, "It is one of the most perplexing problems of my priesthood. I visited Lourdes and Fatima for my twenty-fifth anniversary of ordination. You're in between—wanting on one hand to promote devotion to Mary and on the other of stopping these demonstrations."

"These demonstrations" were three-hour vigils at which the rosary was prayed continuously and during which Veronica Lueken received a visit and a message from the Virgin Mary and/or Christ himself. Lueken told the crowds that God was nearing the end of his fuse, that he had grown impatient waiting for the world to return to prayer, penance, and sacrifice. Dire consequences, including the commencement of World War III and the devastation of earth by a giant, fiery comet known as the "Ball of Redemption," were predicted if humankind didn't shape up fast. Earth was facing the loss of perhaps a billion people if the threatened "chastisement" were loosed upon it. The Roman Catholic Church, Lueken told followers, had been infiltrated by communists, Freemasons, and worse. Thanks to the liberalized attitudes of laity and clergy alike following the Second Vatican Council, the Church was being brought down from within.

Soon, the group found that the church grounds had been fenced and declared off limits for the purposes of their gatherings. No problem. They moved the meetings to a nearby traffic island—a wide median across the street from the church. Neighbors continued to complain of debris left behind by worshipers and of the generally disruptive atmosphere of the meetings. Some of the confrontations between pilgrims and homeowners culminated in fistfights. On April 1, 1975, a delegation from the Bayside Hills Civic Association and a handful of elected officials from the area requested action from the local police commissioner. The police, however, were convinced that Lueken and her followers were protected by the First Amendment and that officers had no right to evict worshipers from the public space where they were then gathering. The police department was by that time in the habit of dispatching a contingent of officers on each vigil night to keep the peace between Lueken's followers and incensed local homeowners. The department had a hundred officers present for the group's next meeting.

The neighborhood association's final recourse was to file suit against Veronica Lueken. Subsequent to that, in May 1975, an agreement was struck between the visionary and members of the Bayside Hills Civic Association in the chambers of state supreme court justice Joseph J. Kunzman. Lueken agreed to hold the prayer meetings elsewhere, and Judge Kunzman issued a court order barring Lueken's followers from congregating on or near the grounds of Saint Robert Bellarmine Church. This was OK with Lueken, as the Virgin Mary had, in the end, given her approval for the gatherings to be transplanted to nearby Flushing Meadows-Corona Park.

Flushing Meadows, home of the U.S. Open tennis championships and a two-minute walk south from Shea Stadium, had been the site of the 1965 World's Fair. The area in the park where the group chose to congregate is known as the Vatican Pavilion. Michelangelo's *Pietà* had been displayed there during the fair, and Pope Paul VI had given a blessing from the spot during a 1965 visit to New York. Commemorating the papal visit is a low stone dais and a large semicircular stone marker and bench. Flushing Meadows offered Lueken and company spaciousness and freedom from concern over harassed (or harassing) neighbors. The stone platform of the Vatican Pavilion serves to this day as a stage for the ongoing vigils of Our Lady of the Roses.

The vigil I attended in June was the capping event of a weekend billed as the 26th Anniversary Pilgrimage. For four days Baysiders had holed up at the La Guardia Marriott, sharing meals and daily Latin Masses. On the vigil day they were bused en masse to the park to pray and parade and revel in the presence of the Virgin.

I bused myself from La Guardia to Flushing and walked into the park from its eastern edge, wending my way toward the Vatican Pavilion through fields of extremely serious soccer players. Unlike my elementary-schoolers (the only soccer players I had ever previously witnessed up close), these were full-grown men, some near middle age, shirts off, running full out, tacking upfield at unbelievable speed, filching the ball from each other with surgical precision. Kids wearing in-line skates were everywhere, some rinking around in what looked like an empty reflecting pool, some coasting idly along the park's sidewalks. Like most of New York, at least in its better moments, Flushing Meadows reflected a multiplicity of generations and of cultures grown accustomed to sharing the crowded urban space with a certain measure of expedient harmony. Older people shared benches or walked dogs; young couples strolled with babies; a toddler on Fisher-Price skates dangled from her dad's arm, her legs scissoring furiously beneath her. The park is a nice mix of open, mown meadows and wooded areas thick with oaks and maples. Jets to and from La Guardia ripped overhead with abrasive regularity every three or four minutes, halting conversations and coming within a decibel or two of causing actual ear pain. In the middle of the park stands a fountain featuring the Unisphere, a large framework globe with the continents on it in sheet metal, surrounded by jetting fountains of water. Two criss-crossing rings trace orbits around the globe, making the whole thing look like a giant model of an atom.

I heard the pilgrims at the Vatican Pavilion before I saw them. They were praying the rosary. As I neared the pavilion, I spotted the telltale hats of the Baysiders (Mary had told them in 1974, "White berets for the men, blue for the women," and, as with most of her directives, they seem to observe that one scrupulously). A male voice boomed over a p.a.: "May I have your attention, please. We have two priests hearing confessions. A Franciscan priest can hear confessions only from Spanish-speaking people. The monsignor can do it in English, Spanish, and Philippine."

The pavilion had been transformed from a simple stone dais and bench into a shrine. The group's portable fiberglass Virgin, a life-size statue of Mary in a white, gilt-edged robe, had been decked in a crown and blue cape with a high gold collar, and been given the place of honor in the center of the platform. A rosary and crucifix hung from her neck, and a larger rosary had been threaded over her outstretched hands. Beside Mary was a crucifix on a staff. Three large candles stood in front of her, surrounded by flowers. Banks of votive candles flanked the statue. At either end of the stone bench, perched high, sat a three-quarter-size angel, blue with pink and yellow wings, on his knees and facing in Mary's direction. Two women in full veils and white gloves knelt on either side of Mary, facing the crowd. Every few minutes the women were replaced by two different kneeling women—a rotation allowing as many women as possible the privilege of kneeling beside the statue. Also flanking the central statue were two flags under plastic slipcovers: the Stars and Stripes on the left and the papal white and yellow on the right. A large banner had been hoisted behind the whole affair. It read "26 years of Grace and Peace. 26. June 18, 1970–1996."

The crowd was several hundred and building rapidly. Buses arrived regularly, spewing fresh arrivals onto the site. Lawn chairs spread in a wide and growing semicircle before the shrine. Men in white berets, white shirts, white gloves, and sky blue ties with crucifixes around their necks (seemingly the official garb of the more or less official shrine volunteers) were everywhere. Some had walkie-talkies clipped to their belts. A priest in black with a finely embroidered green stole around his neck worked his way among the crowd, slinging holy water in every direction; people held aloft their sacramentals, hoping the holy water would hit them.

A long line of pilgrims formed and snaked slowly past the statue of Mary. Two shrine volunteers stood beside the statue; one held out the cross from the oversize rosary draped over Mary's hands for devotees to kiss. The other held a bell jar inside of which stood a foot-tall crucifix; it too was proffered for a kiss by each passing pilgrim. Described as "the crucifix of Veronica," it had been owned by the visionary, kissed by the Virgin, and used to bless the crowds during past vigils. A third volunteer stood by with a bag of tissues and wiped the articles after each kiss.

The prayers of the rosary continued for most of the evening, interspersed with prayers to Saint Michael and a variety of litanies and petitions. As the crowd grew, the outer ring of participants seemed less interested in joining in the prayers than in socializing. I sat for a while on a low wall at the edge of a dry, circular fountain a good way back from the shrine. Some of the faithful shared my seat and ate tour-provided box suppers or smoked or just chatted with one another.

"There's this church in Roanoke that makes the Eucharist out of honey bread," a fat man with Pierre Salinger eyebrows said to a small woman in a red dress and blue beret. "I asked somebody who worked at the church what was in it, and they said flour, water, salt, and honey."

Both shook their heads in a gesture denoting sad disbelief.

"And the bishop does it that way too! It's supposed to be nothing but flour and water," he added, summarizing the Church regulation they both no doubt knew well.

The woman countered with a story of confrontation with her parish priest over the issue of laypeople distributing consecrated hosts. "I called him on the phone and I told him, 'That's wrong, that's wrong, that's wrong. It's WRONG! It's only supposed to be done in cases of emergency!'" She did not report her pastor's response to this counsel.

The fat man said that Saint Linus, the second pope, had decreed that women should wear a head covering in church and that no other pope had ever rescinded that order. "So women who don't cover their heads in church are going against papal wishes," he concluded. "My wife always wears the blue beret to church."

A man next to me in a blue-and-white-striped shirt and black slacks, tattoos on his arm, was shooting pictures of clouds, his Polaroid SX-70 tonguing out one milky white photo after another. A companion seated beside him asked, after every picture, "Didja get anything on that? Didja get something on that one, Jay?"

I turned for a while and watched a pretty black teenager in cutoff denim shorts and a red halter skate wide circles inside the empty fountain behind me. She swayed from side to side, leaning smoothly into each alternate contraction of her powerful leg muscles, using gravity and the tension of centripetal and centrifugal forces as a purchase from which to propel herself forward. She was a good enough skater that she didn't have to think about what she was doing. She seemed happy just to be there. She was oblivious to the prayers and chatter and kitschy pageantry unfolding around her.

Photographs of Veronica Lueken in ecstasy invariably show her head tilted back nearly far enough to smooth out her generous double chin, her face often shiny with sweat. Straight black bangs protrude from beneath a white, shoulder-length lace chapel veil. Her bulging eyes focus skyward, and she smiles broadly. Followers who stood near her at these times report that Veronica did not blink while in ecstasy—a period of time often stretching to thirty or forty minutes. Neither rain nor snow nor flashbulbs discharging in her face could draw so much as a twitch, it is said. Veronica conveyed the visual component of each apparition to the gathered faithful as she witnessed it. The imagery was evocative and colorful but typically tinged with elements of gloom.

"The sky is a very deep blue this evening," one message begins, "and all about the trees there is a glimmer of star-like light . . . like diamonds are glowing all about the trees. I can see Our Lady coming forward. Her skirts are being caught in the wind. Oh, She's so beautiful! I can see now, coming out of Our Lady's gown in the front—I don't know; it's, it's very startling—I see a heart, a very large, red, pulsating heart coming out upon Our Lady's chest. And there is a short sword that has a silver handle like a cross, and it's into the heart and coming out the bottom. I can't look upon it . . . it's horrible . . . it's like a human heart being pierced by a knife."

After sighting the Virgin or Christ, Veronica would receive a message, which she immediately conveyed to those gathered. There is little of sweetness, mercy, or gentleness in the whole canon of messages received by the Bayside visionary. Favorite themes include the following:

1. The aforementioned decline, if not the outright head-long-to-perdition collapse, of Roman Catholicism. "I gave you My human life upon earth, and what have you done?" Christ sputters. "You crucify Me again in My own House. My Church! For what? A renewal? And what are you renewing? What is your renewal? What are you renewing? Have you found fault with My way? You have brought into My House all manner of WHIMS and FANCY, giving in to your carnal natures. Will you stand before Me as My representatives and say that your teaching has been PURE in My sight? I WILL SPIT YOU OUT AND CAST YOU INTO THE FIRES!"

2. The pernicious expansion of Russian communism. "Unless the bishops and the Holy Father in unity with all the bishops of the world, unless they consecrate Russia to My Mother's Immaculate Heart, the world will be doomed! Because Russia will continue to spread her errors throughout the world, raising up wars and carnage and pestilence and famine. Is this what you want, my children? What communism means is liars and murderers, deceivers straight from the bowels of hell."

3. The any-day-now threat of worldwide war and natural disaster. "Within this century this Ball [of Redemption] will be sent upon mankind," Mary told Veronica. "Look up, and see what lies beyond your windows: a Ball that is fast hurtling toward earth! It will be here within this century, if not sooner." (Sooner than within this century? Lueken's Mary is not a master of English syntax.)

4. The decline of America's traditional reliance on and trust in God and the consequent devastating effect on the once rock-solid American family. "Like a cancer, many areas of your country have become polluted by witchcraft, the worship of Satan, cannibalism, murder, and all manner of idol worship. My children, you must understand the realism of the existence of Satan in your world. Guard your families; protect your homes. They must become a fortress for your family, for when your children leave, they are subjected now to all of the agents of hell."

Perhaps most rankling to Church authorities has been the continual insistence of Lueken and her followers that the Church hierarchy is infected with sin and the heresy of modernism. "The Red Hats have fallen and the Purple Hats are being misled," one message charges. "Rome is in darkness. Conform to the new mode and you will die on the vine." [Key: Red Hats=Cardinals, Purple Hats=Bishops, New Mode=the post–Vatican II Catholic Church.] Supposedly miraculous photographs taken at the shrine—most of which look like long nighttime exposures laced by the scrawling paths of moving points of light—have been variously interpreted by the visionary as depicting, symbolically, the bishops and cardinals of the Catholic Church. In one picture they are described as ducks going downstream "following the current of the world rather than fighting the modern trend." Another interpretation sees the same blobs of light as rats. "Our Lady says that the cardinals and bishops are burrowing like rats into the foundations of the church . . . questioning its sacrosanct dogmas, reevaluating its teachings on morals."

In their zeal to renounce the changes wrought on the Catholic Church in the wake of the Second Vatican Council, Baysiders have asserted—at Mary's insistence—that the pope who presided over three of Vatican II's four sessions, Paul VI, was in fact subdued and held captive in the Vatican by renegade cardinals and was replaced for many public appearances by an impostor. A video marketed by the shrine, *The Miraculous Story of Bayside*, outlines this plot that Mary has called "the deception of the century."

On the video, a stilted, unsmiling narrator—balding, nervous, and continually glancing to stage left as if for help—states, in all seriousness, "Our Lady said that they used an Italian actor, with the best of plastic surgeons, to create this impostor. Our Lady told us that they injected Pope Paul VI himself with drugs to dull his mind and paralyze his legs. Our Lady even went so far as to name the three cardinals mainly responsible for this evil, Masonic, communist scheme. Their names: Cardinal Casaroli, Cardinal Benelli, Cardinal Villot. We were told in the message that many of the bulls and documents that came from Rome in this time period did not come from the pen of Pope Paul VI, but came from the pen of Benelli and Villot."

I met up with the shrine's director, Michael Mangan, just as several hundred pilgrims were being moved into their places for a procession that was about to get under way. I had been scanning the crowd for Mangan since my arrival, unsure whether I would recognize him based only on a small photograph I had seen in one of the ministry's newsletters. He wasn't hard to spot. He was talking earnestly to a reporter, clutching a black satchel in one hand and gesticulating freely with the other; he looked for all the world like a businessman in a hurry. I introduced myself as soon as he broke away from the reporter. He shook my hand eagerly, his brow furrowing in a fleeting facial gesture connoting sincerity and seriousness. He produced from his satchel a small green and gold sticker that read "26 Years of Grace & Peace—Our Lady of the Roses Shrine" and, with a politician's deftness, patted it into place above my shirt pocket. He was happy to talk to me about the shrine, its future, and the controversy surrounding it.

Mangan is not an old man. A reasonable guess would put him at thirty-eight. His dark hair recedes significantly, lending his forehead a height and prominence that make him look smart. His eyes are dark but are warmed by a frequent and easy smile. That night he wore black slacks, a white shirt, and a white beret with ST. MICHAEL written on it in green. A blue tie embroidered with the letters OLR (Our Lady of the Roses) and a crucifix hanging from a cord around his neck completed the ensemble. Our eyes were level as we talked, and he was not shy about looking straight into mine. He nodded as I asked my questions and answered them without hesitation.

I asked first what it was that convinced him that the Bayside apparitions were truly heaven-sent.

"Let's put it this way: The Church gives us the criteria or a litmus test as to determining the authenticity of a message. One: Are the messages in conformity with faith and morals? Bayside, absolutely. Bishops, theologians, everyone has admitted that—everyone who's been objective and open, that is. They may not like the message, they may not believe it, but they cannot deny that there's nothing at Bayside against Catholic faith and morals.

"Number two: What are the fruits? Well, we have testimonies, we have spiritual cures. People who have been away from the Church for ten, twenty, thirty, forty, fifty, sixty years—and we just got a recent testimony of *seventy* years— have come back to the Church. Who else could do that but the Mother of God, Our Lady of the Roses? In these latter days she's calling her children and reaching out to them. And there have been many other things, fantastic cures, *physical* cures. People getting out of their wheelchairs, cancer cures, diabetes, strokes—you name it—smoking, alcohol and drug addiction, the whole thing. But Our Lady has said, 'I will not grant everyone a cure,' and that's because she wants to sanctify us and cleanse us. She wants us to carry our cross because it's a means of growing in virtue and growing in character.

"Three: What is the state of the seer herself? Well, I knew the seer; I knew her very well. We were on very intimate terms; I spoke with her daily on the phone, and she was a very normal, stable woman. She had a psychiatrist examine her years ago; he said that there were no symptoms of delusion or any psychotic problems or anything of that nature. And I knew that anyway; I could see that.

"Another determining factor would be the prophecies themselves. Some of these, the bulk of the prophecies, have not been fulfilled, but some have. And how would this woman know unless these messages originate from God? For example, on September 13, 1978, just before Pope John Paul I died, Our Lady said, 'Pray for your new pope; there is a foul plan afoot against him.' It was like, what, thirteen, eighteen days later he was dead?" (John Paul I died September 28, 1978, one month after his election to the papal office.)

Mangan continued: "And I think most people—people who have studied these things—know that he was murdered. He was done in. Our Lady said he was given a glass of poison."

In light of Veronica Lueken's death the year before my visit to Bayside, I was curious how long Our Lady of the Roses could remain a viable draw. I asked Mangan how the future of OLR looked.

"Oh, very bright," he said with enthusiasm. "The prospect is very bright. Your first name again?"

"Mark."

"Mark. Very bright. Just like Lourdes and Fatima didn't cease when the seers died—and Christ, when Christ died the apostles continued with the work and it flourished." He smiled contentedly, contemplating, I imagined, the very bright, flourishing future. "Same thing here. No difference."

"Does anyone in the group receive visions now?" I asked.

"No. No, no. This is it. No one else will do it. We're waiting for the fulfillment now of these prophecies, and we believe it to be very close. The signs are all around us."

"I'm curious about the hats, the ties, the gloves," I said.

"We have been directed to wear this," Mangan said, reaching up to tap his beret, "by Our Lady and Our Lord. This is the Saint Michael beret. Saint Michael is the defender of the faith. And of course we're asked to call on him in these latter days, what with all of hell literally loosed upon earth. Our Lady said that the demons and Satan himself is loosed from hell, and that's why you have all of this craziness and mayhem and bloodshed and murder and molestation, all of these terrible things happening today. And this is our protection, the Saint Michael beret—as well as our crucifix, the brown scapular, our sacramentals; we're asked to wear those too."

"Are they *symbolic* of that protection?"

"No, no, no. These are actual instruments of grace. We don't adore these, of course, but these are certainly instruments of grace. And certainly something like this," he said, indicating the crucifix hanging at his sternum, "symbolizes Christ's redemptive act. These are all very powerful."

"And I've noticed the women wear blue berets."

"The blue hat is representative of Our Lady's color: blue. She's gathering her blue army, as it were. And of course, Our Lady has asked that the women wear the head coverings during the holy sacrifice of the Mass. Also, the blue hat is a sign of the act of submission of a woman to her husband. Saint Paul speaks about this—that the father is the head of the household and that the woman is the helper, and that these are the roles that God has designed for his creatures. Certainly man and woman are equal in spirit. I want to make that clear, and that should be understood. But in terms of their roles and responsibilities, God has ordained as such."

The berets—white or blue—are available via mail order from Our Lady of the Roses. Sizes are large and medium, and the price is eight dollars plus shipping and handling. I know this because I am on the Our Lady of the Roses, Mary Help of Mothers mailing list (a list that, according to Mangan, contains some fifty thousand names), and the group's catalog arrives at my home regularly. Also available are compilations of past messages (Mary: "You must read all of the messages given from Heaven through the past years, or you will not be saved"), Bibles, books, sacramentals (scapulars, rosaries, "blessed" rose petals), audio- and videotapes, and photographs (a 16" × 20" color photo of Veronica Lueken in ecstasy will set you back $44.95).

"What about the gloves?" I asked.

"Yes, uh, they are for the procession. Our Lady has asked that we wear the white mittens—Our Lady called them mittens; we would call them gloves. It's just a sign of decorum and appropriateness, of dignity given to the procession."

I asked about the group's expectations regarding the eventual building of a shrine and basilica.

"The original site at Saint Robert Bellarmine Church in Bayside will be the site of the basilica," Mangan said. "There's going to be a *big* basilica. And the waters will come up, just like at Lourdes. This *will* be approved. It's just a matter of time. I mean, Lourdes and Fatima, La Salette—they all took time."

I didn't ask it, but an appropriate question at this point might have been: "How much time do you have?" In a declaration dated November 4, 1986, then Bishop of Brooklyn, Francis J. Mugavero, stated the diocese's position regarding Bayside in terms that could hardly be called ambivalent. "I . . . wish to confirm the constant position of the Diocese of Brooklyn," wrote Bishop Mugavero, "that a thorough investigation revealed that the alleged 'visions of Bayside' completely lacked authenticity." The declaration went on to impute the Bayside messages as "contrary to the teachings of the Catholic Church" and warned that Catholics were "hereby directed to refrain from participating in the 'vigils' and from disseminating any propaganda related to the 'Bayside apparitions.' They are also discouraged from reading any such literature."

"How do you square your group's activities with the local diocese's attempts to discredit these apparitions over the years?" I asked Mangan.

"In all due respect," he said, unfazed, "it doesn't seriously concern us. We recognize the bishop's authority, by all means, as a shepherd of Christ, but canon laws 1399 and 2318 were abrogated in 1966 by Pope Paul VI, and what that means, in very simple terms, is that you can frequent any apparition, you can disseminate the literature, as long as there's nothing—there is this one stipulation—as long as there's nothing against Catholic faith and morals. And I challenge anyone to tell me where Bayside is against Catholic faith and morals. That's why we tell people, 'No one can claim you're disobedient or in error or that you're thumbing your nose at the ecclesiastical authorities; you're not. You have every right. It's your constitutional right, it's your divine right, it's your religious right. God is telling you to come here, because great punishments are going to descend upon mankind, and you need to come here and arm yourself with grace.' "

It was apparent that their minds were made up.

Mangan asked which other apparition sites I had been to. I named a few and asked his opinion of them.

"Well, when it comes to apparitions, we are of the same voice as the Church," he said. "Be careful. For every true apparition there's five hundred that come down the pike that are bogus, they're impostors, they're frauds. You have to be extremely careful. I mean, twenty-six years . . . [He tapped the sticker above my shirt pocket.] I think we've shown a lot there. This is the oldest one in the United States. This is it, baby. A lot of these other apparitions are ten, fifteen years old—ten or fifteen *months* old." Again he tapped my sticker. "Twenty-six years. I think that's pretty impressive."

A shrine volunteer approached and signaled for Mangan's attention. He had to go. He smiled at me and shook my hand as we parted.

"God bless, Dan."

"Mark," I corrected.

"Mark. OK. You look like a Dan."

As Mangan and I were talking, a couple of hundred people had lined up for the procession around a portion of the park grounds—actually, just a few laps around the grassy island on which the Vatican Pavilion is situated. Non-processing pilgrims had staked out good spots along the route from which to watch, dragging lawn chairs, coolers, etc., up near the road's edge. The assembled crowd began to shuffle forward. A woman stood in the back of a pickup truck next to a video camera on a tripod, filming the passing pageant. At the front, a priest in a floor-length black cassock, white gloves, and white Saint Michael beret led the parade, holding aloft a processional crucifix atop a staff. Next to him was another priest, a Franciscan, judging from his rough brown habit and rope belt. Behind the priests came two young boys with meticulously combed black hair, wearing the black cassock and white surplice of the traditional altar boy. Each bore a blue votive candle the size of a jelly jar held in a gimbal of sorts on top of a short gold pole. Next, a small band of women walked with a 26TH ANNIVERSARY banner. Then more women with candles on poles. Behind them came fourteen more women, each bearing a large, framed illustration of one of the stations of the cross hanging from her neck, like the front half of a sandwich board. Each of the station-bearers wore white gloves except five and eleven. Five had forgotten her chapel veil as well and had made do with what looked like a paper towel. Eleven (Jesus Is Nailed to the Cross) was a distractingly pretty blonde who—the others will forgive me—looked entirely out of place.

Other highlights of the procession: two little girls, no older than five, in blue berets and long dresses, holding bouquets of yellow, purple, and pink roses surrounded by baby's breath; a statue of Saint Thérèse, wearing a black veil over a dark yellow cape, with an oddly greenish pallor to her face, held aloft on a litter by six men; the shrine's main Mary statue, also on a litter, also carried by six men; a variety of large, fringed banners, hung like standards from high poles, that included portraits of Mary, Saint Michael, Saint Robert Bellarmine, Saint Joseph, Pope John Paul II, Saint Thérèse, and Veronica of the Cross herself, apparently in ecstasy (this one captioned: "A Champion of Heaven, Veronica of the Cross, Prophet of God. 1970, June 18"); the American flag and the papal flag, still sheathed in plastic; and a giant rosary, as big around as a trampoline with beads the size of softballs, carried by nine people, led by a nun holding the crucifix.

The last quarter of the procession was made up of attendees who just wanted to tag along. They chatted and looked around as they walked, not really joining in the prayers being recited by the others. It took over ten minutes for the entire group to wind its way once slowly around the grassy island. They took three laps, and the front of the parade had to continually put the brakes on in order not to lap the stragglers bringing up the rear.

When the procession ended, the makeshift shrine was reconstructed back at the pavilion. All the statues and flags were put back in their original spots, and since the sun was setting, lights were positioned to illuminate the shrine. Mary was lit from below, casting her shadows upward in a slightly ghoulish Boris Karloff effect.

By this point in the evening the head count was somewhere around three thousand. That was the estimate made by local

police, and it seemed reasonable to me. Not a bad turnout
for a Tuesday evening, especially considering the condition
of the visionary, i.e., absent by reason of death. Weekend
crowds, according to Mangan, were usually even more impressive. The prayers being led from the microphone at the
pavilion did not cease until nearly eleven o'clock. Many of the
faithful remained rooted in one spot, praying fervently all evening, but many wandered the edges of the crowd, chatting,
eating, renewing past acquaintances. All in all, the Bayside
crowd struck me as less contemplative than the crowds at
some apparition sites I'd visited. Maybe it had something to
do with the location, but the Our Lady of the Roses experience seemed less about deep, meditative prayer than about
attending the event itself. Hundreds of the pilgrims had arrived from relatively faraway places via bus. Perhaps the long
ride had contributed to their gabby, peripatetic dispositions.

Attendees who were in a shopping mood were not disappointed either. Merchants had set up shop at the bottom of
a grassy slope behind the Vatican Pavilion. Two men sold
statuary from a minivan to three-deep crowds straining to get
a look at the goods. They were hawking plaster angels, Marys,
and Jesuses of various sizes ($12 for a small crucifix, $60 for
a two-foot-tall Mary) and doing a brisk business.

Shrine literature and paraphernalia—from rosaries to
bumper stickers—were also available. While looking through
the available books and pamphlets, spread around in cardboard boxes on the grass, I overheard two men nearby trading
conspiracy theories. Each was voluble and fervid, straining to
invoke in the other a full appreciation for the subject of his
particular monomania. They were walking all over each other
conversationally. I introduced myself and asked what it was
that had them so worked up. They were both happy to have
a fresh ear.

Each had a characteristic rhetorical style. The first, a
chubby redhead in a blue T-shirt, enunciated with precision
and imparted conspiratorial emphasis to certain words or

phrases by way of small, knowing chuckles (e.g., "In the can-
ons of the Council of Trent, I believe, it says that if any pastor
changes the rite of Mass or introduces a new rite, let him be
anathema, which means accursed. And Pope Paul said, 'I am
introducing a *new rite* of Mass' " [derisive, knowing chuckle
here]). He also made annoying sniffing noises way too often.
The second, a tall man with glasses, long hair, and a camel
London Fog jacket zipped to his Adam's apple, made his
points with more force, talking rapidly and sometimes stepping up on the curb beside us as if to give his arguments more
punch by achieving a temporary height advantage.

As I discovered, they were worked up about almost everything. I asked how they had become interested in the
Bayside phenomenon. London Fog answered first.

"I was into the charismatic movement as a Catholic," he
said. "And then I subsequently left the Catholic faith for the
Pentecostal movement, which I now believe to be a heresy. I
was studying in an Assembly of God graduate program, and
I asked the Protestant professor, 'What are the viewpoints of
Communion?' And he said, 'The Catholic viewpoint is transubstantiation; the Lutheran viewpoint is semi-presence; and
for the rest of Protestantism it is symbolism.' Then I asked
him, 'What's the oldest viewpoint of Communion?' and he
said, 'The Catholic viewpoint, transubstantiation, actual presence.' I came back on that airplane a changed man—my mom
had been praying for that for years. Then I met a traditional
priest. He's old, about seventy-five. He preached about hell,
he preached about the Catholic faith like it should be, and
from there on I just sought after the faith. And after my wife
left, about two years after the separation, I learned about the
Tridentine Mass, which is the Mass of centuries. The Tridentine Mass was said for approximately fifteen hundred years,
maybe even longer."

The Tridentine Mass is the Latin rite of the Roman Catholic Mass as codified and standardized by the Council of
Trent in 1570. It was *the* Catholic Mass until the new Roman

Missal, promulgated in 1969 as a result of the Second Vatican Council, introduced the Novus Ordo Missae (New Order of the Mass). The Tridentine is the Mass that Catholics mean when they talk about "pre-Vatican II Mass." It is the Mass many Catholics, mistaking form for substance, had a hard time letting go of after the Church began its program of sweeping liturgical modernization following the council. (There survive several factions of erstwhile Roman Catholics who refuse to acknowledge the validity of Vatican II and the changes wrought in its wake. One of these groups, the Society of Saint Pius V, runs a church and school not far from my home. I was curious enough to attend a Mass there one Sunday, but was so bored and mystified by the end of the first hour of hyper-Tridentine ritualizing that I left shortly after the homily. Families stood stiffly, women with heads covered, children eerily well behaved, as a haze of incense smoke dimmed the sanctuary, enveloping the priest and his phalanx of altar boys like a sea fog.)

"Seventeen hundred years," insisted Redhead. Hard sniff.

"OK, seventeen hundred years," London Fog acquiesced. "Then, suddenly, in 1962 or 1963, around the time I was born, the Vatican Council decided the Tridentine Mass was no longer to be said." He was indignant, as if the affront had been meant for him personally.

"Saint Pius V," he continued, "who was pope at the time of the Council of Trent, said that if anyone would alter the Mass—if anyone changed the sacred Tridentine rite—he said they would incur the displeasure, or wrath, of God, and of the holy apostles Peter and Paul. In God's eyes there cannot be a 'New Order' of the Mass because Saint Pius V, who was a *saint*, after all, already declared that the Tridentine is our Mass.

"And bishops in this country have been shutting parishes down that start to say the Tridentine Mass. I'll give you an example. In Harper's Ferry, West Virginia, a priest there started to say—with permission of the bishop—the Triden-

tine Mass. Within three years there were so many people coming to the Mass that the diocese shut down the parish for no
viable reason. The bishops said something lame about parking
problems or something like that. A lot of the bishops in this
country don't want to reinstitute the Tridentine Mass. They
don't want to return to it. And I'm not gonna judge the
bishops, but I'll tell you this: Some of them in this country
have been influenced by socialism, Masonry, modernism, and
heresy, and they need to repent and turn back to God and
offer the Holy Tridentine Mass. The Mass we have today is
deficient. It's not what pleases God almighty. I have to say
this: What right did they have to take my birthright away? It
was my Catholic birthright, and they took it from me. They
stole my right!"

I wanted to hear more about the Masons. I asked him to
explain the Masonic connection he had alluded to.

"For one thing," he said, "the cardinal who led the commission for the new Mass is suspected of being a Freemason.
So therefore, his intentions were most likely diabolical."

"It's also suspected," Red threw in, "that Pope Paul VI
was being blackmailed by a few Masonic cardinals."

"The Masons infiltrated the Vatican," London Fog explained. "It's a known fact that at least a hundred prelates in
Vatican City are Masons. That in itself is anti-Catholic. In
eighteen-something, Pope Pius IX, I believe, uncovered a secret document written by the Freemasons, called the *Alta
Vendetta*. In that document the Masons said, 'We will no
longer attack the Church from without, like Luther or Calvin;
we will put our men within the church.' Those men are now
bishops in the Roman Catholic Church somewhere, but we
don't know which ones or where they are. They're not really
Catholics; they're on the other side. They want to destroy the
Catholic Church, destroy Christ's church, and they're like rats
that have burrowed their way in. And that's not the only
problem: We've also had infiltration of socialists and homo-
sexuals into the Catholic clergy."

"But what are the Masons hoping to accomplish?" I asked London Fog. "Why would they go to the trouble?"

"They want a one-world, ecumenical organization. They want to put the Catholic Church under the Masonic leadership. They want a one-world, ecumenical church that doesn't conform to traditional Catholic teachings. They want it to be watered down, they want it to be worldly; they don't want Christ's teachings."

"They want more than that," Red asserted. "There's a person I know who stole a Masonic handbook, and it has a satanic black mass in it. The higher-up Masons, the thirty-third degree and above, are satanists, openly. Some of them have actually come out and said, 'We are a satanic church.' You can't blame the Masons that are of first degree to about thirtieth degree. They think they're running a charity organization; they're there for the business contacts, whatever. After they hit the thirty-third degree, they go through a ritual; a man brings out a crucifix and puts it on the floor and says, 'Step on it.' If you step on it, they bring you to the thirty-third and higher degrees. If you *don't* step on it, they say, 'Oh, *good*, we were just *testing* you. We wanted to see if you were a good Christian,' and then you never go any higher in the organization. For instance, I can't remember his name, but whoever it was that ordered the bombing of Hiroshima and Nagasaki, he was a Mason. As a matter of fact, Hiroshima and Nagasaki were the two most concentratedly Catholic cities in Japan. They were also not the original targets for the atomic bombs, but this Masonic, demonic president of ours said, 'No, bomb *these* two cities.' They were all civilians, they were all Catholics, and they were all martyrs. They got wiped out because of this Mason that hated the Catholic Church."

"So," I ventured, "you think it all comes down to the influence of Satan?"

"Absolutely," London Fog answered without hesitation. "There are many facets, many groups, with one common goal: Destroy the faith, destroy the Catholic Church, collapse it, bring it to the point where it's underground—which it's virtually gotten very close to—and then at that point the world would be ruled for a brief period by an Antichrist leader, and an ecumenical Church that denies Christ's teachings."

"Yeah," Red agreed, and sniffed. "But it's not only the Masons. There's the communists too. It's still spreading. Russia's falling apart was all a sham. It's an illusion. They're run by the KGB underground. Gorbachev is actually still running Russia. They've still got over forty thousand nuclear missiles. They produce a nuclear submarine every few weeks. They could literally wipe out the United States within a matter of minutes—*without* a counterstrike. There are Russian soldiers in the United States now. They're all across the country."

At the mention of Russian soldiers, an old woman standing nearby piped up. She was nearer to four than five feet tall, and looked quintessentially grandmaternal. She wore a red-striped skirt and blazer. An orange lace veil floated atop her full head of silver hair.

"They're all around," she said, her eyes narrowing happily above a wide, warm smile. "Submarines. They had a warhead in an abandoned subway, and Jesus and Mary mentioned it to the seer; the seer mentioned it to the shrine workers, and we wrote to Washington and informed them. I wrote to the CIA and told them about it. They found the warhead. Otherwise we'd've been gone." She looked down after making her point and shook her head dolefully.

Red looked at the woman, and they exchanged a glance as if conferring about how much it was safe to tell me. Finally, Red spoke again.

"There are communists all the way up in this country."

"All the way up," echoed the woman.

Red continued, "Some of them have been involved in murder, involved in cocaine dealing, and—"

"Money laundering," the woman interjected.

"I could show you proof on a lot of this stuff," said Red.

"But every person who's come up and said something has died. Nineteen witnesses came forward, nineteen witnesses died . . ."

"Died," said the woman.

"Witnesses to what?" I asked.

"To the government dealing cocaine and being involved in murders," Red answered.

The woman spoke softly. "It's coming out little by little. Little by little."

"And," I pursued, "the whole collapse of the Soviet Union that happened a few years ago was not real?"

"It's a complete farce," Red answered. "An illusion. There are Soviet soldiers—nuclear prepared, chemical-warfare prepared—in this country right now. When they made the anti-chemical warfare treaty, Russia pulled a loophole. They didn't put down their chemical weapons as part of the treaty. So therefore, they weren't bound by the treaty to stop producing these chemical weapons. They've got a hundred and twenty-six underground chemical-weapons factories in Russia that are actually the size of cities but they're not on the maps. They're made airtight underground so that if something goes wrong, they can just [here Red makes a lid-screwing motion as if closing a valve] shut it off; the thing dies in there and it's done with. There's a powder, I can't remember the name, but one ounce of it will kill over a thousand people."

"One ounce," echoed the woman.

"They could just fly over the people and drop this stuff out; if it touches your skin, you're dead."

"You're dead," said the woman. "They have it. Veronica Lueken said that Russia is preparing for World War III."

"And the Russians have infiltrated the United States?" I asked, attempting to sort out this rapidly complicating indictment.

"There are communist *soldiers* in the United States right now," Red nearly shouted at me. "It's 'Joint U.N. maneuvers.' That's all they'll say. Russia has a veto in the U.N.;

they're actually one of the few countries that has a veto power over the U.N.'s actions. And that all leads to . . ." Here Red laughed a dry little laugh and stuttered a bit, frustrated by his own inability to convey the enormity of the plot in terms that would make an impact on me.

"Oh, man . . . you really don't understand how deep this goes," he said, and sniffed vigorously. "I mean, it's really ridiculous. The U.N. is promoting one-world government, but it's not even the Russians, it's not even the communists, not even the modernists—"

"It's *Clinton*," the woman croaked angrily. "Clinton. I'm not afraid to say it! He sold our country down the river to the U.N.!"

"Clinton's just a pawn," Red asserted.

I waited for the revelation, but he had apparently decided to play his cards close to the chin, perhaps not wishing to become the twentieth dead witness.

"To put it in a general way without actually naming names," he said, "study up on world banks. Just study the subject and you'll find some interesting things." This inside info was imparted with a conspiratorial half smile and a knowing nod. I said OK, but doubted whether I'd have the time or inclination anytime soon—say, within this lifetime—to tackle the subject of world banking.

Red had said all he was prepared to say, and he and London Fog turned to each other and resumed their conversation at the point I had interrupted them.

The woman had not said her piece yet, though. She told me she had followed the Bayside apparitions since the beginning, flying to New York from her home in California at least once a year. She echoed Red's sentiments on just about every point, except that the way she had heard it, in order to advance to the thirty-third degree, a Mason—instead of stepping on a crucifix—had to kill someone.

She had other concerns as well. "The UFOs—this is a big joke, about our government, and about people—they claim that these are good people that are trying to save the earth. Like heck, they are!" Her voice rose, cracking with indignation. "Our Blessed Mother said that they're from the devil's kingdom. They're the false prophets."

"Who?" I asked. "The Masons?" I was getting confused.

"No—UFOs! Yeah, they're nothing but from the devil's kingdom. See, he has his workers, and that's how they travel all over [she swept an arm in front of her, palm skyward] seeking the ruin of souls."

"And they're traveling in things that are mistaken for UFOs?"

"They *are* traveling in UFOs."

"I see. But they're not from other planets?"

"No. The Virgin Mary said there's nobody else living on any planet but the earth. That's why our government's so nuts. Spending all that money to see who's on Mars or Venus. It's a waste of time and money. I sent literature on this to some of the senators, and I don't know what happened afterward, I can't recall, but suddenly the interest in finding people living on Mars and Venus was almost obliterated."

"And you think the letters you wrote might have had something to do with that?"

"Yes. Yes, I do."

She talked longer, much longer, the topics pitching desultorily along semi-predictable lines—communists, congressmen ("I write to all of 'em"), satanists, the Ball of Redemption ("What a terrible thing to look forward to!"), the New Order of the Mass, Communion in the hand, female servers ("The Virgin Mary has verified that the pope did *not* sign the law for female altar girls"), etc., etc., etc.

The amount of energy it takes to nurture and sustain a conspiracy mind-set seems staggering to me, impressive in terms of the sheer quantity of inertia that has been overcome in order to spend one's days fleshing out figments, collecting the literature, networking with like-minded conspiracy buffs (the Internet is great for this), writing impassioned pleas to

Congress. All in the interest of seeing things that most likely are not there, of drawing emphatic lines between people and factions, of keeping "us" radically and ideologically separate from just about any conceivable "them."

The soccer players and skaters and young couples pushing strollers had all gone home by the time the vigil ended. Prayers continued well past dark at the Vatican Pavilion. There was much taking of pictures up near the statues and candles and floodlights—luminous combinations sure to result in enigmatic Rorschach photographs, particularly if snapped by an unsteady hand or with a long exposure. For a while the wind picked up, and volunteers had their hands full keeping the banners from toppling. Near the end, finger-size white candles poked through white cardboard disks like straws through plastic drink lids were distributed among the crowd and lit. A short litany was then recited over and over, during which believers raised and lowered the glowing candles rhythmically: "Our Lady of the Roses, pray for us [the candle was held at chest height]; Mary, Help of Mothers, pray for us [the candle was lowered to the waist]; Mary, Light of the World, pray for us [the candle was raised above the head]." This, as it turned out, was the last ritual of the evening. At the end, a voice over the p.a. told us that the evening's gathering had drawn thirty-five buses and about thirty-five hundred people, then, "Have a good night, safe journey home, may God bless you all." Soon after, pilgrims began packing up and heading home. They talked quietly amid the scrape and slap of folding lawn chairs.

I headed toward the northern edge of the park and Roosevelt Avenue, with the intention of catching a train into Flushing and a cab from there back to my hotel at La Guardia. I walked past the Unisphere; it glowed importantly, like a small planet, ablaze with reflected light. The day's earlier humidity had lifted, and the sky had cleared; predicted rain had never developed. Beneath the broad limbs of trees overarching the wide walkways of Flushing Meadows park, it was cool, dark, and quiet. Queens hummed at the park's edges, but at its center, buffered by acres of trees, grass, and earth, the din thinned and softened to a constant, contented purr.

The courts of the U.S. Tennis Association are situated near the park's northern edge. One of the tennis center's satellite courts was lit to near daylight brightness by white floodlights; as I approached I could hear the steady, dry *pock . . . pock* of a tennis ball being racqueted back and forth. Two women were on the court, and I stopped to watch for a minute. They stood on opposing baselines, both in full tennis whites, stroking the ball to each other easily. They weren't playing a game; they were just warming up, working their ground strokes, forehand and backhand, at what looked like about half speed. They were the kind of players who you could tell had been holding racquets since toddlerhood, and I felt the same pleasure watching them as I had felt watching the teenage skater earlier in the evening—a kind of vicarious satisfaction, a hard-to-pinpoint delight in glimpsing an unself-conscious display of a nearly perfected human skill.

I continued past the tennis center to the train station. I had not eaten since breakfast, so when the train reached Flushing, I slipped into a tavern for a hamburger and a beer, hoping to clear my head a bit after my evening with the Baysiders. The burger was good and the fries were perfect—hot, crisp, and salty. I finished one beer and ordered a second.

"Ya mutha broke ya in right; ya cleaned ya plate," the waiter said as he cleared away my dishes. I finished the second beer and left money on the table.

"God bless you," said the waiter as I got up to go.

Outside, though it was nearly midnight, pedestrians of every description moved with purpose along the sidewalks of Roosevelt Avenue. A few looked as though they had nowhere else to be, but most hurried along, heads down, plainly heading somewhere, plainly not yet there.

CHAPTER EIGHT

✤ ✤ ✤

Beautiful Water, Birds Singing

California City, California

I drove into the high Mojave desert at night, from Bakersfield up and over a four-thousand-foot pass through the Tehachapi Mountains, southern foothills of the Sierra Nevadas. The darkness beyond the edges of the highway was total. Even without visual confirmation, though, the whine of my Nissan's engine, straining to keep up with the demands of its cruise control, told of some fairly drastic and rapid shifts in elevation. I'm a compulsive car-radio button pusher. Punching through the stations on the ride between Bakersfield and the desert, I heard more varieties of Hispanic music than my Midwestern vocabulary can account for.

Once over the pass, the ground leveled and I reached my motel in the town of Mojave, a one-mile straight shot of motels, gas stations, and restaurants. It was nearly midnight, and not a lot was going on. When I rang into the motel office, the clerk came to the front desk from attached living quarters. She left the door open behind her, and through it I could see the stuttering blue flash of reflected TV. A small child called for her to come back.

I was beat from a transcontinental flight and a six-hour drive from San Francisco. I hauled my bag up to my room, flipped on the television, and sat on the edge of the bed to take my shoes off. On the TV screen, two lanky blondes with outsized, synthetically buoyant breasts and wearing nothing but high heels struck poses and grappled each other, moaning in that open-mouthed way that I've always associated with pornography but never with real sex. It was the Playboy Channel. At least that's what I figured, as there was a glossy-haired guy in a dinner jacket watching the women. This is *Playboy*'s idea of sophistication. As interesting as this sort of thing might be when you first happen upon it, I always get a little sad seeing it. I start thinking about the people involved and their parents and families and wondering what sorts of things they used to talk about doing when they grew up and what they think about what they're doing now, and before long the whole thing is about as erotic as a forced march. I was considering those breasts—surgically plumped to near-parodic proportions and destined to remain anachronistically pert as their owners grow elderly behind them—when the phone rang. It was the clerk at the front desk. She had forgotten to tell me when I checked in that my wife had called and left a message. And then the desk clerk had the pleasure of saying to me, a total stranger: "Hope the trip went well. Good night. I love you." I thanked her for the message, turned off the television, and went to bed.

I had come to the desert to see and, I hoped, meet a Mexican–born mystic and visionary called Maria Paula. Since 1989 she had drawn crowds numbering in the thousands to a remote spot twenty-five miles north of Mojave, out in the desert past a small strip town called California City. The crowds came on the thirteenth of every month for prayer and to witness Maria Paula's reception of an apparition and a message from the Virgin Mary. Pilgrims had reported sun miracles, visions, healings, and numerous other miraculous phenomena. The Virgin of her visions has identified herself to Maria Paula as the "Lady of the Rock, Queen of Peace of Southern California." Maria Paula speaks only Spanish, and I had made tentative arrangements to interview her at some point in my visit with the aid of an interpreter.

The messages Maria Paula had so far received via the Virgin had been anything but sunny. Mixed in with admonitions to love one another and pray more frequently and more fervently were threats of pending disaster. The Son of God was coming, believers were told, "to raise up and to purify the whole world. I come to warn and protect you," Mary had said, "because you are my children. There will be great poverty, hunger, and plagues that will hinder your lives. Unrelenting wars, great conflicts between countries, and the entire world will be in communism." God, Mary said, had quite simply had more of mankind's insolence than he could stomach. "Very soon my children," she explained, "you will receive a great surprise from God, who is very angry and tired of the arrogance of the hearts of humanity. . . . It is a very severe lashing that awaits you for your lack of understanding of God, for condemning God, and the destruction of the Holy Catholic Church." In at least one message to Maria Paula, the Virgin Mary identified herself as "Your Mother of Pain."

Mary had also had some unflattering things to say about the Catholic clergy: "Many of them have lost their faith and unity with the Mother of God. The evil one has put all kinds of confusions in their minds and leads them to unknown pathways. . . . My dear cardinal and bishop sons ignore my petition."

I had been told that the regular monthly vigil at the desert spot would begin the next morning around eleven o'clock and that I should plan to arrive early.

Thanks to the flight west through four time zones the day before, I was finished sleeping and out of bed by five o'clock the next morning. Before breakfast I drove in darkness to a spot in the desert a couple of miles north of Mojave to wait for the sunrise. Still farther north, California City appeared as a single strand of yellow and orange pinprick lights laid near the horizon. Through lateral rips in a mass of dark cloud, some stars and the waning moon were still visible. As the light came up, turning to salmon those clouds nearest the sky's eastern edge, the landscape into which I had traveled grew clearer. I was on a wide, flat desert plain more or less surrounded by mountains. The peaks of the Tehachapi range loomed out of the darkness to fill the western horizon, at first seemingly blacker than the night sky around them, until the sun gained some height and revealed them for brown and gray stubbled with occasional clumps of green. Other peaks, breaking the horizon farther away to the north, east, and south, showed bronze, hazy purple, green, and gray. Hills to the south, around Mojave, bristled with hundreds of high-tech windmills—long-bladed propellers affixed to tall white shafts.

The plain was studded with dark green waist-high shrubs that I later learned were creosote bushes. Interspersed among the creosote, and less numerous, grotesquely twisted Joshua trees faded into view in the rising light, bodies wracked and arms raised to heaven—the aspect that had inspired early Mormons to name them for the combative, sun-stopping Old Testament leader. Some looked less like a gesticulating biblical character than a severely arthritic hand, with bursts of palm greenery at the fingertips. A waitress at the pancake house where I ate a short stack a little later that morning told me that Joshua trees were a member of the lily family, that they bloomed white in March, and that they looked especially good under snow, "which it doesn't come often but we do get."

California City is about fifteen miles northeast of Mojave, in the direction of Death Valley. After breakfast and a shower I headed that way, up Highway 14. Halfway between Mojave and California City was a billboard with a portrait of the Virgin on it and an 800 number. The text read "Virgin Mary Speaks to America Today." I figured it had something to do with the Maria Paula apparitions until I called the number; the sign and the phone number belonged to supporters of

Our Lady of the Roses in Bayside, Queens, over 2,400 miles away. Other signs along the way warned of high winds and road closures for those traveling farther north: "120 to Yosemite, closed. Sonora Pass (108) closed. Monitor Pass (89) closed. Passes subject to storm closure." The Tehachapis, clear now in the morning sun, stood brown and sparsely vegetated, at the farthest western reach of a slowly rising plain on my left.

The flatness and relative lack of vegetation of the desert is such that you can see California City from Mojave, and vice versa, even though the two are fifteen miles apart. The entrance to California City is a double-lane boulevard with widely spaced ranch housing on either side. A sign at the city limits says "Welcome to California City. Land of the Sun." The broad dimensions of the street suggest a certain hopefulness on the part of city planners. As it turns out, California City is little more than the east-west boulevard strip and a few straight streets shooting out into the desert in the other two directions, real estate development not seeming to have progressed much more than a quarter or half mile from the main road in either direction. I had been told to proceed through California City to the far side of town before heading north into the desert. I reached Randsberg-Mojave Road and turned left. A few blocks later, I was out of town and driving into the desert wilderness.

The surrounding earth and shrubbery were mostly done in varieties of tans and browns. Creosote bushes and, here and there, sprays of tenacious, weedy grass provided what little green there was to be seen. The sun was still rising, climbing aggressively and burning off the morning clouds. A little way out of town, Randsberg-Mojave turned into Twenty Mule Team Road and went barreling for miles straight into what looked like nowhere. It's an odd feeling to a Midwesterner to drive for miles without seeing any man-made structures. After ten miles of undifferentiated soil and shrubbery, I came to a sign that pointed left and announced: "Our Lady of the

Rock." I took the turn onto an uneven dirt-and-sand road. A couple more turns and a few teeth-rattling bumps later, I pulled up onto a small rise to find cars, campers, pickup trucks, and a couple of buses. This was obviously the spot.

As I parked, a large crow, black and shiny as wet licorice, landed in front of my car and walked back and forth until I got out and slammed the door, at which noise he gained the air heavily and flapped away, low to the ground. The view from the rise was expansive, the sky seemed immense, and the plains rolled out on all sides to hills and mountains on the distant horizons. The Tehachapis turned into the Sierra Nevadas and went fading into the northwestern sky in successively dimmer shades of dark brown and purple.

At the edge of the site, a man and woman were running a coffee and snack stand. It was this man who told me everything I know about creosote bushes. I had expressed some curiosity regarding the desert vegetation and the surrounding landforms. "They put out a poison," he said of the creosotes. "It kills the other plants around them." He also pointed at hills dotted here and there on the surrounding horizon and told me what they called some of the formations and places we could see from where we stood. They had names like Horned Toad Hills, Barren Ridge, Middle Knob, Red Rock Canyon, and Astor Gold Mine.

In the center of the site was a wide clearing where no shrubs or grass grew. Most of the people—early arrivals all—had gathered there near a white wooden cross that was thin and probably twenty feet high, with a small, brown, three-foot-high crucifix tied to it with rope. On top of that was yet another smaller crucifix, black, with a ten-inch corpus. A roughly square zone, maybe fifty by fifty feet, had been staked out with metal fence posts and cordoned off with bright yellow nylon rope. Within the delimited area a crew of five men in white T-shirts and jeans was assembling a pavilion of aluminum pipe and white tent cloth over a raised platform covered with blue astroturf. The pavilion, as it turned out, was a makeshift temple for the purpose of covering a statue of the Virgin, which would make its entrance later, and for keeping the p.a. system—two big black speaker cabinets and an amplifier—out of the way of the weather. Several dozen gallon jugs of water were set in a group near the platform. Some people had backed their cars up in the direction of the site and were having breakfast, their tailgates and trunks open for access to coolers from which they withdrew sandwiches and cold drinks.

The visionary, Maria Paula, was not yet at the site; I was told she would show up around eleven o'clock, in about two hours. Clearly, the work proceeding on the construction of the pavilion was being done in preparation for her arrival. I had no idea what Maria Paula looked like and kept an eye open for likely candidates as I moved around, talking to pilgrims. Had I known what kind of an entrance she would eventually make, I would have been less concerned about the possibility of missing it.

The crowd grew steadily. Blankets were spread and folding lawn chairs were placed around the edges of the cordoned-off area, with new arrivals staking out spots in successive rings outward. Most chatted happily with their neighbors. Some prayed quietly, but it was obvious that nothing official had begun yet.

Many of the Mojave faithful were sharing "miraculous" photographs with one another. Almost every third or fourth person had a fistful of Polaroids and was poring over them while those beside him looked over his shoulder. Even though I had about had it with the pictures, I got close enough to look at a few.

A short, plump woman showed me two Polaroids, both taken directly into the sun.

"We took all these pictures and nothing came out, and then all of a sudden these two came out. . . ."

One had glare that looked vaguely castle shaped. The other was another shot of the "golden doorway to heaven." The door phenomenon, though finally accepted at many sites for what it actually is—the unmiraculous reflected outline of the camera's aperture—still had great currency in the Mojave. It seems the true explanation hadn't worked its way west yet.

"Like a doorway, huh?" I said.

"Yeah. And she's got other pictures that are better."

"You shot that right into the sun?" I asked.

"Yeah, see, like right there, that's a stairway." She pointed to a spot below the golden door and identified it as a stairway. I could see nothing. "I have no tricks on my camera," she said. "It's just a Polaroid, OK?"

Bored with the pictures, and not having the heart to tell them how passé the whole golden door thing had become in the Midwest, I asked the photographer and a friend next to her if they had ever experienced anything else miraculous at the site.

"Um, no, this is my first time," said the friend. "Just the pictures that I've seen of her, you know—and people have been healed, things like that."

"What kind of healings have you heard about?"

"Uh, Maria, what kind of healings have happened?" she asked the photographer.

"Different ones, I don't know," Maria said, suddenly shy. "I'd rather not talk about mine, though."

Nobody had asked about hers, and I was just turning to walk away, ready to assent to Maria's wish not to discuss her personal healing, when she abruptly overcame her shyness.

"OK, I was supposed to have open-heart surgery," she said. "They had already taken the tests and all, and they said I wouldn't live three months if I didn't have the surgery. After I came over here, I passed out one day at work, and the doctors checked and said they found nothing. And I'm a believer now, believe me. 'Cause he had only given me three months to live, and I didn't have it."

"So no need to have the surgery now?" I asked.

"No."

She then pointed across the site to a heavy woman in jeans and a brown shirt. "See her? She's lost a hundred pounds." She suggested the weight loser might have a more dramatic story to tell.

I walked over to where the woman in question stood with her teenage daughter, looking at pictures spread on the trunk lid of a compact car. The photos were being explained, in Spanish, by their owner, a dark, leathery-skinned man in his fifties wearing a red plaid shirt, crisp new blue jeans, and a little wide-brimmed straw hat with black trim. He held a ragged business envelope stuffed with photos and laid them out one by one on the trunk lid, explaining each as he went, pointing with a stubby index finger. The pictures were no more remarkable than others I had already seen, except for two relatively clear portraits of Jesus—with his familiar beard, mustache, and hair—supposedly captured by pointing and shooting into a cloud-filled sky. Most of the others were the standard sky shots with lots of glare and lens flare resulting in the blobby Rorschach patterns I had seen so many times before. Some were Polaroid shots in which it looked as though the emulsion had been prematurely interrupted in mid-development, resulting in unidentifiable paisley-like patterns of black and green and orange. I asked the man if he spoke English.

"A little," he said. His English, as it happened, was about as limited as my Spanish, so the woman with him—the weight loser I had come over to speak to in the first place—acted as interpreter, explaining the significance of each picture as the man laid them out, pointed, and spoke rapidly in his native tongue. He turned one of the pictures of Jesus in the sky upside down and said he could see the devil in the other half of the picture. I tried but couldn't see it. Some of his most involved explanations—amounting to graphic lessons in Christian cosmology—were reserved for the pictures with emulsion smears. The black stripe running along the top of one photo represented our sins. An emulsion smear near it represented hell. Three other smeared spots stood for, in order, suffering, the devil, and Christ. The lesson of this photo, as he explained it, was that we had to go through suffering to get to Christ. He had similar interpretations worked out for each of the other photos in his packet. I stood looking at photos, nodding back and forth between the man and the interpreter, until he had come to the end of the stack and returned the photos to the envelope. I turned once more to the woman.

"Someone told me you had had a healing," I said. "Would you mind telling me about it?"

She was still overweight, despite the alleged hundred-pound weight loss. She wore glasses, had swept-back black-gray hair and a dark complexion. She wore a tan, untucked cotton shirt over blue jeans, and a white rosary hung around her neck. She was reluctant to talk at first, but soon warmed to the subject. I asked how she had first become aware of the apparitions in the desert.

"I had been sick for the past eight years," she began, in perfect English with just a trace of an accent. "I had been seeing doctors in my hometown. They kept on saying I was fat and to stop eating. In reality, in the end I saw a specialist in the city who told me I had three tumors larger than grapefruit and some cysts. The tumors were in the ovaries. I was a big infection, one big inflammation. I weighed three hundred and something, almost three hundred fifty pounds. They really couldn't tell because they couldn't weigh me, they couldn't stand me up. The first time I came here, with my cousin, I was on my second pneumonia bout within three months. I came on April the thirteenth. My husband said, 'Why are you going?' I said, 'I'm going to go die in Holy Mother's arms, or she's going to get me well. One way or the other.'

"All this time I had also been praying for my family. My mother stopped being a Catholic. My sister did too. They're not Catholic anymore. And during the time that I was sick, they disowned me because of being a Catholic. They claim to be born-again Christians. So the first time, after coming here, my cousin asked, 'What did you pray for for yourself?' I said, 'I prayed for the salvation of my family, for all our sick, for blessings upon all of them, especially my children, their spouses, their children, for them to be safe, to get to heaven.' Again she asked me, 'What did you ask for yourself?' and I would say I had prayed for everyone else but not for me.

"She kept insisting that I ask for healing for myself. Well, we kept coming, and one day after the apparition here, someone pointed to the sky and said, 'Look up; we're pretty sure she's up there. Look up.' And I said, 'I can't see. I'm not supposed to be out here in the sun on account of my medicines.' Then I looked and said, 'Well, from the sun I see a big old rosary illuminated all the way to the ground. There's a big cross over us.' And a Spanish lady said, 'Look really good because our Holy Mother's always holding the rosary.' But I said, 'But the rosary's so *big*, how can she hold that big old rosary?' One elderly woman near me said, 'I've never seen her before. Look up and tell me that you can see her!' So I looked up even higher, and she was there! She was *so big*. She was illuminated, her features were illuminated. Her heart was illuminated too, and so big. It was glowing. And the sun became like a little pearl at the bottom of her heart. And the sun, which was a pearl, came out in different rays of color— gold, silver, the reds, the blues. The greens were like gold, like silvers. The rays were all upon us. I said, 'Holy Mother, this sun is shining all over the world. Save all of us because we all want to get to heaven only we sometimes take wrong roads. Forgive each and every one of us.'

"And then my cousin asked again, 'What did you ask for yourself?' This time I told her, I had said, 'Holy Mother, heal me and make me well. Help me to lose the weight so I can have my surgery.' And right now, since then, I've lost almost a hundred pounds. And my sugar has got under control; now I'm only on one pill, and the doctor says that maybe if I lose another hundred pounds, I can have the surgery I need. And the doctor had told me that it was gonna take me I don't know how many years to stop feeling the pain, and I don't feel the pain anymore. When I had the infection, the inflammation, I couldn't put jeans on because nothing tight could touch me, nobody could touch my stomach; it was always hot and infected and inflamed. I was so weak with all the hemorrhaging of all these years, I would be trembling just with the vibration of my voice. And now, praise God, I feel a lot better. And each month I don't know how I'm gonna get here, but I get here."

She makes the trip every month from a small town west of the Tehachapi Pass, riding with her cousins in their truck. On the way over, they pray as they ride.

"If you want to see the Virgin, you have to say three rosaries," she said. "We start praying when we leave the house. Today we started with the chaplet; then we say the three rosaries, the Joyful, the Sorrowful, and then the Glorious mysteries. In between we might mention the mountains or this or that, but mostly our concentration is just on Jesus' life. But this place is beautiful for anybody that has any kind of problems. I've told many people that have been sick, and they've come. It's especially helpful if you're having problems with other people."

She has had copies of her favorite miracle pictures made and passes them out to as many people as she can. "We have taken some of our most blessed pictures early in the morning. We get the gate of heaven, the door. Our Holy Mother's usually in the middle. In one of the pictures that we took, she was so clear, and her heart was red, but once, in one of the pictures, the heart had a little line of red going down like that, and I said, 'Why is my picture like . . . why is the red kind of coming down that way?' I didn't want to say *bleeding*. And there was a lady next to me who told me, 'Because our Holy Mother is very sad from all the abortions and her heart is bleeding.' I said, 'Oh, my Lord!' Of course, it wasn't that clear by the time we got home. In some of the pictures I take she is so clear, yet by the time we get home they're faded. And you can see the mist. Like a mist, you know? Someone said that's because the person that wants to see her has to come, has to pray to be able to see her.

"The pictures are blessed," she continued. "I get the copies and I take them to our local priest. He blesses them and I distribute them. Every little bit of money that I have, it's to make more duplicates and to pass them out and to give directions on how to get to her. Sometimes I think, 'Oh, my God, we're telling too many people!' Because it's hard to get in here. But it's really beautiful!"

At this point, an F-16—the first of many—from nearby Edwards Air Force Base flew over, making a smooth, thick, ripping sound like a prolonged slurp at the bottom of a milk shake. Our conversation paused while the jet went over.

"There's so many stories," she said, shaking her head.

By ten o'clock there were probably eight hundred believers gathered, and the number was growing. There were old people, young singles, young couples with small children, some nuns, some priests, babies, entire extended families. Many of them had cameras—Polaroids, 35mm SLRs, hand-held videos—and were pointing them skyward and shooting away. The air was full of the zipping sound of Polaroids spitting instant photos out of their front ends. One cameraless old woman stared at the sun with the aid of half a pair of sunglasses held in front of her regular glasses. A two-man news crew from Telemundo, a Los Angeles Spanish–language television station, was working the crowd; the talent was smooth and neutral-looking, but the cameraman, with a ponytail and Lennon glasses, wore a fixed expression of bemused incredulity just this side of a smirk. A young man in blue jeans, Ray-Bans, and a white T-shirt with SECURITY emblazoned across the back got the crowd's attention by turning on the p.a. and asking someone to move a maroon Chrysler. Shortly after, I watched as this same man deputized a crew of helpers and handed them each fresh white security T-shirts, which they immediately put on over the shirts they were wearing. Once they were suited up, the security chief directed them in the process of staking out a little pathway into the roped-off area.

"When Maria Paula comes," he explained to his newly liveried assistants, "people usually try to crowd the car, so what you want to do is surround her and walk her in." The others looked at him gravely and nodded.

Preparations inside the yellow-roped area had been completed; the pavilion was up and waiting. Information booths had been erected outside the perimeter of the roped-off area. The sign above one read "Our Lady of the Rock: Information, English" and above the other "Informacion Español." Thirty or forty people were in line at each of the booths. A sign above one said, "Printed messages and photos. To help defray printing costs, a goodwill donation would be appreciated. Thank you." Workers in the booth were collecting money and passing out a suspiciously clear cloud photo of Mary along with a copy of the past month's message. The message warned, "If mankind does not mend its ways, and pray with love the Holy Rosary, the world will not have salvation. All will be lost."

The sky was by this time completely blue, and the air was dry and warm. For the time being, there were no clouds, although they would return in time to be photographed before the end of the day's activities. Having left an Ohio February behind just two days before, I felt out of place, meteorologically speaking, and somehow undeserving of this sudden, unearned summer day.

At ten-fifteen two men within the perimeter began leading the rosary over the p.a. At first it was prayed in English, probably the lowest common linguistic denominator here, but eventually it veered off into a handful of other languages. The people closer to the rope joined in the prayers, but most of

the others were having too good a time milling around, looking at pictures, eating and talking near their cars. More charter
buses showed up (one said LAS VEGAS TRIPS on the sign-
board), dumping cargoes of blinking tourists onto the bright
desert. I looked over the shoulder of one new arrival as he
snapped a picture and showed it gleefully to his friends. There
was a ball of glare in the middle. "It's the Virgin! It's the
Virgin!" he shouted.

Another F-16 thundered hollowly across the blue sky, this
one fairly low. The jet rolled, spiraling forward like a football.
Later in the afternoon a woman told me she wouldn't be at
all surprised if the jets had been scrambled from Edwards AFB
to check out the strange phenomena in the sky over the
desert.

In preparation for Maria Paula's arrival, a band of children,
twenty-one in all, had donned altar-boy surplices with white
rope belts and were gathered near the entrance to the pavilion
area. They were pulled into line by order of height, and stood
waiting. Shortly, a green van made its way onto the rise and
pulled slowly to a stop behind the gathered children. The
crowd noise picked up in anticipation, and everyone stood.
Prayers from the p.a. continued, increasing in speed and volume. The boys from Telemundo, TV camera rolling, joined
the press of pilgrims that had suddenly collected at the side
of the van. Maria Paula sat in the passenger seat, clutching a
crucifix to her breast and smiling at the crowd. She made no
move to open her door.

"OK, ladies and gentlemen," a male voice boomed from
the p.a. "The Blessed Mother's here. Let's give her a welcome
with cheers so we can be blessed by heaven. Let's give her a
warm welcome!"

The Blessed Mother in question was a three-foot-high Our
Lady of Fatima statue, which was at that moment being extricated from the back of the van. Dressed in a bridal gown
and holding a white rosary, the statue was placed on a rose-
covered litter and held aloft at shoulder height by two male

workers in security T-shirts. The children moved into position behind the litter, folded their hands as if in prayer, and waited. The crowd near the van was waved back, and the passenger-side door opened. Maria Paula stepped out.

The visionary was dressed all in white—a white veil over a gauzy white habit. She is short and stocky and somewhat beyond middle age. Her hair is black, her complexion dark. Her face, penetrating brown eyes over a broad nose and a warm smile, is a comfortable, kindly one. She smiled sweetly at those near her as she emerged from the van. Her right hand still clutched a crucifix to her chest. In her left hand she held a silver rosary; around her neck hung a long blue one.

The statue of Mary was then processed in and taken for a lap just inside the ropes, to much applause and clicking of cameras. Maria Paula stood beside the van, flanked by three security men. They looked toward the sun. Pilgrims alternately took snapshots of the sun and of Maria Paula, standing silently, looking up into the painfully bright sky. Some gave their cameras to their children, lifted them overhead, and had them snap pictures of the visionary.

The statue was brought to rest atop a banquet table beneath the pavilion. Maria Paula, her head lifted and eyes locked on the sun, walked slowly through a temporary gate in the rope fence, fell into line with the children, proceeded to the statue, and knelt on a blue plastic tarp laid on the ground before the tented Virgin. The children knelt beside her so that the group formed a semicircular arrangement before the makeshift shrine. Many of the faithful outside the rope knelt also. Maria Paula, still staring at the sun, kissed the crucifix and held it to her heart before speaking—whimpering, really—in Spanish into a microphone. She sounded out of breath, sad, and weak or ill. I couldn't make out a word of it. (I learned later that at this point in the ceremony she was already hearing the voice of the Virgin and was repeating her message word for word.) Suddenly a mind-numbingly loud feedback loop exploded from the p.a. A security man rushed to the amplifier and made a grab for the volume knob. Maria Paula continued to stare skyward; her mouth moved rapidly, but we could no longer hear her. She spoke with great emotion and emphasis, her body rocking gently forward as she leaned into each phrase.

The crowd became very quiet while Maria Paula communed with the Virgin for a good thirty minutes. Half of them watched Maria Paula; the other half stared in the direction she was staring. Some stood or knelt with their arms opened wide; a few grimaced as if in pain. Some sat on the hoods of surrounding cars. Several stood on chairs to take pictures over the heads of the others. Many just pointed. Beside me, a man in a Knights of Columbus baseball cap whispered, "Look at it. There's something turnin' blue up there." A few clouds had wandered onto the scene and covered the sun momentarily, so I took the opportunity to glance up. The bright light stabbed sharply into the backs of my eyes and I quickly looked away, but what I had seen had looked just like clouds in a bright desert sky. And for the next two minutes everything looked like a bright white dot.

Before long the p.a. was back on; Maria Paula sighed heavily and sounded near tears as she continued her conversation with Mary in short, emotive bursts. Some of the kids kneeling with her had grown tired and settled back to sit on their heels; a couple of the younger boys talked to each other furtively.

Eventually, Maria Paula emerged from her ecstasy. She crossed herself, stood up slowly, adjusted her habit, bent down to retrieve her crucifix, and walked over to stand beneath the tent, next to the statue. Some Our Lady of the Rock volunteers who had been videotaping the proceedings approached and spoke with her for a moment on camera. The crowd had come to its feet and pressed forward to the ropes. Maria Paula headed over to greet her flock.

Just then a two-stage explosion of apocalyptic magnitude shattered the quiet desert air—*buh-BLAM!* We all jumped and turned to see what direction the doom was coming from.

Then we heard the telltale sky-ripping gurgle of an F-16, flying over so high it was invisible, compressing the air before
it and strafing the desert with the trailing edge of a conic
pressure wave dragged in its wake—a sonic boom.

That woke a few babies up. I suppose the locals are accustomed to having their teeth rearranged every so often by supersonic aircraft, though I don't see how they could refrain
from jumping every time. We all recovered pretty fast,
though, and everyone was back on the same page in a matter
of seconds. One of the men again approached a microphone
and began leading the crowd in the rosary.

Maria Paula, accompanied by a retinue of volunteers, security people, and cameramen, began working her way
around the edge of the crowd, laying hands on her followers
and praying with them individually. Many people were crying,
both pilgrims and those within the visionary's circle. A large
family of Asians, encamped on a blanket spread just outside
the rope, wept loudly as Maria Paula spoke to them. She
hugged the mother's and father's heads and held them to her
own in a triple head hug, forehead to forehead to forehead.
The couple cried loud and long; Maria Paula did not cry. She
moved on to an elderly woman, hugged the woman's head
to her chest, and stared at the sky, her lips moving rapidly.
When the visionary let go of her head, the woman knelt before her, sobbing sharply. Maria Paula moved on. More hugs
were dispensed; she laid her right hand on some of the pilgrims' heads and traced a cross on their foreheads with her
thumb. With her left hand she grasped one woman—fiftyish,
gray hair, eyes ringed red—by the back of the neck; she
pressed the palm of her right hand to the woman's forehead,
held her for a moment in this chiropractic grip, then released.
The woman's eyes rolled up, then shut. She quivered visibly
before dropping like a felled tree into the arms of those behind her—who, it must be noted, seemed to have been expecting it. They bore her to the ground, where she lay, "slain
in the Spirit," her right hand tapping the earth spasmodically.

Her loved ones ministered to her, fanning her with a hat, holding her still hand.

Others got little more than a grasp of the hand and a smile from the visionary, but seemed satisfied with that. Invariably, if the faithful were not in tears before Maria Paula touched them, they were after. Some held up objects for her to bless, which she did with a vague, cross-shaped wave of her right hand. Many parents shoved their children at her. One young father lifted his three- or four-year-old daughter over the crowd so the girl could touch the visionary's hand. After she succeeded, the father reeled the girl back in, grasped her right hand, and guided her through the motions of the sign of the cross.

It took nearly forty minutes for Maria Paula to work her way all around the edge of the crowd. The prayers of the rosary droned in the background while she visited and prayed with those gathered near the rope. F-16 flyovers continued, and there was one more supersonic concussion ("Oh!" a woman near me exclaimed to a companion. "Another sonic bomb!"). Awhile later, a B-2 "Stealth" bomber winged over us at a relatively slow speed, tipping its wings back and forth as if testing the air; it looked like the Batplane, a black wedge of disaster.

When she finished her rounds, Maria Paula, through a translator, addressed the crowd briefly, thanking everyone for coming and asking that any miraculous healings be reported to the workers in the booths. She was then hustled back into the van, the statue and litter were retrieved and stowed, and the visionary's driver bore her away from the site. The message from the Virgin would be made available on photocopied sheets at the next month's gathering.

Workers began immediately to disassemble the pavilion, the booths, and the yellow rope fence, but most of those gathered made no move toward their cars. There was too much basking in the afterglow for a mass exodus. The whirring and clicking of cameras, if anything, increased after the visionary's departure. People gathered in small groups, sharing pictures and gaping, teary-eyed, at the sky. I stood with one such group that was yelling and pointing excitedly. Without the aid of eye protection of any sort, and with amazingly little squinting, they stared baldly at the sun. Most were crying, though it was impossible to tell which tears were due to the emotion of the moment and which were the eye's reflexive defense at being taxed in this way. The few times I glanced up to try to make out the formations they were reporting, the white glare was too painful and my eyes involuntarily, and almost instantly, averted to the cooler, dimmer desert landscape.

Others gathered around to hear what they were seeing.

A smear of clouds shifted slowly near the sun.

"Oh, my God. Oh, my God!" a woman exclaimed. She spoke English with more than a trace of an Italian accent. "Right there. Right there. The second one. That's Jesus! That's Jesus! That's Jesus!"

"Oh, my God . . ." another woman near her responded breathlessly, weeping, sounding as though she were reacting within a dream.

"That's Jesus! You see? It's moving. Right there! Right there!"

"Can you see the Virgin?" the second woman asked somnolently.

"No, I didn't see the *Madonnina* yet." She paused, then added, "Thank you, Jesus. Thank you, Jesus." She lifted her left hand into the air.

The clouds moved. Several women screamed at once.

"Oh, look, look! There's an angel!"

"Right there! Right here!" Pointing, sighting down an arm.

"There's a leg right there."

"There's the Virgin!" We all strained to see.

"Above the sun?" asked a man trying to make out anything but sun and clouds.

"Right there," one of the women pointed. "You see where the white cloud goes on the bottom? She's on top. She's on top of the cloud. She's coming up a little bit. She has a white veil. She's right on top of the cloud."

"Oh, I see it now." This from another woman in the group. The man still saw nothing, nor did I.

"See? She's bent down. She's got her head bent down, see? Oh, *Madonnina bella. Madonnina.* Oh, God. Oh, God."

"Where?" the man asked. "Is it over this way? Is it a cloud formation?" A couple of the women tried to steer his eyes toward the vision.

"You see where the big light comes up? She's right there."

"What color is it?"

"Gray."

"I still can't make it out."

One of the women turned toward another section of sky. "Oh, there's another one over here; look at that cloud. I don't know what that means, but I'm taking a picture of it."

"Thank you, Jesus."

"Thank you, Jesus."

The Italian woman, having lost sight of the Virgin, scanned the sky sadly, weeping, moaning, murmuring. "*Madonnina* . . . where are you, *Madonnina*? Oh, Jesus . . ."

A woman beside her, rapt, amphetaminic with excitement, still seeing things in the sky, nearly screamed, "Look at it! The baby Jesus in her hand! Right here!" She pointed intently. "Right here!"

"No," the other replied tiredly, "I don't see it now. No . . . *bella* . . . no, I don't see it now. I saw before. Twice I saw it. Just like a picture she looked. Just like a picture. Oh, *Madonnina, Madonnina bella*! You did a miracle before, so bring peace in the world . . . Jesus . . . bring peace in the family . . . for the mothers and all the people in the world,

for the kids . . . Jesus. Virgin Mary, bring joy to my family."
She stopped speaking and cried quietly.

Apart from the clusters of others, one woman stood alone,
moving in the Spirit. She was something less than five feet
and something over two hundred pounds, dressed in a loose
purple muumuu and sandals. Her eyes were closed and her
arms were up, bent at the elbows, palms forward, beating at
the air on either side of her head. Her body rocked and she
staggered, stepping randomly in a more or less circular path.
Once in a while she tipped too far backward and looked ready
to topple at any moment, but she never did. A couple of
nearby pilgrims shot videotape of her as she shimmied in the
Spirit.

Sun gazing continued, and a few lone seekers wandered off
for solitary walks in the desert, but things had begun to wind
down. Sandwiches and drinks were again pulled out of coolers. A chihuahua the size of a squirrel chased three giggling
little girls into a van. Two boys, preschoolers, beat a creosote
bush with sticks. A young couple posed for a picture beneath
the big crucifix. Within thirty minutes of Maria Paula's exit,
the set had been struck: The tent and booths were down,
ropes and posts were up and packed away, and pilgrims had
begun to leave. Within an hour this spot would be just one
undifferentiated plot of ground among millions like it in the
Mojave desert—a parcel of crumbly soil covered with scrubby
vegetation stretching away to bald, striated mountains color-
coded by distance.

On the way back to my motel, I powered down all four of
my rental car's windows and let the desert air—comfortably
warm and dry, smelling subtly vegetative and dusty—wash
through the car and over me. The stereo's seek button found
a Dwight Yoakam song; I let it rest and boosted the volume.
It turns out the desert is one place where country music
sounds really, really good.

I spent most of the afternoon and early evening hanging around my motel room, making notes and watching the movement of life and commerce in Mojave, California, from the balcony outside my front door. It seemed mainly to be a matter of semitrailers cruising up and down the main drag and people going into and coming out of restaurants and gas stations. I was waiting for a phone call. A representative from Our Lady of the Rock ministries had half promised me an interview with the visionary, but we had not settled on a time or place. In a call to the ministry a couple of hours after Maria Paula's departure from the scene of the vision, I had been told to sit tight; they had to think about it.

The call came at seven p.m. Could I come right now? I assured the unidentified caller that I could, and I was given directions to the ministry's headquarters. I was to travel back to California City, drive through to the far side of town, and look for an apartment complex just on the edge of the desert.

"You'll know it," the caller said. "It's the second to last building. After that it's just black."

Driving across the desert expanse in the dark toward California City was a much different experience than driving into Mojave the previous night had been. The first time I had not known the terrain that surrounded me in the blackness. Now I knew that I was rolling across an immense flat basin, its distant edges delineated by dreamily stark and high mountains. The fact that I could not see my surroundings but knew them for what they were—mainly vast and empty—caused my scalp to tingle with a sense of some unspecified dread. I have always had a similar reaction to vastness, particularly in natural settings that seem endless, unvariegated, and vacant. I suppose it's a low-level version of agoraphobia. (A recurring dream has me adrift in a small inflatable raft on the glossy blue-black surface of the sea at nighttime. A low moon skips the beam of its reflection across a swath of the sea. My thoughts on the raft are not about which direction land lies or how I am going to get to it; I am concerned only with the unthinkable depth of the water below me and the expanse of starless navy blue sky above. Suspended between those two overpowering realities, conscious of my existential ridiculousness just in terms of sheer scale, I curl up in the bottom of the raft and try to hurry sleep.)

I was met at the apartment (which did indeed stand on the edge of California City, with the desert at its back) by a young man I had talked with by telephone from Cincinnati. He welcomed me into a nicely furnished and decorated two- or three-bedroom unit on the second floor. A videotape of the day's festivities in the desert was running on the television.

"Would you like a cup of tea?" someone shouted from the kitchen, where several women and a young girl were working busily. "Coffee?"

"Coffee would be great," I said. "Thanks."

Maria Paula entered the living room from the back of the apartment. She was dressed, from neck to foot, in a brown habit; over her head was draped a white, sheer veil. An oversize rosary hung around her neck. She crossed the room and shook my hand. I said I was happy to meet her, and she nodded and smiled shyly at me but said nothing. The young man told me what I already knew.

"She does not speak English," he said. Maria Paula looked at me and shrugged, still smiling. "You can talk with Maria Paula and her spiritual director, Father Javier, downstairs, in his apartment. He will translate for you." Someone handed me a cup of coffee. The visionary then led me outside, where we descended the stairs to the apartment directly below. She rang the bell.

The door was opened by a dark-skinned man who did not speak but ushered us inside. The doorman immediately retired to one of the apartment's back rooms, and I did not see him again. Father Javier, a handsome young priest with dark hair combed straight back, glasses, and a black blazer over a white shirt and gray slacks, was waiting for us in the living room. He rose from the couch, reached for my hand, and introduced himself. He then motioned Maria Paula into a seat adjacent to the couch and me onto the couch beside him.

The apartment was immaculate. Religious art was placed tastefully throughout the room and included an image of Our Lady of Guadalupe, a portrait of the "Divine Mercy" (Jesus with red and white rays emanating from his chest), a picture of the pope, and a two-foot-tall statue of Jesus.

They had only one question for me before we began our conversation. Had I been sent by the bishop? I assured them that I had not, and we began a conversation that lasted about an hour, with Father Javier acting as translator.

Born and raised in Mexico, Maria Paula neither reads nor writes, Father told me. "She is a simple person," he said. I found the visionary warmly communicative and eager to answer all of my questions. She spoke quietly but with great conviction. Occasionally, in her haste to make her responses clear to me, she attempted a phrase or two in English. Father Javier chuckled when she did this, tickled, as he expressed it, by her "simplicity and spontaneity." Maria Paula's long white veil was pushed back off her head and draped over her shoulders during our conversation; its ends lay in her lap, and she fiddled with them occasionally to give her hands something to do. She seemed happy and smiled often, the right side of her upper lip lifting slightly higher than the left, tilting the expression to one side.

I asked her to tell me how this had all begun. Father Javier relayed my question, and Maria Paula leaned forward in her chair to respond. Father gave me her answer. The responses as reported here are mostly as they eventually emerged in English from the mouth of Father Javier. The visionary and I tossed him questions, answers, and clarifications, and he did the best he could to keep the traffic flowing in both directions.

"She has a girl, a daughter, who had leukemia. The apparitions started taking place when her daughter was three years old. She was feeding her daughter when suddenly this girl stands up and she starts seeing our Blessed Mother."

"No, no," Maria Paula interrupted with a correction.

Father listened.

"OK," he continued, "nobody knew that it was our Blessed Mother. The girl saw a bright light that bothered her a lot. And then the girl said, 'Mommy, I see a lady in the light.' Three times her daughter said she had seen our Blessed Mother, uh, the lady.

"Then one day, in intensive care, the daughter told Maria Paula that she was dying. There, at that very moment, the miracle occurred. She came back to life, and the girl said to Maria Paula, 'Mother, I saw Jesus Christ.' At the same time, there in the hospital room, Maria Paula and the girl saw a special light in the room. A bright light. Then after several days, when she was recuperating, the little girl was looking out the window and she was praying. Maria Paula was curious, wondering what the girl was looking at. Maria Paula didn't see anything—just light, natural light, from the window. So the little girl told her, 'Mother, the very nice lady told me that you have to repent for your sins and consecrate all your children, and start praying as much as you can.'

"The little girl told her, 'Mother, the lady told me that you have to go to the mountain to pray. You will find, on top of the hill, a kind of reservoir that contains water.' So she went to the top of the hill that her daughter had said, looking for the reservoir. She didn't find it right away, but from May to the middle of June, she was going every day trying to find that reservoir.

"Then, on July twenty-second, she found the reservoir. Later, on July twenty-fourth, was the first time Maria Paula saw the Blessed Mother."

"What year was this?" I asked.

"Nineteen eighty-nine is when she first saw the Blessed Mother."

"Tell me about when she first saw Mary."

"On the day she found the reservoir, she went back home and started praying before an altar that she had built. She was kneeling. She was very tired and she fell asleep. Around three o'clock in the morning, she felt a presence of someone. She felt that someone was calling her, and she opened her eyes. What she saw was a big cloud and then in the middle, on the cloud, she saw the cross, and she saw Saint Francis of Assisi, Saint Thérèse of the Child Jesus, and a big angel. Saint Francis of Assisi was holding in his hands four hosts, little hosts. Saint Thérèse was holding a piece of rope, white rope. The angel was holding a kind of cup filled with oil. And Jesus Christ told her, 'Come up. Come forward.' Jesus asked her, 'Are you going to be faithful and obedient to my Blessed Mother? Will you follow my footsteps? Will you be humble and obedient to what I'm going to ask you to do?' She answered, 'Yes, my Lord, I will obey and do what you ask me to do.' Jesus Christ then took the cup from the angel and poured it on her head. 'From this very moment,' Jesus said, 'you will be named Maria Paula.' Her real name was Julia. When this happened, Jesus Christ gave her a white robe. Then Jesus was silent for a couple of seconds. He looked directly into Maria Paula's eyes—he has very clear eyes—and he told her, 'You will find me on the streets. You will find me in those who are abandoned, those who are oppressed, those who are forgotten, those who are blind and paralyzed'—people who suffer in general. And then everything disappeared."

As she talked and as Father Javier relayed her tale to me, Maria Paula leaned farther forward in her chair, her eyes lit with pleasure at the retelling of her story.

"She thought she was in a dream, but it was not a dream," Father continued. "This was around four o'clock in the morning. She then left the house, holding a statue of our Blessed Mother, her rosary, and a bottle of holy water, and she went back to the top of the mountain. She fell once. She left her shoes. At one point on her way up the mountain, she recalls very clearly that she found herself walking in darkness. No light. She tried very hard to grasp the branches—the hill was hard to climb."

Maria Paula illustrated, with flailing, grasping motions, her arduous ascent up the hill.

"She felt something like thorns under her feet, and she could see a serpent, a snake. It was horrible. [The visionary grimaced at the memory.] A big snake, a large, big one. She felt that the serpent was going to bite her, and though she can't explain how, she suddenly walked very, very quickly to the top of the hill. When she got there, she knelt and was not able to speak. She was having a hard time breathing too. As she knelt, she felt a presence behind her back, but it was not a good presence—it was an evil presence. She felt that she was paralyzed. Her thinking was functioning not very well. She tried to cry out loudly, but she couldn't. She tried to get up to get the bottle of holy water—she had dropped it—but she couldn't. She tried to look behind her but couldn't. At that very moment, like this—" Father Javier snapped his fingers—

Maria Paula, anxious to convey the experience herself, spoke directly to me in broken English. "There was a beautiful water, look like air, and the birds singing, beautiful, and smell very fresh, look like branches and flowers and water. . . ."

Father Javier: "She could hear the sound of water and birds singing. She says it is very hard to try to describe, but it was very beautiful, what she experienced. She continued trying to look behind her, but then she heard a voice from heaven that said, 'Don't look back; look at me and you will be safe. I am the Mother of God, Our Lady of the Rock of Southern California, the Queen of Peace of Southern California. I come to bring peace and love for these people who need it so much. Maria Paula, I want you to come every single day at six o'clock in the morning. God our Father has sent me to console all the people here.' That's the way she started. Our Blessed Mother's request, since then, has been for prayer, conversion, penance, to pray the rosary especially, and for the consecration of all of us to her Sacred Heart.

"Every day at three o'clock in the morning," Father Javier said, "she kneels to pray. Every single day she prays from three o'clock in the morning until eight o'clock, and our Blessed Mother appears to her sometime during her prayers. Before she goes to the desert every thirteenth, she is in her room praying, preparing herself. She knows it is time to go to the desert when she feels very clearly something like a command in her heart. She always hears a voice that says, 'Maria Paula, it is time for you to go to the desert.' When she is at the apparition site, the first thing she sees is a big light in the sky, and then a big angel. She says this big angel prepares the people to receive the Blessed Mother. Then she starts seeing a cloud, and in the middle of the cloud is a bright light, and then our Blessed Mother appears."

"And how does the Blessed Mother appear to her? Three-dimensional or flat like a picture?" I asked. Father Javier conveyed my question to Maria Paula, and she answered, pointing at me.

"She sees our Blessed Mother like she's seeing you right now. Very human, only transparent."

"So it's not like a picture?"

"No. Is not a picture. She's a real person. Our Blessed Mother moves her lips when she talks to Maria Paula. She also sees our Blessed Mother move her fingers."

"How is she dressed?"

"She wears a big white robe made of, like . . . silk. But very simple and beautiful. She covers her head with a blue mantle."

Maria Paula illustrated this point by pulling her long veil over her head, wrapping both ends beneath her chin and draping the ends over her shoulders.

"She never sees a crown on her head, but there are a lot of lights around her head. Her eyes are very blue, blue, beautiful blue; you can't even describe it. The color of her mantle matches with her eyes. And she holds a rosary—a big, long rosary with big beads. When our Blessed Mother is using the rosary with her hands, the rosary is turning gold; it's very beautiful."

Like Ray Doiron, the Belleville visionary, Maria Paula's only experience touching the Virgin has been to kiss her—on the feet and hands.

Also like Ray Doiron, Maria Paula has been given a glimpse of hell. "Our Blessed Mother told her, 'Maria Paula, I need you to see this, and that way you will pray more for your brothers and sisters on earth.' And then our Blessed Mother parted her mantle, and Maria Paula saw hell."

The visionary's face clouded as she described the vision. "It is horrible," Father said. "A lake of fire, horrible. She sees many people. She's seen all kind of horrible animals there, snakes, and a lot of people. She hears a lot of people crying —desperate people. She can't even describe the horribleness and desperation. Maria Paula has told me that she thinks more people would repent and be converted if they could see this vision. Once she asked our Blessed Mother, 'How come you don't let more people see this?' 'Maria Paula,' the Blessed Mother answered, 'the people would die right away [finger snap] of depression.' "

"Just from seeing it?" I asked.

"Uh-huh."

"I know I'd rather not see it," I admitted.

"I don't want to see it either," Father Javier agreed. "I want to be in heaven."

As it happens, Maria Paula has also seen heaven. "In heaven there is only joy," Father said, "joy, happiness, rejoicing, and angels and saints. And always she sees our heavenly Father—but she cannot see his face, only his hands, his fingertips, and his feet. She sees a small part of the chair, the throne, and no more."

The visionary spoke, in English. "There is all light. In the middle of the light I look in to angels. Very much angels, big angels and the small ones. All kinds of angels around God the Father."

"She has been to heaven two times," Father Javier continued. "It was an experience so beautiful. She felt like she was flying. She felt that she had a hand holding her. Somebody was taking her to that place." Maria Paula illustrated by spreading her arms as if imitating an airplane. "When she got to that place, she saw something like a runway, like where the airplanes land, and much light. And these people who were holding her hands, they pulled her down, right onto the stomach." The visionary patted her belly.

Father Javier and the visionary both laughed loudly at Maria Paula's description of the landing. "Anyway," Father continued, "she wanted to stay in that place, but a voice came from the heavenly Father, 'It is not your time yet. Go back.' "

My last question of the evening was one to which I already knew the answer: "Has the Church expressed an opinion on Maria Paula's experiences?"

Father thought for a moment before answering. "What the Church says . . ." he began, and then recast the thought. "The Catholic Church, as you know, is very, very prudent. She has to investigate quietly and prudently. The Church here in the diocese of Fresno is still investigating about this case of Maria Paula."

In a letter issued to the priests of the Los Angeles Archdiocese in September 1995, five months before my visit to the desert, Cardinal Roger Mahoney had made it clear that the "Our Lady of the Rock" phenomenon did not enjoy Church approval. "I must indicate to you that this movement cannot be given support by the Church," the letter reads. The cardinal alludes to doctrinal and canonical irregularities but offers no further details. He concludes with a recommendation: "Well-intentioned individuals and groups who have become involved in this movement might be encouraged to join a recognized Marian movement such as the Legion of Mary."

We talked awhile longer, until the conversation waned to

an exchange of closing pleasantries. As I readied myself to leave, Father Javier summed up by stressing Maria Paula's devotion to the course her life had taken. "This lady only sleeps maybe two hours every night. She prays a *lot* and, as you can see right now, she doesn't feel tired. I have to sometimes say to her, 'You have to go to sleep,' and she does it, under obedience. She obeys me, of course, because it wouldn't be a good sign if she didn't. But I think she prays most of the time, night and day, night and day. And she sees our Blessed Mother every single day. In my personal opinion, she is a very authentic visionary." Maria Paula smiled at me warmly.

After the interview Maria Paula and I walked out of Father Javier's apartment together. I thanked her for taking the time to meet with me, and she smiled. We nodded good night, and she rustled up the stairs to the apartment where I had found her.

I turned north out of their parking lot and drove away from California City and Mojave, into the desert. I had mentioned to Maria Paula and Father Javier that I meant to drive into the desert to see what it was like after dark. The visionary had warned me to be watchful and intimated that sometimes "bad people" were in the desert at night, particularly up near the apparition site. "What kind of bad people?" I asked. "Satanists," she answered.

Satanists or no, I wanted to see the desert at night, and I wanted to see the stars. About five miles out of town, I pulled to the gravel shoulder of Twenty Mule Team Road, got out, and sat on the hood of my car. Around me the desert was supremely dark and quiet. I could see the lights of California City, a slight glimmering strip of yellow and orange on the southern horizon, but nearby I couldn't make out much beyond twenty or thirty feet from the car. I leaned back on the windshield and looked up into a night sky city dwellers don't often get to see, deeply black and pricked by a million points of shimmering starlight. The familiar constellations were there, but a fabric of lesser stars lay between and behind them—the great gauzy swath of the Milky Way. Two or three times my peripheral vision caught the faint white dying streak of a falling star, always just too late to look directly at it. From that vantage point, the human urge to frame a cosmology around this nightly wonder suddenly seemed the most understandable thing in the world. I was tempted to begin outlining one myself, then and there—with the goal, of course, being to imagine a place for oneself amid such a display, to be able to lie on one's back, surrounded to all horizons by the glitter of infinity, and feel unquestionably at home.

CHAPTER NINE

✦ ✦ ✦

Darkness and Devils
Necedah, Wisconsin

One of the most unnerving religious attractions in the United States exists on a plot of what used to be farmland near the small town of Necedah, Wisconsin. The farm was purchased in the mid-1940s by the Van Hoofs, Godfred (Fred) and Mary Ann, who worked and lived on it with their seven children. As an agricultural enterprise, the Van Hoof farm was never much of a going concern; the house was ramshackle and the land was sandy and ill-suited for successful cultivation. It is as a shrine to one woman's grotesque and oddly enduring private revelations that the property has enjoyed its variable reputation for nearly the past fifty years.

On a brittle-cold day in December, I drove to Necedah to visit the shrine and to keep an appointment I had made via telephone with Joe Schelfhout, the shrine's caretaker of twenty-nine years. I drove northwest from Chicago beneath a cloudless blue sky through flat-to-rolling farmland that had been lightly dusted with snow. The setting sun to my left dipped behind a low parabola of cloud that edged up over the horizon like a purple-gray bowl, golden rimmed, threatening to cover the world.

The terrain around Necedah, nearly halfway up and in the

middle of the state, was flat and stark, and had received more than a dusting of snow. Gray farmhouses surrounded by black, leafless trees loomed against the pale landscape, and a hard, shifting wind blew snaking wisps of snow across the highway. A handmade sign nailed to a telephone pole advised: "Jesus—Don't Leave Home Without Him." Another sign, this one a small billboard, let me know I was nearing my goal: "Queen of the Holy Rosary. 14 Grottoes. Free Admission." In Necedah, population 743, municipal Christmas decorations hung on telephone poles lining the main street and framed the businesses at the town's small center—a barbershop, a restaurant (The Skillet), Schultz' Super Market, and a tavern (Down the Hatch). It was hard to imagine what this town had done with the rock festival–size crowds that had come, over forty years ago, to see and hear Mary Ann Van Hoof.

After overshooting my turn at the far edge of town, I doubled back and found my way to the road that led to the shrine, at which this sign was posted:

QUEEN OF THE HOLY ROSARY, Mediatrix of Peace, Mediatrix Between God and Man, Welcomes you to Her shrine. Open 24 hours daily. Free admission. Guided tours. Slide presentation. Free literature, 9am–9pm. Place of apparition, please dress modestly.

The road ran past dark stands of barren trees, empty fields, and a small country cemetery. By the time I had reached the shrine itself, the sun had set and the light was going fast. I found the information center, parked, and crunched across hard snow toward the lighted building.

Inside a small room on one side of the stone building, an elderly man in a brown leisure-suit blazer and a black, flapped hunting cap sat on a metal folding chair. His head rose from his chest when I knocked on the door's glass, and he motioned me in and introduced himself as Ray Schelfhout.

"Joe's my brother," he said. "He's the caretaker here."

As it happened, Joe was home eating supper, but Ray said Joe had not forgotten I was coming to talk with him and that he would be back soon. In Joe's absence, Ray geared up to tell me about Necedah himself. "I've been close to the shrine ever since 1950," he told me as he began fishing around through stacks of pamphlets, brochures, and photocopied pages on a back counter in the little room.

"Sit down," he said. I sat on a metal chair at a kitchen table that occupied the center of the small space. We were in the caretaker's room, attached to one side of the information center proper. The room's walls were stone and cement, its floor plan loosely trapezoidal. A loud furnace blower kicked warm air into the room from an overhead duct. When it occasionally stopped blowing, the buzz of two fluorescent light fixtures and the electric grind of a kitchen clock on the wall behind me rose to meet the sudden silence. Brooms and rakes stood in one corner, beside a coat rack. Shelves on the wall opposite me held a variety of books, pictures, and statuary, including five two-foot-tall plaster versions of the Queen of the Holy Rosary, as envisioned by Mary Ann Van Hoof. The Virgins held their arms outstretched toward me; their necks were long, erect, and creamy white, their eyebrows slightly arched. The statues wore an expression, it seemed to me, of almost aggressive pleasantness. A bulletin board beneath the shelves held a frozen flurry of papers, a calendar, and a picture of Pope John Paul II. Behind me, on a low ledge below the room's windows, stood racks of rosaries and plastic bottles filled with water.

Ray found what he was looking for, a pamphlet entitled *Messages, 1950.* He pulled a chair up to the table and slid the booklet across to me. Its cover illustration was an aerial photograph of the Van Hoof farm taken on August 15, 1950. In the photo thousands of pilgrims are converging on the farm from all directions and swarming over the property. The crowd gathered at the Van Hoofs' that day, estimated at one hundred thousand souls, has been called the largest in rural Wisconsin history.

Mary Ann Bieber married Fred Van Hoof in 1934, four months after answering his ad for a housekeeper in the *Wisconsin Farmer and Agriculturist*; at twenty-five, she was sixteen years Fred's junior. After spending the first years of their marriage as sharecroppers in the Southwest, the Van Hoofs moved to Necedah and attempted to make a go of the farm. In photographs from the period, Mary Ann is large-boned and severe-looking, her eyes wide open behind wire-rim glasses, her dark hair swept up and piled atop her head. A broad forehead, thick lips, and a prominent jawline justify her description by a 1950 *Newsweek* reporter as a "plain, strong-featured woman." Although baptized into the Catholic Church in infancy, Mary Ann had not practiced the faith until after her marriage to Fred, an active Catholic. Once settled in Necedah, the Van Hoofs became regulars at the local parish of Saint Francis of Assisi.

On the night of November 12, 1949, something extraordinary happened to Mary Ann Van Hoof. She had a vision—an experience that, as it turned out, would provide the passage from her first life, as the hardworking wife of a tough-luck farmer, to her second, as a seer and a focal point for the religious yearnings of thousands upon thousands of anxious and hopeful pilgrims. Mary Ann's encounter that night was the first in a nearly thirty-five-year run of mystical experiences that would continue until her death in 1984. The Necedah apparitions and the events surrounding them constitute America's largest, oldest, and most historically significant apparition series. Mary Ann Van Hoof set the standard for the singularly American, apocalyptic, conspiracy-driven genre of private revelation, and there are stylistic echoes of Necedah in some of the most popular apparitions occurring today, including, perhaps most obviously, Conyers, Georgia, and Bayside, New York. The Necedah series has also been the source of more divisiveness and controversy than any such series I know of.

Mary Ann was lying in bed that November night, wide awake, in pain, and worrying about her family. Her health had been poor for years, and she was at that time suffering from heart problems and a recurring kidney ailment. She was afraid her illnesses were preventing her from properly caring for her husband and children, and she prayed that Jesus and Mary would make her well enough to at least tend to her family. In the midst of her prayers she heard a noise outside her bedroom, which she at first assumed had been caused by one of the children having come downstairs. The noise stopped in the little hall outside her bedroom door. Mary Ann glanced into the hallway and saw a figure standing there. She at once realized it was too tall to be one of her children; at the same instant she was struck by the realization that she had not heard this person descending the stairs.

Mary Ann was frightened and began reciting the Hail Mary. As she did so, the figure moved toward her, into the bedroom, and stopped near the bed. The seer noted that the apparition wore a veil and was dressed in blue. Nearly paralyzed with terror, perspiring and unable to cry out, Mary Ann finally turned her back on the phantasm and lay looking in the opposite direction, trembling until, a few minutes later, she steeled herself to look back over her shoulder. The specter was gone.

Worried that he might not believe her, she didn't mention the experience to her husband for several weeks. When she finally did, he did not react with skepticism but instead asked how the figure was dressed and in what color. It was Fred who then first suggested the identity of the night visitor.

"Why, it sounds like it was the Blessed Virgin Mary," he said. Fred also had an idea what the Virgin might have had in mind. "I think it has something to do with the wickedness of the world," he ventured.

Now Mary Ann had a fresh worry. If Fred was right, she

had turned her back on the Virgin, and she spent a great deal of time over the next few months fretting about that and praying for forgiveness. If the Virgin would forgive her, Mary Ann prayed, she would do whatever was asked of her.

The next mystical experience occurred on Good Friday, April 7, 1950. Again Mary Ann was lying in bed, unable to sleep thanks to her physical problems. She heard a voice and assumed it was her oldest daughter talking to one of the other children—that is, until she heard the words, "My Child."

"I was startled," the visionary wrote of the experience, "so pushing back the cover to listen, I saw to my surprise the Crucifix hanging on the wall at the foot of my bed was all aglow with the strangest light and the Corpus twice as large as it should be. But to hear such a sweet voice frightened me very much."

The voice was that of the Virgin. It had been she, the Blessed Mother told Mary Ann, who had appeared in the bedroom the previous November. The Virgin urged Mary Ann to pray ("pray, pray, pray hard") and left her with a mission. She was to approach the pastor of Saint Francis parish, Father Sigmund Lengowski, and request that he tell his parishioners to pray the rosary every evening at eight o'clock, "for prayer only will help you." The Virgin let Mary Ann know that she would return after this commission had been completed. "When your Mission is fulfilled, I will be back but not in this room, but where and when the flowers bloom, trees and grass are green."

The Van Hoofs shared the news with their pastor, who agreed to alert his flock to the request and asked to be kept abreast of any further developments.

In her memoir, *Mary Ann Van Hoof's Own Story of the Apparitions of the Blessed Virgin Mary*, the visionary records her third mystical encounter, the first full-blown apparition and message from the Virgin, with characteristic attention to details of the moment. It was noon on May 28, 1950, Pentecost Sunday; she had rounded up the family and was herding them into the kitchen for Sunday dinner. "Just as I was opposite the kitchen door," she wrote, "I stooped over to brush a mosquito off my leg and as I did so, I noticed a flash of light. First I thought a car had driven up and the light flash was from reflection of the windshield." She looked out the door, in the direction of the flash, and was surprised to see a blue cloud hovering behind a stand of four ash trees in the yard. She was overcome with a feeling of elation and felt herself drawn to the cloud. "Joanne [the visionary's thirteen-year-old daughter] tells me my face had a very strange expression and that I walked out slowly with my hands extended."

As Mary Ann neared the trees, the cloud moved in front of them, and suddenly Mary appeared. She descended to a spot about two feet off the ground and hovered there, appearing to stand on a small cloud or pillow. She was dressed in blue and white and held her arms out to the visionary. Mary Ann noted that the Virgin held a white rosary with a gold chain and gold crucifix. The corpus on the crucifix, however, was flesh-colored "with a sort of strange glow coming from it." In addition, the visionary noted, the wounds on the corpus looked real. "The blood looked like it was ready to drip from it," she wrote.

Mary Ann knelt to hear the Virgin's words. The response to Mary's initial request for prayer had not been up to her expectations. With certain notable exceptions (primarily consisting of the visionary's friends and relatives), the community had not reacted as the Virgin had hoped. "Only ten percent are devoted and say the Rosary very devoutly," she complained. As a consequence of this rebuff, Mary Ann Van Hoof herself would have to pay. "You, My Child, must do penance for your people and community who failed to do as requested on Good Friday," Mary told her. The visionary was told to attend Mass for fifteen days, to fast every day, and to go to Mass on five first Saturdays "in honor of My Immaculate Heart." Her physical pains too, she was told, would continue

"as a sacrifice for sinners." Thus was sealed Mary Ann Van
Hoof's fate as a "Victim Soul," a vicarious sufferer (à la Veronica Lueken and, not so incidentally, Jesus himself) working to make restitution for the sins of the world, a role she
would accept for the rest of her life.

Before departing, the Virgin let Mary Ann know what to
expect in the way of future visits. She would return for the
following two days and again on June 4, June 16, August 15,
and October 7. Though 1950 would prove to be Mary Ann
Van Hoof's most celebrated year as the Virgin's mouthpiece,
visions, messages, and other mystical encounters would continue for the rest of her life.

The next day's apparition was again at noon. A purported
miracle occurred during that vision that is still offered today
by Necedah supporters for the consternation of doubters. The
Virgin reportedly lifted Mary Ann's rosary from her hand to
touch it to her own, and two of Mary Ann's children claimed
to have seen the rosary suspended in midair. The message that
day warned of persecutions to come—both personal and
global. For her own good Mary Ann was to seek the counsel
of trusted persons and, above all, to persevere in faith, love,
and prayer. "The enemy of God," Mary warned, "is creeping
all over America." We were to return to clean living, sacrifice,
regular attendance at Mass, and prayer in order to overcome
the onslaught of Satan. And as the children of Fatima had
reportedly been told, we were to pray for the conversion of
Russia. Mary Ann was then instructed to write to the pope,
Pius XII, and let him know the contents of the message. During this vision Mary Ann was asked to kiss Mary's foot. "To
my surprise," she wrote, "it was warm and felt like real flesh,
soft and velvety." The Virgin also proffered her rosary's crucifix for a kiss. Mary Ann did as she was told, but not without
some difficulty, because the corpus, wounds and all, looked
unappealingly realistic.

During the following day's apparition, Mary asked the visionary to mark out a perimeter around the spot where she

stood, an area that would from that time be known as the Sacred Spot. She also requested that a statue be erected on the spot in her honor.

By the end of the third vision in May, word had begun to spread, and twenty-eight people gathered to witness the June 4 event, among them the Van Hoofs' pastor, Father Lengowski. Again, the Virgin urged prayers for the conversion of Russia. She also directed the visionary to bless the attendees by touching the crucifix of her rosary to their foreheads.

Before the next apparition, the Van Hoofs were visited by three priests, one of them the editor of the diocesan newspaper. This priest, according to the visionary, questioned her sternly about her experiences. "He tried to trap me," she later wrote, "but was unable to do so." Before they left the house, the three priests reportedly shut themselves in a dark room with Mary Ann's "Good Friday" crucifix to see if it would glow for them. It didn't.

On the morning of June 16, the Van Hoofs awoke to find strangers waiting in their yard. The family went to church and on their return found even more people awaiting the visionary and the visit from the Blessed Mother. The crowd continued to build throughout the morning, many of the pilgrims approaching Mary Ann and begging her to pray over them. After one woman had burst into the Van Hoofs' home, weeping hysterically and claiming she had been miraculously cured of asthma, Father Lengowski placed a guard at the door to keep out strangers. As the crowd pressed closer to the house, volunteers strung ropes in an effort to establish a line beyond which pilgrims could not venture. Shortly thereafter, the bulkhead door to the cellar collapsed beneath the weight of six pilgrims who had stood on it in hopes of getting a glimpse inside the home. One, a "heavy-set" woman, broke her ankle and had to be carried from the property for treatment.

By noon more than a thousand pilgrims were gathered and waiting. Mary Ann had brought the formerly glowing "Good

Friday" crucifix to the Sacred Spot with her, and when Mary appeared, she asked the visionary to bless the crowd with it. Next, the Virgin requested that in addition to the statue mentioned in a previous vision, a shrine too be built in her honor. She then reiterated her plea for more prayers and, to drive home the point, revealed to Mary Ann a glimpse of what the world could expect should her request for prayers be ignored. The scene that unfolded before the visionary's eyes was of a bustling city that had been leveled, as if by a nuclear disaster. Buildings, trees, and people had been pounded to rubble, and bodies (and body parts) filled the streets. One mutilated survivor reached heavenward in a gesture of belated supplication just before "his internals burst forth with blood and grime all over him." The Blessed Mother then turned her attention to the assembled pilgrims and, through the visionary, admonished them to clean up their lives, to remember the Ten Commandments, and to pray harder—especially, once again, for the conversion of Russia.

Before the vision Father Lengowski had told Mary Ann to ask for a sign of some kind from the Virgin in order to substantiate the visionary's claims. Mary Ann twice asked for the sign; both times the Virgin acted as if she had not heard the request.

By the next apparition, August 15, the Van Hoofs' mail was being delivered in large bags. Mary Ann was besieged with prayer petitions and requests that she wear pilgrims' rosaries, scapulars, and medals during the apparition. Believers, some of whom had begun assembling the day before the apparition, attempted to get close enough to the visionary to touch her with their rosaries. Wreaths and flowers arrived from all over and were piled around a life-size "Our Lady of Fatima" statue that stood atop an altar at the center of the Sacred Spot. Temporary snow fencing was erected at various points around the property in the interest of crowd control. A p.a. system was strung around the farm. Food and drink stands went up in outlying fields. A television crew constructed a camera platform in the cow yard, and writers and photographers arrived from *Newsweek*, *Time*, *Life*, and the *New York Times*.

Pilgrims camped out or slept in cars on the Van Hoof property and surrounding farms the night before the apparition, keeping Mary Ann awake through the night with their praying and singing and chatting. She arose at dawn "in a daze" and washed her face to refresh herself at least that much before she and Fred were driven to town for early morning Mass. The Van Hoofs arrived at Saint Francis to find the church stuffed with pilgrims, with more waiting in line to get in. To accommodate the faithful, the bishop, against his inclination, had authorized the celebration of the Mass every half hour throughout the day. The Van Hoofs were hustled into a side door and seated near the front of the church. Immediately after Mass cameras began flashing and the crowd surged toward the visionary. Police were called to help, and Mary Ann and Fred dashed like Beatles from the church to the car before making their way back to the farm amid the stream of pilgrims surging in the same direction.

By midday, according to state police estimates, one hundred thousand people, drawn from all over the continental United States and beyond, had assembled on the Van Hoof farm. The crowd included about a hundred priests and nuns, who had been provided front-row positions adjacent to the Sacred Spot. Pilgrims at the throng's outer edges stood nearly a half mile away. The late summer sun blazed indifferently, and the wind kicked up clouds of sand and dust from the barren fields. At noon the visionary emerged from her house in a blue linen dress and white shoes. She carried a rosary and her "Good Friday" crucifix, and her husband and children trailed behind her. The Virgin appeared to Mary Ann dressed in dazzling white and with a message much the same as in past months—a call to prayer and a warning about a satanic, communist conspiracy threatening to engulf America. Mary declared, inscrutably: "More than three-thirds of the nations is now covered with the enemy of God. . . . Black clouds are coming over . . . America. . . . Alaska is the first stepping-stone. Remember—the Pacific Coast!" One contemporary newspaper account described the message as "at times incoherent" and "rambling and studded with incongruities." Finally, the Virgin urged prayers for America's politicians, in particular for Wisconsin's Catholic senator, a man who had "made big wrongs" but remained capable of "great good," Senator Joseph McCarthy.

The last of the 1950 apparitions had been predicted to occur on October 7. Pilgrims began gathering at the farm by October 4, but this time the crowd would peak at around thirty thousand. Early on the morning of the seventh, many in the gathering crowd claimed to see the sun spin as it reportedly had at Fatima. It was by no means an experience common to all attendees, however; Mary Ann Van Hoof herself tried to look, but saw nothing out of the ordinary and said it made her eyes hurt.

When the Virgin appeared, the visionary saw a giant rosary floating over her, its beads "as big as baseballs." Mary Ann described the oversize beads as transparent yet somehow showing all the colors of the rainbow. The colors were "churning," and rays of light streamed from the beads. This time the Virgin began with a report on rosary recitation in North America; though the United States was seriously lagging, it seemed Canada had taken Mary's pleas to heart, and as a result Canadian prayers were up by seventy-five percent since the previous July. Mary then returned to the subject of the shrine, giving explicit instructions for its design and features. Next, she hinted darkly to Mary Ann that "the Enemy would like to close your mouth forever," and warned her never to go with or eat food prepared by strangers. In remarks directed to the gathered pilgrims, Mary again stressed the deficiency of their worship and supplication thus far. "Stop your mockery of Our Lord," she thundered. "Stop it!" As clouds continued to gather over America, the one weapon powerful enough to stop the pernicious advance of the enemy remained the rosary.

The Virgin told Mary Ann that she would be with the visionary in years to come on all the anniversary days of the 1950 apparitions. She was also more explicit about the arrangement by which Mary Ann Van Hoof would be made to suffer for the sins of her community. She was to feel the pains of Christ's Passion every Friday between November 17 and Christmas and again throughout Lent of the following year. (Regular such sufferings through the weekends of Advent and Lent would continue to afflict the seer for more than thirty years. In many subsequent messages the Virgin would refer to Mary Ann Van Hoof, in the third person, as "the Victim.")

At the end of the October 7 message, the visionary took three steps backward, passed out, and fell stiffly to the ground, banging her head on a statue. A few minutes later, she was revived and helped to her feet and into the house, where she fainted a second time.

Ray Schelfhout had been involved with Necedah since the beginning. "When there was twenty-eight people out here, on Trinity Sunday, 1950, I was one of those twenty-eight," he told me. There is a picture of Ray taken in the 1950s in a book I bought at the shrine that night. In the photograph he is a thin, serious, almost glowering young man standing in bright sunlight. He wears pleated pants, a white shirt, and a wide, too-short necktie.

The night I met him, Ray was an old man. The backs of his long, thin hands were marbled with dark veins; the skin on his face was loose, and his earlobes hung low and slack. His gray-green eyes were sheltered by pure white eyebrows. Beneath his sports coat he wore a dark zippered cardigan and a Green Bay Packers necktie over a blue and brown plaid flannel shirt. The earpieces of his glasses were wound with tape where they touched his temples.

Ray had stood beside Mary Ann Van Hoof at noon on August 15, 1950, the day one hundred thousand people showed up at the farm. He told me about that day, looking at the tabletop as he talked, but raising his eyes to meet mine each time he wound up a point.

"It was the hottest day in years. Not quite as hot as last year. Not quite. Last year it reached 105. It was close, though. Mr. McEvoy, who was head of the state traffic police, said to himself at eleven o'clock that morning, 'With a crowd this size, we should have a hundred casualties here today due to the heat.' And he said, 'It's pushing one hundred thousand now.'

"Mary Ann came out about twelve noon, as she was shown the sign of the mist above the ash trees, which was her signal. I was right up close by with her. I heard Mary Ann say, 'Oh, please, not that . . .' when she was told by the Blessed Mother to get up and speak to the crowd. She said, 'Oh, please, not that. *You* tell them.' And the Blessed Mother said, 'You will repeat as I say.' Mary Ann had the Good Friday crucifix in one hand and a rosary in the other, and she repeated sentence for sentence everything Mary told her to say. When she spoke of war—and I was in the services for three years, I know what cannon fire sounds like—I heard a thunderous noise, like cannon fire in the distance.

"The crowd, of course, was very intent on her words. There was a cross section of people there—elderly, sick, children in mothers' arms, some were on stretchers, some were in wheelchairs. When it was over, I ran into Mr. McEvoy, the traffic officer. He was down at the restaurant, having himself a malted milk. He said, 'Somebody handled that crowd today and it wasn't us.' There were no bumped fenders. Twenty thousand cars, 134 buses, seven special trains, and a couple of airplanes. There were no casualties. None.''

Just then the door opened, and Ray's brother Joe walked in from the cold, back from supper and wrapped tightly in a heavy coat with a big fur collar turned up around his neck. His eyes were deep-set and peered out beneath the bill of a black cap. I rose for introductions, and we all sat down. Joe took a seat at the far end of the table without removing hat, coat, or gloves. As Ray continued talking, Joe's chin rested on his chest and he looked at his hands, which lay in his lap. A couple of times he became so quiet I thought he had gone to sleep, but then he would surprise me by suddenly piping up with an affirmation of something his brother had said or to elucidate a particular point.

"We still celebrate the anniversary days every year," Ray went on. "And the Blessed Mother has been here on these anniversary days, as she said she would. I haven't missed a single one. And there's always, *always* evidence of her presence. It takes various forms, but follows the general pattern. Of course, the crowds are not big now due to all of the persecution, but again, with world events confirming the messages, and with the many experiences that people have had over the years, they keep coming back."

"Where does most of the persecution come from?" I asked.

"It comes from the clergy—from those who, as heaven said, should be the very strongest supporters. And of course, from other people as well. But Mary Ann suffered persecution too. In '51 Mary Ann started suffering. Actually, it was already happening in Advent of 1950. She started suffering the Passion of Our Lord, and I witnessed it myself for thirty years."

As Ray touched on the subject of Mary Ann's reenactments of Christ's torture and crucifixion, it was clear that the memories he was recounting still resonated deeply for him some forty-six years later. He paused, seemingly in an effort to quell an emotion rising within him; his eyes appeared on the verge of welling up.

"As regards the Passion," Ray said, "Mary Ann said at first

you think you cannot take any more, but then you find as time goes on you can."

Following the apparition of October 7, 1950, Mary Ann's mystical experiences grew more frequent, if less public, and the messages became more urgent and doleful. Intimations of a grand worldwide conspiracy were offered in indirect and telegraphic fragments: "I saw a very brutal looking man in common clothes . . . the head of the Conspiracy of our water-fronts and airfields. I also saw an object drop from an airplane and a large forest burst into flames." In an April 1953 vision she witnessed the explosion of a hydrogen bomb; it annihi-lated the core of a large city, and victims miles away were left partially incinerated and twisting in agony. The blast seared Mary Ann's throat and left a nauseating taste in her mouth that lasted for a month. She had visions of other saints, including Saint Francis, Saint Thérèse, and Saint Joseph. She saw popes, priests, nuns, and laypeople. Quite often the apparitions—almost without exception darkly tinged and troubling—were inscrutable even to the seer herself, but she apparently accepted many of them as episodes of clairvoyance, depicting actual events occurring over a distance of time or space. She was shown visions of battlefield carnage in Korea —decaying corpses of American boys denied a proper burial. In one vision of a Korean prison camp, an "American boy" had been maltreated by his captors to the extent that "his feet had been frozen off at the ankles. The guard forced him to arise and stand on the bones." In another such "psychic" vision she watched from the backseat of a car while a young couple in the front argued over a baby that rode between them on the seat. The man stopped the car and stalked away in anger; the woman shook the baby until it cried, then pressed her hands to the infant's throat and strangled it. Mary Ann claimed she was given glimpses into the private lives of some of her neighbors—teenage girls sneaking around with young men ("Those dirty girls . . ."), men flocking to local taverns, adulterers, immodest dressers, sinners of every stripe.

At times Mary Ann's confusion about the swirl of voices and visions surrounding her seemed ready to overwhelm her. The Virgin's rhetorical style—oblique, threatening, "lovingly" bombastic—and the profusion of "signs" given in the visions as often as not left Mary Ann depressed or perplexed about the exact nature of the work that was expected of her. "One did not ask 'What do you mean?' like you would from an ordinary person," Mary Ann wrote. Many of her visions were accompanied by extreme pain and ended with the visionary's blacking out and having to be carried off to bed.

Mary Ann's "suffering" came as promised. Her reenactments of the Passion took place behind closed doors, but a group of observers was usually on hand to witness the phenomenon. Typically six to eight people—doctors, priests, helpers—would crowd into the small eight-by-ten bedroom where Mary Ann lay. The bed was draped with rosaries and scapulars, and religious pictures and statues were placed throughout the room. All eyes were on the visionary as the three-hour ordeal began. "The sight we saw," one observer noted, "was too magnetic to look away." At the stroke of noon Mary Ann's body stiffened. Her arms shot straight out from her sides "as Our Lord was nailed to the cross." Her legs straightened suddenly, as if jerked into place, and her feet too were then "nailed" into position, one atop the other. Mary Ann's point of view reportedly shifted throughout the experience—sometimes it was she who hung on the cross; sometimes she raised herself slightly in bed, her arms still outstretched, and moved her head and eyes as if she were viewing the crucifixion of Jesus. The expressions of pain on Mary Ann's face were described as hard to watch but even harder not to. Her eyes were opened wide and rolled from side to side; it was reported that she did not blink once during the three hours. Her jaw hung loose, moving continuously, and her tongue wriggled in her mouth. Her lips were "parted to the extreme and twisted in pain." Her breaths came in gasps and pants or in long, rattling inhalations. Sometimes her mouth moved silently, as if forming words; sometimes words were heard, though often they were in a language no one present understood. She lifted a shoulder and pulled to one side or the other as if to tear herself from the nails, her entire body convulsing in an effort to wrench free from the cross. It is claimed that on two occasions, in 1951 and again in 1952, stigmata of the crown of thorns—red, pricked wounds—were manifested on Mary Ann's forehead. She later began to prophesy during the trances and offered luridly detailed, minute-by-minute accounts of Christ's suffering—"The swollen eyes! The bleeding Mouth! The hole in His Forehead where He had hit a rock! The matted slimy Hair!"

Beginning in Advent of 1951, Mary Ann experienced abdominal pains and "constant" vomiting. Nothing she ate would stay down. A little experimentation revealed that the only things she could ingest and hold on to were coffee, tea, orange juice, and 7-Up. According to her own account, she ate no solid food for twenty-four days leading up to Christmas 1951, with no ill effects. A phenomenon known as inedia, such prolonged abstention from solid food is not unknown in the history of Christian mysticism. Mary Ann's purported inedia recurred during many subsequent Advent and Lenten seasons.

Though Ray has been a firm supporter of Mary Ann Van Hoof's claims for nearly a half century, he told me he had originally approached Necedah in a skeptical frame of mind.

"I was living in Appleton at the time, and I had just got back from a visit to Fatima when this happened, so I came up here with very strong reservations. If I could find anything wrong with it, I was not going to bother. I was going to stay with Fatima, which was approved. But the more I looked, the more I listened, and the closer I got, the more I realized that this had to be from God. After all, what was she asking for? The sacraments daily, pray the rosary, wear your scapular, support your priests, clean out the schools, sisters should go back to wearing their habits and living their lives as they previously had before these modern changes came. The Church should go back to the true Mass as it was given to us by Christ himself. We were asked to obey the Ten Commandments, and we were told that God does not give laws that are impossible. Everybody can and should obey the Commandments. If we did return to them, in our schools, we'd have an altogether different climate here education-wise, home-wise, and church-wise. It would happen."

Ray was also of the opinion that Mary Ann's purported status as a stigmatist would assure her claims a favorable judgment by the Church someday.

"In all the history of the Church," Ray said, "almost two thousand years, there has not been a stigmatist that was not a true mystic, visionary, or seer. So when the Church finally comes to bring the truth out, I think that point will weigh very heavy in Mary Ann's favor."

Ray had also been impressed by the claimed "sun miracle" of October 7, 1950, both because, he said, it substantiated Mary Ann Van Hoof's experiences as supernatural, and because it seemed to be a sign linking Necedah to the more famous series of the Virgin's appearances in Fatima, Portugal. On October 13, 1917, at Fatima, the sun was reported to have spun like a pinwheel and plunged wildly toward earth, prompting many of the seventy thousand gathered for the Virgin's final appearance to the three shepherd children to drop to their knees and beg for mercy. When it returned to its accustomed place in the sky, the previously rain-soaked crowd and the ground on which they stood had been dried and warmed.

From the end of the table, Joe spoke, without lifting his gaze from his hands: "I was here October the seventh, 1950. Rained real hard. The people's clothes got all wet, and twelve o'clock noon the sun come out and started to spin and telescope to the earth, threw different colors off. People were on their knees, wondering what was going to happen next. I seen that in 1950. Their clothes dried so rapidly they forgot they were wet."

What most accounts of Fatima and the original "miracle of the sun" fail to mention, however, is the fact that—as on October 7, 1950, in Necedah—there were those in attendance at Fatima who heard others in the crowd exclaiming about a miracle in the sky, yet saw nothing out of the ordinary themselves.

An even stronger link between Fatima and Necedah, though, was each Virgin's preoccupation with Russia and the communist threat. Following World War II, Fatima had become well known throughout the United States in part because of what was believed to be Our Lady of Fatima's strong stance (hence, God's stance as well) against communism. And despite the recent dismantling of the Soviet Union, Ray expressed little confidence that communism was any less of a threat today than it had been in 1950.

"One of the prophecies, of course, was 'Alaska's the first stepping stone. Remember the Pacific Coast.' Now, the Bering Strait is twenty miles across from Russia to Alaska. If that was frozen over, they could move troops, they could move materials, and so forth. And with our military being sent to Bosnia and Haiti, and how many other places—and our equipment is over there too—what would we have left here to stop them? What? And Russia has *not* been converted. The country of Russia has *not* gone back. Sure, there's some slight indications that it could be happening, but heaven said that Russia will be converted only when enough people pray the rosary every day. If you took a survey of the average Catholic parish, I think you might be shocked to find the low percentage of the families that are saying the rosary every day."

Reaction to Mary Ann Van Hoof from diocesan officials, led by Bishop John R. Treacy of La Crosse, was, from the beginning, cool. Initially described as "highly questionable," her claims were thrown into serious doubt following the August 15 vision and its rambling, equivocal message. The bishop initiated an investigation in June 1950, sending priests to the apparition events as observers and calling the visionary in for questioning on several occasions.

In April 1952, Bishop Treacy ordered Mary Ann to report to Marquette University Medical School for a ten-day stay in order to undergo observation during her period of suffering. While in the hospital, she was fed fruit juice and coffee—the substances on which she claimed to sustain herself during these periods—and lost weight at a rate commensurate with such a diet. Her head and hands were bandaged, and sharp objects were removed from her room. No stigmata appeared.

A member of the bishop's investigating committee who had accompanied Mary Ann to Marquette, Father Claude H. Heithaus, afterward discussed the results of the study with the press. According to Father Heithaus, three psychiatrists observed Mary Ann's "suffering" trances and diagnosed the convulsions as self-induced, neurotic behavior resulting from "hysteria and repressed sexual anxiety." Father Heithaus called the visionary's feverish writhings a "disgusting performance."

For a few months early on, Father Heithaus had been a believer in the seer's claims, but reportedly began to doubt when he witnessed Mary Ann disobeying her spiritual director and accepting gifts of money from pilgrims. Father Heithaus said that after the onset and popularization of the visions, the heretofore tumbledown Van Hoof farm had been newly outfitted with an electric refrigerator and stove, a freezer, and a heater, as well as a new car and tractor.

The investigating committee turned its findings over to Bishop Treacy, and in June 1955 he issued this statement:

Because of the continued promotion of the claims made by Mrs. Mary A. Van Hoof of Necedah, Wis., we, by virtue of our authority as Bishop of the Diocese of La Crosse, hereby declare that all claims regarding supernatural revelations and visions made by the aforementioned Mrs. Van Hoof are false. Furthermore, all public and private religious worship connected with these false claims is prohibited at Necedah, Wisconsin.

This episcopal censure did not stop Mary Ann's visions, and although the large crowds of 1950 never returned, a core contingent of believers were not dissuaded by what they considered the bishop's "opinion." Eventually several hundred of the faithful moved to the area, populating a portion of Necedah's outskirts that would come to be known by locals as the "Shrine Belt." The shrine itself grew to include a dozen small block and stone buildings displaying paintings and statuary that depicted the visions and prophesies of Mary Ann Van Hoof. Plans were drawn up for a "House of Prayer," a church-size building of the sort the Virgin had asked for.

The seer's "sufferings" continued, as did the apparitions and messages on anniversary days. The messages themselves, as the years went by, devolved into a mire of conspiracy-charged, anticommunist, racist paranoia touching on everything from Elvis Presley to nuclear fallout. The visionary spoke continually over the years of "Yids"—"mongrelized" Jews who were poised to take over the world through a murky international banking scheme. Television, rock 'n' roll ("Satan's own beat"), the United Nations, food preservatives, water fluoridation—all were subversive elements planted by satanic forces in order to anesthetize America, to blind us and our children to the gathering thunderhead of world domination by the "Yids," the Russians, or the "Red Chinese." "WAKE UP, AMERICA!" the Blessed Mother warned repeatedly. Soviet planes and submarines were moving ever closer to American shores, according to the Virgin, who issued reports on communist subterfuge and troop movements through the mouth of Mary Ann Van Hoof. (The "Sub Report" for December 2, 1956, is typical of the lot: "1 sub at the Aleutians, 2 subs near Cuba, 1 sub near Key West, 1 sub near Hawaii.") Satanic minions, called "Grand Masters," were in place around the globe—one or two to a country, all watched over closely by an iron-fisted "Supreme Grand Master"—weaving intrigues of such knotty complexity that anyone trying to unravel the plot would "never get to the center of it." The eventual outcome of the conspiracy, as best I can understand it, was to be the establishment of a "One World" government with the common people, you and me, pressed into service as slaves.

Joe lifted his head and spoke again, this time looking straight into my eyes. He looked a lot like his brother, but with greener eyes and a more pointed nose. His voice was shakier than Ray's, though, and his breathing seemed labored. He held a handkerchief with which he frequently wiped his nose.

"It tells us here in the messages that we have a battle today between the Christian people and those people that are trying to destroy Christianity. In the messages she tells who they are, how they're fooling, how they're tricking, and how they're misleading us Christian people. She tells us how displeasing it is to God and what to do to correct it. The devil is all in back of it. The devil has got a lot of power, and he's going to give us more problems in the future. He's trying to destroy Christianity. And in order to destroy Christianity, he has to get our Catholic Church. In order to get our Catholic Church, he has to get our religious leaders—bishops, priests, nuns. He knows their weaknesses, and he's got bishops, priests, and nuns doing things today you never thought they would be doing.

"The main thing here at Necedah is the messages. Sure, we've had all different types of cures here—heart, cancer, blindness, crippleds, many spiritual cures. We have unusual pictures that people take, we have phenomena of the sun, we have rosaries that change color. We have a lot of proofs that this is all true, but the main thing is the messages. The messages are telling us that something is coming, and it's terrible. What's coming is scary. Heaven is trying to help us, but it's still coming.

"They're warning us, see. That's why these messages are so important. That's why the Mother of God is appearing all over the world. We're getting a lot of signs—floods, tornadoes, earthquakes. I don't know what's all gonna come. But if we try to please the Blessed Mother and Our Lord, if we can show 'em some interest, some cooperation, they're gonna guide us, they're gonna protect us, they're gonna help us. They're gonna put us in the right place at the right time. The messages tell us ways of helping ourselves in the future."

All of Mary Ann Van Hoof's revelations and messages were painstakingly recorded and transcribed by faithful helpers in anticipation of the day when the Catholic Church would decide to take another look into the Necedah apparitions.

The Church did open a second investigation of Necedah in September 1969, under Bishop Frederick W. Freking, and five months later condemned the cult all over again. This commission upheld Bishop Treacy's original decree and, in addition, noted that the visionary's testimony was contradictory, that her life offered no evidence of the kind of positive impact that a genuine apparition might be expected to have, and that the messages contained questionable accusations against Church and government leaders. Members were "hereby instructed to cease all activities regarding the promotion of their cause" and to close down the shrine. When the Van Hoof group did not comply, Bishop Freking's next step, in May 1975, was the imposition of a formal interdict (a form of censure short of excommunication) against Mary Ann Van Hoof and six other officers of For My God and My Country, Inc., a corporation founded to promote the cult. The interdict had the effect of denying its recipients all of the Catholic sacraments except Confession.

The new pastor of Saint Francis of Assisi church in Necedah, Father James Barney, seconded the bishop's motion by refusing communion to any area Catholics who were unwilling to renounce their connection with the Van Hoof cult. In a standoff one morning before Mass, Father Barney issued a challenge from the sanctuary—"I asked the loyal and obedient Catholics to approach the altar and asked the rest of them to leave. . . . After about a minute, they did." As had every other instance of official Church censure, though, this latest salvo from the clergy seemed only to harden the resolve of the Necedah supporters.

Perhaps because of its history of poor relations with the official episcopate in La Crosse, the Van Hoof group's next move was to seek out a bishop of its own. In May 1979, an announcement was made that the Necedah shrine had been ceremonially consecrated by a man claiming to be an archbishop, one Edward Michael Stehlik, archbishop and metropolitan of North America, American National Catholic Church, Roman Catholic Ultrajectine (a splinter of an offshoot of a faction that broke with Rome in the eighteenth century). Bishop Freking denied Stehlik was an ordained Roman Catholic bishop. "Hence," Freking wrote, "any jurisdiction that he may exercise in this area is entirely self-proclaimed. For the guidance of the faithful, it should be noted that this action on the part of Mrs. Mary Ann Van Hoof and her followers . . . definitely establishes that they are no longer affiliated with the Roman Catholic Church."

Freking was not the only one leery of Stehlik's qualifications. A December 1979 news report that aired on an ABC affiliate in Milwaukee attacked his credentials and questioned the character of Van Hoof's "archbishop" and some of the clergy who served under him. According to the broadcast, Stehlik had been excommunicated by the Old Catholic Church for, among other offenses, wearing "witchlike" clothing at church services and "babbling incoherently." After a year of critical scrutiny from the press over the matter of his credentials, Stehlik quit his church in January 1981, returned to the Roman Catholic Church as a layman, and declared the Van Hoof apparitions a sham. He left a successor, Francis diBenedetto, who ran things until May 1983, at which time he too resigned from the Old Catholic Church, returned to the Roman, and, like Stehlik, claimed the Van Hoof apparitions had been a hoax.

Contemporary newspaper accounts indicate that the departure and denunciation by the group's own clergy did more to shake up the cult membership than any action by the official Roman Catholic clergy ever had. By one account, two-thirds of the members defected in the wake of Stehlik's and diBenedetto's pullouts. Cult children returned to public schools, and some families moved out of the area entirely.

Many expected the death of Mary Ann Van Hoof in March 1984 to signal the cult's demise. Although membership did decline in the mid-1980s, the group, if not exactly thriving, survives to this day. One estimate puts the number of Van Hoof adherents living in and around Necedah at more than three hundred, with an estimated several thousand supporters scattered around the country. Prayer vigils are held on shrine grounds throughout the year, in celebration of various church feast days as well as on the anniversary days of the Virgin's 1950 appearances to Mary Ann Van Hoof.

The shrine today comprises more than a dozen life-size dioramas depicting the subjects of Mary Ann's visions; the information center and gift shop; a private Christian school; a home "for unfortunate men"; a pageant grounds on which the Holy Family's journey from Nazareth to Bethlehem is reenacted on the first Saturday of every December; a replica of the original Van Hoof farmhouse (the original was destroyed by fire in 1959); and the concrete foundation of the "House of Prayer," the large heart-shaped church originally commissioned by Mary in 1950 and currently still under (painfully slow) construction.

"They finished the main floor of the House of Prayer last

year," Ray told me. "Some of the side walls and the supporting columns are there now. The steel has been ordered,
as I understand it, and the supporting columns will be finished next year, about thirty of them. They'll hold up the
mezzanine and the roof. The building's half a block long and
a quarter of a block wide, and the estimate for the seating
capacity is around two thousand, including the mezzanine
and the main floor. It's being built in the shape of a heart,
and it will have seven altars, for seven Masses at one time.
Confessions will be heard in different languages, which indi-
cates that people will be coming here from foreign countries
as well as from our own."

I asked about the projected completion date.

"It's hard to say," Joe answered. "It said in the messages
that we'll get our House of Prayer when we earn it. Just what
does heaven mean 'when we earn it'? Maybe there isn't
enough prayers being said. Maybe what's happening in the
Church is displeasing. Heaven knows how fast it is being
built. If they wanted it faster, they'd have more help for us.
That's what we're short on—voluntary labor and voluntary
donations."

I told Ray and Joe I was interested in seeing what there
was to see on the shrine grounds before heading back to Chicago. Ray handed me a color brochure describing the shrine
and the scenes depicted in the outbuildings. Then they loaded
me up with other pamphlets and books, shook my hand, and
invited me to come back whenever I liked.

Outside, the temperature had dropped below zero, the
wind blew hard, and the sky was black and cloudless. The
Orion constellation was vaulting the horizon, like a high-
jumper clearing the bar, and a sallow three-quarter moon,
swollen and sluggish, floated idly behind the trees.

The outbuildings house depictions of a select few of Mary
Ann Van Hoof's visions and are arranged in roughly circular
fashion around a paved path. Each scene features realistic, full-
size figures and is set within its own small stone building with

a floor-to-ceiling window spanning the front. The dioramas are well lighted from within, and the various figures, props, clothing, and painted backdrops all look to have been created by professional artists and sculptors.

The first scene on the path is the Last Supper. The entire cast is present, including Judas, who looks away from Jesus and frowns dyspeptically. Jesus stands in his traditional center spot at the table, on which rest plates of bread and a roasted lamb on a platter.

The building next to the Last Supper depicts the First Mass, which, as explained in the brochure Ray had given me, "was offered about an hour later in another part of the room" in which the Last Supper had been held. The cast is the same as in the previous diorama, but in this scene the meal has become formalized as the Catholic Mass. A small gold chalice stands on the table in front of Jesus and each of the apostles. Judas is no longer seated at the table, but lurks nearby, in a corner of the room, clutching his stomach, his face dark and grimacing.

Other dioramas include a depiction of Francis "Mother" Cabrini, the first American citizen to be canonized by the Roman Catholic Church, draped in black and standing on a small shelf above an altar ("She promised," the brochure noted, "before it became a law, to go with us if we drive fifty-five miles per hour, not over sixty"); the Holy Family on an apparently quiet evening at home, Mary at her spinning wheel and Joseph and a preteen Jesus messing around with some carpenter's tools; and Mary Ann Van Hoof herself in a sky blue dress, in mid-vision, kneeling at the Sacred Spot.

As I made my way around the grounds, I could hear, over the tossing of the trees, the crisp popping of a flag in the wind. I eventually came to it, an American flag, run up a pole and flapping like mad in the evening's sharp gusts. Beneath it, standing in the open air, lit from beneath and staring straight ahead, were statues of presidents Washington and Lincoln, both of whom had figured in Mary Ann's ecstatic narratives as iconic Ur-Americans. Between them, standing atop a cloud atop a globe, was Jesus, left hand on his heart, right hand raised in blessing.

Behind the presidents, the unfinished concrete and exposed reinforcement rods of the in-process House of Prayer ran along one side of the circle of dioramas. Mary had explained that its Valentine-shaped floor plan was meant to "honor My Divine Son's Sacred Heart and My Immaculate Heart, to entwine with the hearts of men." The foundation of the House of Prayer butts up beside the four ash trees, which will be visible from inside the building through a glass wall at one end. The Sacred Spot itself, a few feet away, will actually be enclosed within the church. A statue of the Virgin as she appeared to the visionary will be suspended above the Sacred Spot.

I knew as I stood facing the presidents and the footings of the House of Prayer that to my right loomed the shrine's centerpiece; I could see it out of the corner of my eye. Given pride of place amid the circle of dioramas, it depicts Christ's crucifixion as envisioned by the seer. I had glimpsed it earlier as I got out of my car, and while I knew I would eventually have to get in close and take a look, it's the sort of thing you have to let your vision sneak up on in order to keep your head from swimming when you first look at it.

It is numbing in its luridness. Jesus is depicted life-size on the cross. His body is a mass of wounds—bruises, cuts, and splashes of blood too numerous to count. His knees look as though they're nearly worn through. His fists are half clenched, his mouth is open, and his eyes are rolled skyward in an expression that's a perfect mix of shock, agony, and resignation. This is the first representation of the crucifixion I have seen in which the act of nailing Jesus to the cross appears to have been superfluous. The artists and sculptors who created it were guided by marks Mary Ann Van Hoof made in red and purple crayon on a four-foot version of the corpus during a 1955 vision in which she was shown the "rips, tears, blood and bruises inflicted by the scourgers." She described the corpus of her vision as "very beautiful." A sign posted beneath the crucifix includes this quote from Psalms: "They have pierced my hands and my feet. They have numbered all my bones."

The wind pushed stiffly at my back as I stood staring at the crucifix. I had reacted the way I sometimes do after, for example, turning a page in a magazine to an unexpectedly gruesome photograph. The first response is an internal double-take, the quick, tingling pulse of a wave of mental nausea. Next, though, comes an urge to look closer and to keep looking (sometimes accompanied by an almost palpable inability to look away at all), an impulse to study the image until the initial revulsion is overcome and the object resolves, finally, into the benign mundanity of its constituent parts, thereby losing its power to shock the imagination.

I looked at the mutilated, torn, and impaled body long enough to take the scene apart in that way and see it for what it was—the reflection of a gibbering, chaotic figment crouched in deepest shadow within the walls of one pitiable human mind.

After that it felt OK to turn my back on the scene and return, through the darkness, to my car.

Epilogue

One of the oldest Marian prayers of Western Christianity, the Salve Regina, or Hail Holy Queen, dates from the eleventh century, when it was composed by a monk known —probably not to his face—as Herman the Cripple. The prayer, recited at many of the apparition sites I have visited, is little more than an anguished plea for some measure of heavenly consideration and succor:

> Hail, holy Queen, Mother of mercy, our life, our sweetness and our hope. To thee do we cry, poor banished children of Eve. To thee do we send up our sighs, mourning and weeping in this valley of tears. Turn, then, most gracious Advocate, thine eyes of mercy towards us. And after this our exile, show unto us the blessed Fruit of thy womb, Jesus. O clement, O loving, O sweet Virgin Mary.

I know the strength of the religious impulse. And I have some idea why so many millions have embraced Mary through the centuries. In many ways she's easier to warm up to than her inscrutable son. And by virtue of her having once been one of us, she is generally thought to be more sympathetic, more understanding of human weakness and suffering. In the messages received by many modern-day visionaries, hers is the voice of tenderness and restraint playing alongside God's threat of retributive violence against earth and humanity, like a mother sheltering her children from the father who's come home at day's end with a black look in his eye. One of Mary's many titles (and one of my favorites, both for the rounded pleasantness of its sentiment and for the pure physical pleasure of pronouncing it) is *Consolatrix Afflictorum*, she who consoles us in our afflictions. In the image of the comforting mother that lies behind this and similar names for Mary, pilgrims—many of whom no doubt flee a world of troubles to journey to apparition sites as often as they can afford—have found a source of hope. And with hope as rare as honesty here at the frayed end of the millennium, I sometimes find myself wishing, for the pilgrims' sake and for my own, that the numerous, and increasing, reports of apparitions, revelations, and miracles could be true, or at least more credible than they seem.

But wishing never has been enough. And though I have looked closely, I have seen no miracles.

Those who would counter that the gathering together in prayer of thousands of believers constitutes the real miracle are simply mistaken about the meaning of that word. A phenomenon, as we can see most clearly in a case such as Mary Ann Van Hoof's, is decidedly *not* the same thing as a miracle, no matter how popular it may be or how salutary are its effects on the lives of individual believers.

Those who might claim that I have not perceived miracles because I have not looked with the eyes of "faith" may, in a sense, be correct. But no matter how nuanced, that argument has never seemed to me anything other than a case of the horse being planted firmly behind the cart.

Apparition enthusiasts, it seems to me, are doing what most everyone else has been doing for the last several thousand years—trying to bring a little orderliness to bear on this notoriously disordered existence. Like plenty of other religious ideas, fervor for private revelation seems to be less about faith than about control, a grasping for easily enumerated (if not so easily defended) ideas about the order of things. For every person capable of thriving in and even deriving pleasure from a world as mutable and capricious as ours, there seem to be a thousand others who find life's ambiguity, its fundamental obscurity, intolerable.

Bibliography

Literature available on the subject of Marian apparitions is copious and of wildly varying quality and credibility. Of the works consulted in the course of my research, most of which are listed below, a few stand out as superior tools for readers interested in plumbing the subject to greater depths.

Sandra Zimdars-Swartz's *Encountering Mary* has set the standard for balanced, scholarly treatment of the phenomena of Marian visions and the dynamics of the growth of their popularity among communities of believers. If you read only one more book on the subject, this should be the one.

No more succinct and helpful presentation of the Catholic Church's position in regard to claims of private revelation is to be found than in Benedict Groeschel's *A Still, Small Voice*. Father Groeschel distills the essence of Augustin Poulain's *The Graces of Interior Prayer* and offers sound guidance for readers seeking answers.

Michael P. Carroll's *The Cult of the Virgin Mary* offers a tightly constructed and thought-provoking argument for a Freudian basis of Marian piety. His speculations on the psychological underpinnings of our era's most popular Marian apparitions are eye-opening, if potentially scandalous to believers.

Though only tangentially related to the subject of Marian apparitions, *The Physical Phenomena of Mysticism*, by Herbert Thurston, is a sublimely creepy compendium from the outer fringes of Roman Catholic lore—everything from stigmata to miraculous corpses. This book is out of print but well worth searching for in the stacks of your local library. Makes Stephen King read like A. A. Milne.

Ashton, Joan. *Mother of All Nations*. San Francisco: Harper and Row, 1989.

Brown, Michael H. *The Final Hour*. Milford, Ohio: Faith Publishing, 1992.

Carroll, Michael P. *The Cult of the Virgin Mary*. Princeton, N.J.: Princeton University Press, 1986.

Catechism of the Catholic Church. Liguori, Mo.: Liguori Publications, 1994.

Catholic Encyclopedia. New York: Robert Appleton, 1912.

Children of Mary, comp. *Roses from Heaven*. Vol. 2. Orange, Tex.: Children of Mary, 1990.

Christian, William A., Jr. *Apparitions in Late Medieval and Renaissance Spain*. Princeton, N.J.: Princeton University Press, 1981.

Connor, Edward. *Recent Apparitions of Our Lady*. Fresno, Cal.: Academy Guild Press, 1960.

Delaney, John, ed. *Woman Clothed with the Sun*. New York: Hanover House, 1960.

For My God and My Country, Inc., comp. and ed. *Revelations and Messages*. Necedah, Wis.: For My God and My Country, 1971.

Gallery, John Ireland. *Mary vs. Lucifer*. Milwaukee: Bruce Publishing, 1960.

Green, Charles Henry. *We Saw Her*. London: Longmans, Green, 1953.

Groeschel, Benedict J. *A Still, Small Voice*. San Francisco: Ignatius Press, 1993.

Hancock, Ann Marie. *Wake Up America!* Norfolk, Va.: Hampton Roads Publishing, 1993.

Laurentin, René. *Our Lord and Our Lady in Scottsdale*. Trans. Doris Laguette and Ernesto V. Laguette. Milford, Ohio: Faith Publishing, 1992.

The Mercy Foundation. *I Am Your Jesus of Mercy*. St. Louis: Mercy Foundation, 1994. Videocassette.

Messages from Our Heavenly Mother to Her Children. 1995. Available from the People's Prayer Group, Breese, Ill.

Miller, J. Michael. *Marian Apparitions and the Church*. Huntington, Ind.: Our Sunday Visitor Publishing Division, 1993.

The Miraculous Story of Bayside. Rev. ed. Bayside, N.Y.: Our Lady of the Roses Mary Help of Mothers Shrine, 1986. Videocassette.

New Catholic Encyclopedia. Washington, D.C.: Catholic University of America, 1967.

Nickell, Joe. *Looking for a Miracle*. Amherst, N.Y.: Prometheus Books, 1993.

Odell, Catherine. *Those Who Saw Her*. Huntington, Ind.: Our Sunday Visitor Publishing Division, 1995.

Our Loving Mother's Children, comp. *"To Bear Witness That I Am the Living Son of God."* Vol. 1. Newington, Va.: Our Loving Mother's Children, 1991.

Peers, E. Allison, trans. and ed. *The Complete Works of Saint Teresa of Jesus*. 3 vols. London: Sheed and Ward, 1957.

Poulain, Augustin. *The Graces of Interior Prayer*. London: Routledge and Kegan Paul, 1950.

Rahner, Karl. *Visions and Prophecies*. New York: Herder and Herder, 1963.

The Riehle Foundation. *I Am Your Jesus of Mercy*. 2 vols. Milford, Ohio: Riehle Foundation, 1989–90.

Swan, Henry H. *My Work with Necedah.* 4 vols. [Necedah, Wis.]: For My God and My Country, 1959.

Thurston, Herbert. *The Physical Phenomena of Mysticism.* Chicago: Henry Regnery, 1952.

Walsh, William James. *The Apparitions and Shrines of Heaven's Bright Queen.* 4 vols. New York: T.J. Carey; London: Burns and Oates, 1904.

Wilson, Ian. *Stigmata.* San Francisco: Harper and Row, 1989.

Zimdars-Swartz, Sandra L. *Encountering Mary.* Princeton, N.J.: Princeton University Press, 1991.

DUTTON

SPIRIT GUIDES

☐ **THE WISDOM TEACHINGS OF THE DALAI LAMA by Matthew E. Bunson.** This extraordinary volume gives us access to the universal wisdom expressed in the teachings of the revered spiritual leader of Tibetan Buddhism and provides a powerful philosophy for our trouble times. With magnificent simplicity, the Dalai Lama offers his perspectives on peace, love, religion, justice, brotherhood, and human rights and reveals a clear path to spiritual growth and enlightenment.
(279275—$12.95)

☐ **SPIRITS OF THE EARTH** *A Guide to Native American Nature Symbols, Stories, and Ceremonies* **by Bobby Lake-Thom.** This is a practical and enlightening resource that includes dozens of fascinating animals myths and legends, as well as exercises and activities that draw upon animal powers for guidance, healing, wisdom, and the expansion of spiritual influences in our lives.
(276500—$13.95)

☐ **GUARDIAN ANGELS & SPIRIT GUIDES** *True Accounts of Benevolent Beings from the Other Side* **by Brad Steiger.** Along with dozens of compelling eyewitness accounts and real-life histories, this fascinating book includes techniques that may enable you to "hear" more clearly the soft whispers of angelic guidance and messages in your life. (273587—$9.95)

Prices slightly higher in Canada.

Visa and Mastercard holders can order Plume, Meridian, and Dutton books by calling
1-800-253-6476.
They are also available at your local bookstore. Allow 4-6 weeks for delivery.
This offer is subject to change without notice.

PL301

DUTTON   **PLUME**

BOOKS TO INSPIRE

☐ **THE LESSONS OF ST. FRANCIS:** *How to Bring Simplicity and Spirituality into Your Daily Life* **by John Michael Talbot with Steve Rabey.** Beautifully designed and illustrated, this book combines deep spiritual insight with the offer of a saner, less complicated way of living. The inspiring example of a beloved, profoundly human saint provides gentle guidance to peacefulness and joy in a hectic age. (943145—$19.95)

☐ **MOTHER MARY SPEAKS TO US by Brad Steiger and Sherry Hansen Steiger.** Inspiring and comforting, this beautifully written book reveals the miraculous experiences of everyday people who have seen, spoken with, and been healed by Mary, Mother of Jesus. Here, too, are her words of guidance, penance, and compassion recorded by those privileged enough to hear them.
(941258—$19.95)

☐ **PAPAL WISDOM:** *Words of Hope and Inspiration from John Paul II.* **Compiled by Matthew E. Bunson.** The selections in this unique and invaluable collection reflect the heart, the mind, and the soul of one of the most important and influential figures in the world today and one of the most eloquent and inspiring popes of all time: John Paul II. (941193—$14.95)

Prices slightly higher in Canada.

PL261

DUTTON

 PLUME

YOUR INNER SELF

☐ **ABOVE AND BEYOND** *365 Meditations for Transcending Chronic Pain and Illness* **by J.S. Dorian.** Daily companion that combines inspiring quotations with positive words from the author, a survivor of cancer, heart disease, and lupus. With a reassuring meditation for every day of the year, it is a sourcebook of strength and courage for anyone facing the challenges of a chronic condition or acute illness. (276268—$9.95)

☐ **BECOME HAPPY IN EIGHT MINUTES by Simon Reynolds.** Simple, powerful steps to improve your mood quickly. Drawing on a unique combination of visualization, neurology, spirituality, and biochemistry, this essential guide provides six simple steps to elevate your mood instantly and if practiced over time, lastingly. (274885—$9.95)

☐ **SHORTCUT THROUGH THERAPY** *Ten Principles of Growth-Oriented, Contented Living* **by Richard Carlson, Ph.D.** A stress consultant teaches the ten easy principles of growth-oriented, contented living and reveals how traditional therapy often interferes with the healing process. "A wonderful book of 'shortcut nuggets' that lead the way to changing our attitudes so that we may choose happiness."—Gerald Jampolsky, M.D., author of *Letting Go of Fear* (273838—$10.95)

☐ **THE IMMUNE POWER PERSONALITY** *7 Traits You Can Develop to Stay Healthy* **by Henry Dreher.** The author reveals that the key to mind-body health is not avoiding stress, but developing personal strengths for coping with hard times. We can cultivate seven traits of resilience that help us fight disease, and keep us robust and vigorous. "Excellent . . . a valuable guide to achieving personal immune power."—Bernie Siegel, author of *Love, Medicine and Miracles* (275466—$13.95)

☐ **INSTANT CALM** *Over 100 Easy-to-Use Techniques for Relaxing Mind and Body* **by Paul Wilson.** This book offers the easiest, most effective relaxation techniques ever assembled in a single volume. They include age-old methods from many different cultures, and exercises from the most up-to-date scientific research. By removing your immediate anxiety, these techniques can help you regain perspective on life as a whole, enabling you to lower your tension level for the long term. (274338—$11.95)

☐ **FACING THE WOLF** *Inside the Process of Deep Feeling Therapy* **by Theresa Sheppard Alexander.** This extraordinary book vividly and vibrantly recreates the first eight sessions in a course of therapy from the points of view of both the patient and the therapist. The method is Deep Feeling Therapy, an offshoot of the Primal Therapy developed by Dr. Arthur Janov to allow the patient to directly confront and "go through" buried traumatic experiences of the past so as to gain freedom from their power to cripple the emotions and poison life. (94060X—$20.95)

Prices slightly higher in Canada.